God's
Incredible Plans for Me:

A Memoir of An Amazing Journey

*My dear Haskell & Iris,
Thanks for being a part of my journey these many years.
Be blessed and inspired as you read of God's goodness.
Love & best wishes!
Shirley
September 24, 2017*

Shirley C. Iheanacho

Xulon PRESS

God's Incredible Plans for Me:
A Memoir of An Amazing Journey
by Shirley C. Iheanacho

Printed in the United States of America.

ISBN 9781498498586

www.xulonpress.com

Dedication

With profound gratitude to my Heavenly Father, I dedicate this book to my parents, Cecil DaCosta and Myril Howell; my husband, Morris; our daughters, Ngozi, Chioma, and Akunna; our precious grandsons, Nikolas and Timothy; and to all who will read these pages.

"It's in Christ that we find out who we are and what we are living for. Long before we first heard of Christ,. . . He had his eye on us, had designs on us for glorious living, part of the overall purpose he is working out in everything and everyone"
(Ephesians 1:11, *Message*).

Acknowledgments

The author gratefully acknowledges the combined efforts of family and friends who helped to make this book possible. Extra special thanks and appreciation go to my husband, Morris, for his encouragement, cultural contributions, editorial advice, proofreading skills, and for his patience and understanding when the preparation of this book took much time and attention away from him. Special thanks go to my daughters, Ngozi, Chioma, and Akunna, for the gift of motherhood and for providing inspiration and priceless input. My siblings, Everette, Halstead, Rudolph, Edison (deceased), Neville, DeLoras, and Cynthia were always there for me. My visionary parents, Cecil and Myril, gave love, wisdom, nurture, and training that provided the foundation for who I am today.

For honest critiques, insightful suggestions, editorial expertise, and overall guidance, I am deeply indebted to Dr. Melvin Peters, Pastor Everette Howell, Dr. Akunna Iheanacho, Dr. Roy E. Malcolm, Chioma Iheanacho, and Ngozi Bolton. Thanks to Dr. Rowland Nwosu, Shirley Scott, and Dr. Clarence Hodges for their input in the beginning stages of this book. Special thanks and appreciation to Pastor Howell for the historical data about the Howell family. Thanks also to Dr. Peters, Pastor Howell and Dr. Iheanacho for their tireless assistance and persistent nudgings that propelled me to complete this book. Thanks to Dr. Oliver Davis for his editorial input. Profound gratitude and appreciation go to Ms. Lauren Griggs for her editorial proficiency that significantly enhanced the final product. Special thanks to Kaven Ible for taking the time to proofread the final draft.

For inspiration, encouragement, and prayers, my appreciation goes to Dr. Katie Arnette, Clementine Collins and Marilyn Wallace, my faithful and supportive prayer partners; Dr. Jean Blake, Dr. Sylvia Barnes, Kaven Ible, Joy Peters, Paulette Johnson, Dr. Ursula Benn, Thelda Van Lange Greaves, Jocelyn Thomas, Polly Anders, Dr. Chukudi and Evelyne Izeogu, and the late Thelma Prime who didn't live to read this book.

Thanks to Chuck May for his untiring general support, tenacity, and photo assistance; also to Nikolas Trofort, my grandson, for his help with the computer and photos. To my inspirers, prayer warriors, and anyone who held up my hand as I traveled my journey, thank you. Although your name may not have appeared in this book, you are dear to my heart, and I thank God for you. Continue to touch lives and make a difference.

Finally, thank you, dear reader, for allowing me to share my story with you.

"Bless the LORD, O my soul; And all that is within me, bless His Holy Name! Bless the LORD, O my soul, And forget not all His benefits" (Psalm 103:1, 3, NKJV).

Endorsements

Anyone who cherishes family or longs for a happy family in spite of the many challenges to family these days will find inspiration and hope while reading these pages written from the heart of its author. Shirley knows from personal experience that life is not lived in the isolation of a goldfish bowl, but true character of any family is developed as it successfully copes, on a daily basis, with all the many challenges impacting family members.

You will have difficulty to put down this book once you start to read.

Clarence E. Hodges, Ph.D., Retired

Former General Conference of SDA and NAD Executive

U.S. Department of State Executive

White House Personnel Consultant

This book is a captivating narrative of my dear friend, Shirley Howell Iheanacho's journey through a challenging, fulfilled, and exciting life. Her life has not been in vain as demonstrated by the many lives she touched along the way. I invite you to accompany Shirley through this life journey; your life will not be the same.

William A. Murrain, Esq.

Chief Operating Officer

MBA Wellness Centers

President, Murrain Associates, Inc.

Shirley Cyrene Howell Iheanacho is a woman of passion. Everything she does is with meticulousness and gusto. As you read her life story, you will laugh, cry and have "Aha" moments. You will appreciate the spiritual wisdom this woman of faith has developed in her relationship with the Creator of the Universe who knows each one of us intimately. From the beginning to the end, you will understand that He has a life plan for you, too.

Kaven L. Ible, M.S.

Friend and Former Co-worker

Retired Administrative Assistant to the Provost and Senior Vice President

Oakwood University

Foreword

G *od's Incredible Plans for Me: A Memoir of An Amazing Journey* is a book for everyone. The great Redemption Plan formulated in the beginning by God includes all humanity who, through faith, accept the divine invitation to participate. In this book, the writer reveals how her commitment to follow God's leading has strengthened her spiritual journey.

She was encouraged by family, friends, and colleagues to share her experiences as an international student, spouse, parent, administrative secretary/assistant to four Oakwood University presidents and the provost, speaker, author, and prayer warrior. Her supervisors eloquently lauded her for the skillful, faithful, and professional manner in which she fulfilled her duties and responsibilities. In this publication, Shirley shares her memoirs as an encourager, prayer warrior, writer, and an international speaker and singer.

Her journey, however, was not devoid of the dark valleys of pain and illness. By faith, she journeyed on living confidently in God's hands. She counts it a joy and an honor to share her memoir of an amazing journey.

> "Precious memories, how they linger on
> How they ever flood her soul
> In the quietness of the midnight
> Precious memories still unfold,
> forever etched in the halls of [her] mind."

(Adapted from J. B. F. Wright's song "*Precious Mem'ries*.")

Roy E. Malcolm, Ph.D.

Retired Professor and Former Academic Dean

Oakwood University

"Glorify the Lord with me; Let us exalt His name together" (Psalm 34:3, NIV).

Introduction

A very long time ago, on the breezy, paradise island of Barbados, in a quiet country place called Sweet Field, a bouncing 7½ pound baby girl was born to Cecil DaCosta and Myril Elaine Howell. There was great rejoicing at the birth of their first daughter whom they named Shirley Cyrene (pronounced Cerene). This is the story of that baby girl's life journey.

Pulling back the curtain of my memory, I am humbled and awed to catch a fresh glimpse of the great God of the universe orchestrating events in my life and placing people, circumstances, and situations in motion to bring about His plan for me. It's fascinating how He put together each piece of the puzzle to form a beautiful picture. In His love and mercy, He took me to places and allowed me to reach heights I never imagined in my wildest dreams that I could have attained and made my life rich and full.

Reflecting on my journey, I am awestruck at God's providential leadings. Over the years, I have come to realize that He created me for a purpose and that He had great plans for me, which I was unaware of as I was growing up in Barbados and Trinidad. What He says in Isaiah 55:8-9 is true, "For My thoughts are not your thoughts, nor are your ways My ways," says the Lord. "For as the heavens are higher than the earth, so are My ways higher than your ways, and My thoughts than your thoughts" (NKJV).

My journey has not been without challenges, heartaches, pain, sickness, joy, and laughter. Sometimes, the negative circumstances in which I found myself have caused me to question: "Lord, why me?" During the times when God showed me favor, I was transported through scenic mountains and verdant valleys with myriad evidence of God's unfathomable love and faithfulness.

Right before my eyes, He has opened doors that were securely locked, torn down seemingly impenetrable barriers, removed roadblocks, and granted me safe passage to proceed. While battling sickness, near death experiences, fear, and despondency, I have cried out to Him in my midnight hour, and He has heard my cry and rescued me. God has a way of showing up right on time. In many instances, He has shown up before I had the presence of mind or the sense to call on Him.

Although I've made wrong choices, botched up, messed up, and fallen into and out of the pit of sin countless times, somehow, God has never turned His back nor given up on me. His hand of mercy has always raised me up, and His arms of love have held me close. He "made my feet like the feet of a deer," and helped me to climb mountains of difficulties (Habakkuk 3:19, NIV). In my weakness, He was my pillar of strength, and He carried me when I couldn't carry on.

You and I are children of the highest God who has known all about us even before we took our first breath. He loves us with an unfathomable love, and He's interested in the most intricate details of our lives. His plans for us are grand and awesome: "to prosper us and not to harm us, to give us hope and a bright and wonderful future" (Jeremiah 29:11, NIV).

There is no guarantee that the journey will be without challenges and disappointments, pain and suffering. We live in a sin-sick world, and bad things do happen. I know from personal experience that, one day, you can be on your mountaintop of ecstasy with everything going well, and the next, there may be only chaos and confusion. Sickness, pain or bad news can come crashing down on you, shattering all your well-planned dreams. God can use the disappointments and difficulties life brings your way to generate the energy and the fortitude necessary to propel you to reach higher heights that you might not have accomplished otherwise.

Through it all, the Lord has promised to be with us (Isaiah 41:10, GNT). He has the power to work out all things together for our good (Romans 8:28). Trust Him, then, patiently wait as He causes you to soar above the clouds on wings as eagles, to run and not become weary (Isaiah 40:31), and to ride upon the high places of the earth (Isaiah 58:14). Yes, we serve an incredible God who does incredible things!

I thank God for the opportunity to share this memoir of His phenomenal blessings, and I pray that it will bring glory to Him and inspiration to you.

"I will praise You, O LORD, with my whole heart; I will tell of all Your marvelous works.
I will be glad and rejoice in You; I will sing praise to Your name, O Most High"
(Psalm 9:1-2, NKJV).

Table of Contents

Chapter 1

God's Gift of Family

B rad Henry, former governor of the State of Oklahoma, penned these profound words, which I will use to introduce my story: "Families are the compass that guides us. They are the inspiration to reach great heights, and our comfort when we occasionally falter."

Join me as I share a few vignettes of my family, upbringing, and incredible journey from where God took me, a child from a little island in the Caribbean, to this point in my life. I will begin with my mom, Myril Elaine Howell. "What is Home Without a Mother?" is the title of a song written by Alice Hawthorne, and I consider it appropriate as I share highlights about my mother. In families, we owe what we are or hope to be to our Heavenly Father, but good mothers are a close second.

Myril

Myril, pronounced Mee'-rill, whom we affectionately call Maah, was born on February 4, 1916, in the parish of St. Lucy, at a place called Grenidges on the island of Barbados. She was one of four children born to Eileen Warner Griffith and Edmund Francis Skinner.

It was a very challenging time in which she grew up. Two years prior to her birth, World War I began which adversely impacted the lives of the people on the little island. Life was hard, and unemployment, poverty, and dreaded diseases were prevalent everywhere.

In her pre-teen years, Myril attended St. Lucy's Elementary Girls' School located a few miles from her home but didn't go beyond the fifth grade. God blessed her with wisdom far beyond her years, and her natural intelligence and great wit and wisdom have upheld and sustained her family throughout our lives.

Myril Elaine Howell

As a teenager, she was fortunate not to have to work on a plantation, or to depend on a man for "favors," as was the practice back then. Her mother, a skilled seamstress, taught her, along with other young women, how to sew. Also, her mom's sister, Dora Adams, lived in the U.S., and she frequently sent money and boxes of clothes to the family to keep them dressed in the latest fashions.

Before Myril became a Seventh-day Adventist, she occasionally accompanied her sister, Cynthia, to the Pentecostal Church in a nearby village. She said that they liked the church because they enjoyed watching people "get the power" (the Holy Spirit). It was exciting for them to see worshippers dance, clap, and roll around on the floor. This changed when she and her best friend, Eva, attended evangelistic meetings conducted by an Adventist pastor and committed their hearts to the Lord through baptism. They became members of the Checker Hall SDA Church in St. Lucy.

Myril considered herself to have been a well-behaved girl, but she admits that she occasionally got into trouble. She and Eva nicknamed one of the church elders "Moses" because of his pious and serious attitude when he entered the pulpit. One day, when "Moses" stood up to preach, Myril said to Eva, "Look at Moses!" Both of them laughed, unaware that the elder had overheard them. When Myril got home from church, she learned that "Moses" had already gone to her house and complained to her mother about her behavior. Her mother confronted her with the elder's accusation and expressed deep disappointment in her behavior.

She gave Myril an unforgettable whipping and concluded with these words, "I put dis nice dress on you and send you to church to listen to de preacher, not to talk and laugh in church." Myril confesses that, from that day and for many years, she hated the elder. She later forgave him, and they became good friends. In a tribute to her he wrote, "In her early teens, she chose the path of development to become an honorable lady."

During this time, a young man in his twenties by the name of Cecil DaCosta Howell was influenced by the Greaves brothers, Edgar and Eric (prominent members of the Checker Hall SDA Church and the community), to become a Seventh-day Adventist. After his baptism, he was recruited to work as a colporteur, now called literature evangelist, to travel to the islands of Antigua, St. Martin, St. Eustatius, Saba, and Anguilla to sell religious books. His peers described him as an energetic colporteur. He and Urbane Francis are recorded in history books as the individuals who initiated the first SDA church group organized on the island of Anguilla.

When Cecil returned to Barbados after his stint as a missionary, he never returned to colporteuring. His father, a trained carpenter, taught him carpentry, which he mastered. One day, a friend of Myril's family told her mother, Eileen, about a young man who made very good cabinets (called "wagons" in those days) for only six shillings. This young man was Cecil. On the recommendation of the friend, Eileen purchased a cabinet from him. More than 84 years later, Myril still keeps dishes, cups, glasses, and other items on that cabinet.

Myril was in her teens when she first met Cecil. He occasionally passed by her house to visit friends who lived nearby. One day, her mother asked him to come in and help her with Myril's grandfather who was experiencing severe pain caused by a hernia. Myril's beauty and charming personality must have captured Cecil's heart during this initial encounter, because his visits to her house became more frequent. Her mom noted that something was growing in Cecil's heart for her daughter, and she questioned him about it. Eileen told him that if he was interested in her daughter, he should write a letter to her father expressing his feelings. So, he did.

Myril's father read the letter and asked her what she knew about him and if she loved him. She confessed that she did, and a meeting was convened to discuss the contents of the letter. Her dad told Cecil that she was very young and that nothing should be done to cause her to err. Cecil assured her father that he would comply with his wishes. (Everette told me that recently, she was reminiscing about those days and asked him what "to err" meant.) Cecil proposed to Myril, and she accepted his invitation to become his wife. They were married in 1934 at the Government Hill SDA Church. He was a 27-year-old ambitious carpenter, and she an 18-year-old, starry-eyed seamstress.

In 1935, Myril and Cecil became the proud parents of their first child, a son, whom they named Everette. A set of twins soon followed, but they didn't survive. She still talks about this painful experience in her life. A few years passed and another son was born whom they named Halstead.

During this time, two events seriously threatened this little family. They owned a dog named Ginger who was a watchdog. One night, Ginger began to bark loudly and refused to stop as he walked in the direction of a large tank of water near the house. Cecil couldn't stand the dog's continual barking, so he decided to go outside, against his wife's advice, to see what was causing the dog to bark.

Myril placed Halstead between two pillows and followed her husband to discourage him from going out into the darkness. He urged her to go back inside the house and reassured her that he would take care of the problem. Myril returned to the house, but Cecil continued outside where he encountered three men hiding behind a breadfruit tree. They attacked and beat him. He suffered broken ribs and a dislocated shoulder and was hospitalized; fortunately, he survived. The three men were arrested and sent to jail. The reason for this beating was never discovered.

The late 1930s proved to be a challenging time for the young couple and their rapidly growing family, as well as for the citizens of Barbados. Conditions had become so dire that, with seemingly no other way to correct the situation, the people decided to riot to obtain a better standard of living. Cecil was visiting Bridgetown, the capital city, when the riots broke out. He was overcome with fear and frantically tried to discover a means by which he could escape from the city as quickly as possible. He boarded a bus that took him as far as University Hill, still quite a distance from his home. To get away from the rioting and shooting, he decided to go home via the seashore, so he took off his shoes, carried them in his hand, and walked and ran on the beach, away from the rioting and shooting. Thankfully, he arrived home safely and shared with his wife the chaos and confusion that was going on in the city.

By 1940, World War II was at its peak in Europe, and it impacted the lives of both rich and poor as far away as the British colonies in the Caribbean. The few resources available on the island were being sent to support the war effort thousands of miles away. Molasses, sugar, and cotton that were cultivated on the island were produced to be shipped to England.

Merchant ships, which typically brought foodstuffs and other goods to the islanders, were now assigned to war personnel or restricted by the German submarines that seemed to be everywhere. The situation became worse when a German submarine torpedoed *The Cornwallis*, a merchant ship, while it was unloading cargo in the Bridgetown port. Rationing of food quickly became the order of the day. Families were issued coupons or tickets according to their size. Staples such as rice, sugar, cooking oil, and kerosene were very scarce commodities and, even when available, the unemployment situation made it extremely tough for poor families to purchase necessities.

The dark nights grew darker because people were forbidden to use light at night to avoid being seen and, possibly, bombed by enemy planes flying overhead. Simple survival was all that anyone thought about or could hope for. "Cut and contrive" were words repeated often. "Make do with what you have" was a phrase uttered by parents as they told their children there would be no supper that evening.

It was in this atmosphere of stringent circumstances that I was born. Although a welcomed addition to the family, I was another child who needed to be fed and clothed during a difficult time. According to Everette, if I was not fed, changed, and put to sleep as I demanded, my voice could be heard just as clearly as the air raid sirens that went off from time to time. Unlike Halstead, who didn't like his mother's milk, I loved it and nursed until I was 13 months old, the longest time of any of Myril's children.

Our family continued to grow rapidly, and, in 1941, Rudolph, a premature baby, arrived and needed much prayer and attention. Myril's doctor warned her about the impact her continuous pregnancies could have on her health and that of her offspring. His warnings went unheeded, and Myril continued to have babies with no ill effects to either her or my siblings.

By 1942, World War II had kicked in ferociously. Added to this terrible turn of events was a drought, which made it impossible for crops to grow. The situation that existed at the time was so severe, that with so many mouths to feed and so little income with which to do it, my parents had to make some very tough decisions. Cecil heard that the Americans were operating a military base in Trinidad and were recruiting skilled workmen. He applied and was accepted. He departed for Trinidad leaving Myril in Barbados to manage their young family. Fortunately, her mother lived a short distance away and was able to lend a hand. A few months after working at the base, Cecil learned of job opportunities available at Caribbean Training College, a Seventh-day Adventist institution, and he transferred to that campus where he assisted with the building of a new dormitory. For nine months, Cecil worked hard and sent money back home to support his family.

Conditions began to improve, so he decided to return to Barbados. His family continued to grow, and four more children were born after Rudolph: Edison, Neville, DeLoras, and Cynthia. Together, Cecil and Myril worked untiringly to care for their large family. Such slogans as "A little with content is great gain," and the tried-and-true, "You have to learn to cut and contrive," were often repeated.

As a dedicated mother, homemaker, and seamstress, Myril learned to survive hardships by mastering the art of "snipping, stitching, cutting, and contriving." For example, she patched and re-patched Cecil's worn-out pants, and when he could no longer wear them, she would cut off the legs of the pants and make them into short pants for Everette. I too experienced Myril's cutting and contriving when I attended high school. When my one school uniform became too faded, my mother made me pick it to pieces; and she turned it inside out and made it into a new uniform. She was astute and knew how to stretch every dollar to make ends meet.

In addition to all the other hats my mom wore, she was our family physician and pharmacist. As a result of her expertise with home remedies, we seldom went to the doctor. If we complained of a stomachache, she gave us a dose of castor oil. Sometimes, our dad added a little lime or orange juice to reduce the awful taste, but it didn't help much. If we sustained an injury to our finger, and it looked as if it might become infected, Myril washed it with water and sterilized it with kitchen salt. One treatment usually did the trick. She made her oatmeal and soap poultices for other injuries. The leaves of the cassava (yucca) plant were used to reduce fever. Milk from the aloe plant relieved stomach pains. Soursop leaves, steeped in boiling water, helped to reduce the debilitating effects of the common cold. What's amazing about these homemade remedies is that they all worked!

Myril's vision that we wouldn't always remain in our little country village propelled her to prepare us daily for the rigors of a bigger world. We learned to wash and press our clothes, clean the house and the yard, keep our one school uniform clean and tidy, take care of the animals, and be of good behavior. Any reports from neighbors that any of us had been disrespectful or mischievous always reached home before we did. That was where the slogan, "Spare the rod and spoil the child," was revered. A child must not be spoiled, so the tamarind rod, leather belt, or some other corrective instrument was always readily at hand and put to good use.

Myril taught us many biblical principles which governed our lives as we matured, and we have endeavored to pass these values on to our children. She was blessed with a forgiving heart and encouraged us to practice forgiveness, as well. She would admonish, "What's the point of being a Christian if you can't forgive your neighbor?"

In addition to taking care of her children, Myril was involved in church-related activities. She loved to sing and sang in the choir and with other groups; she also served as a deaconess and children's Sabbath School teacher at Checker Hall SDA Church and Boscobelle SDA Church. When the going got tough, she sang songs like: "His eye is on the sparrow," "O wait, meekly wait and murmur not," "Wonderful love, wonderful love, wonderful love of Jesus." To this day, she continues to hum her favorite tunes around the house.

During my recent visit to Barbados, she volunteered to explain to me how she came to be called Maah. She said she sent her two toddlers, Everette and Halstead, to visit her mother, who lived close. When they returned home, they stood outside the door and yelled, "Merle, open the door!" She was shocked to hear them call her "Merle," so she immediately talked to her husband about it. They both agreed that they couldn't have their children call her by that name. They came up with two acceptable names, and of the two, they chose "Maah." She also shared how her name changed from Merle to Myril. From birth, she had been called Merle, and she thought that was her official name until she applied for a passport to travel to the U.S. It was then she discovered that the official name on her birth certificate was Myril. It's been Myril ever since.

Although Maah, at approximately five feet tall, is the shortest person in the Howell clan, what she lacks in physical stature, she makes up for it in wisdom. She is known to repeat many favorite proverbs such as: "Life is like a wheel. You may be up now, but the wheels turn. Do good while you're up so that when you're down, someone will do good unto you." "Time waits for no man." "A stitch in time saves nine." "Where there's a will, there's a way." "As long as there's life, there's hope." "Don't burn your candle at both ends." "Waste not, want not." "Half a loaf is better than no bread." "You can't have your cake and eat it too." " Learn how to cut and contrive." "Don't count your chickens before they hatch." "Put aside a little something for a rainy day." "Take care of the pennies, and the dollars will take care of themselves." "Be sure your sins will find you out." "Two wrongs don't make a right." "You can run, but you can't hide." "If you don't have a horse, ride a cow." "If you think you are better than others, don't act like them."

Maah has a heart of gold and a special caring touch, which she willingly shares. At the end of Sabbath service, it is customary for her to greet people and inquire about their families. She notes who is missing and tries to find out why. Once, I overheard her tell a young man that she hadn't seen him at church for two weeks. He hurriedly explained, "No, Miss Howell, I was only gone for one week; the other Sabbath, I was downstairs helping someone." She looked at him seriously and said, "All right, but I don't want you to miss coming to church, you hear me, young man?" Respectfully, he replied, "Okay, Miss Howell."

She is an ardent supporter of young people and relishes their company. She has the art of making them feel good about themselves; and they, in turn, make her feel young at heart. It is her strong desire to help them grow to be upstanding citizens, to strive for excellence, and to serve God faithfully. Humbly, she expresses gratitude to God for her little part in molding lives for Him.

Whatever church assignment Maah's children or grandchildren are involved with, she considers it her responsibility to assist them with the appropriate input. On one of my visits to Barbados, Neville invited me to preach at Boscobelle Church. Maah heard about it and inquired about the title of my sermon. I told her that I was still working on it. Immediately, she said, "You should talk about 'In Times Like These.' Tell the people that Jesus is coming soon! And you must move your hands (gesticulate) when you talk." She demonstrated just how I should do it. Although I didn't follow all of her advice, all went well.

In December 1996, family members traveled to Barbados for a surprise tribute in her honor. Letters, poems, and pictures were solicited from family, friends, former pastors, presidents, and others. Among them were letters from the late Elder Robert Folkenberg, former president of the General Conference of SDAs; Bill Clinton, former United States president; and Drs. Calvin B. Rock and Delbert W. Baker, former presidents of Oakwood College (now University). Maah was touched and blessed by the many expressions of love that she received.

Tribute to Maah 1996

Over the years, Maah has traveled to the U.S. on numerous occasions to spend time with her children and grandchildren, as well as to attend graduations and weddings. They consider her a lot of fun and cherish fond memories of the wonderful times she spent with her family and how she exuded so much warmth and love.

Maah at Oakwood

In 2010, family members gathered, again, in Barbados to celebrate Maah's 94th birthday. At the end of the special church program, Neville, head elder of Boscobelle Church, invited her to give a few remarks. With a resolute voice, she responded: "The race is not for de swift nor de battle for de strong, but he who endures to de end." She concluded by expressing her deep gratitude to God for sparing her life to witness this moment.

Afterward, the family gathered at Maah's house for fellowship dinner. Some of us ate outside under the huge mahogany tree and shared secrets about our formative years, the revelations of which brought shock and much laughter. At one point, Maah stood up, put her hands on her hips, and said, "How come I never heard these things before." Everette quickly responded, "Because you were too busy making babies." We all laughed out loud.

In July 2014, family members came together for our family reunion. It was a time of fellowshipping, greeting, bonding, sharing past experiences, playing games, and having fun. Even at the age of 98, Maah kept up with all of the festivities. We enjoyed fun, food, and fellowship, but, most of all, we reveled in rich and abundant spiritual blessings.

Howell Family Reunion

At the end of the worship service the following Sabbath, a young man came to where Maah and I were sitting and said, "I am here today because of Sister Howell. She taught my friends, who are sitting back there in the church, and me when we were in kindergarten Sabbath School. She told us things that we haven't forgotten. She is a wonderful, sweet, Christian lady, and we love her."

Later that afternoon, family members ate a delectable meal and had wonderful fellowship at Rudolph's house. During this time, some of us recalled amazing stories from our childhood days. I gave a special tribute to our parents on behalf of the family and shared information about Daah that was new to some family members.

Eunice, Halstead's daughter, worked tirelessly to organize the reunion celebration, as well as the Sunday afternoon fun activities for all age groups, from the youngest to the oldest. There was lots of merriment. My two oldest brothers, Everette and Halstead, 79 and 75, respectively, participated in the lawn mower race. Much excitement and laughter were generated as family members enthusiastically cheered them on. Everette won, and his prize was a congratulatory kiss from Audrey, his wife of over 52 years. My husband, Morris, enjoyed himself immensely as he participated in some of the games.

One thing that I observed during this visit was that Maah is still a proud lady. I was holding her hand as we walked in the front yard; suddenly, she pulled her hand away and said, "Don't hold my hand. I don't want the people in Fustic Village to think I can't walk by myself."

Maah's 100th Birthday Celebration

Thursday, February 4, 2016, will go down in history as an auspicious and unforgettable day in the lives of the members of the Howell family. Myril Elaine Howell, the matriarch of our family and God's precious gift to us, celebrated her 100th birthday. She was surrounded by the Governor General of Barbados, His Excellency Sir Elliott Belgrave; children, grand-children, great-grandchildren, parish officials, loved ones, and friends.

Maah's 100th Birthday

Excitement was in the air. Much time and energy went into planning the details of this day, and it had finally arrived. Before the arrival of His Excellency, the Governor, strict adherence to the protocol outlined by his office was followed so that we would exhibit the proper behavior when he arrived.

At the appointed time, everyone gathered at the home of Dr. Halstead Howell for this momentous occasion. His Excellency presented Maah with a gift from Her Majesty, the Queen of England, with these words: "From one Queen to another." The personal gift from him and his wife included a beautiful floral arrangement and a bottle of wine. Following his glowing remarks, he invited family members, parish representatives, and friends to give tributes in Maah's honor. It was indeed an enjoyable experience to hear complimentary comments about Maah's life and the tremendous impact she has had on everyone.

Pastor Danforth Francis, president of the East Caribbean Conference of Seventh-day Adventists and the chief representative of the Adventist Church on the island of Barbados, brought greetings. His greetings were significant to our family because Pastor Francis' father, Urbane Francis (now deceased), had been a dear friend of Maah and Daah for decades. His Excellency closed the reception with toasts to Maah, and I was invited to give the vote of thanks. Everyone who participated in and attended this significant milestone enjoyed themselves. It was a grand occasion. The reception was followed by a celebration at which people continued to lavish love, appreciation, gifts, flowers, and well wishes upon Maah.

The birthday celebrations continued through Sabbath, February 6, at the Boscobelle SDA Church. Maah was honored by family, church members, and friends. Children, grandchildren, and great-grandchildren participated in the Sabbath School program. Family members sang two songs for the worship service, and Everette preached. He concluded his message with the following words; "Indeed, 'Success is not measured by the number of things you have accomplished in life, but by the obstacles overcome in achieving success'" (Adapted from Booker T. Washington's quotation in his book, *Up From Slavery*.) "God made a promise to Jacob, 'I am with thee and will keep thee in all places whither thou goest, and will bring thee again into this land, for I will not leave thee until I have done that which I have spoken to thee of' (Gen. 28:15, KJV). To this promise, Jacob responded by committing his life to God. Today, as a family, Myril's family, we do the same, in the name of the Father, the Son, and the Holy Spirit, AMEN."

Maah's Celebration at Boscobelle Church

Maah's long journey has not been without its pitfalls and instances of grief and pain, but, with God's help, she has successfully navigated the trials and tribulations, and survived to graduate from the school of hard knocks. She also graciously embraces the joys and blessings that she has experienced. We give thanks, praise, and the highest honor to our Heavenly Father for guiding, blessing, protecting, and sustaining her to enjoy and celebrate her auspicious 100th birthday. Glory to God!

Maah continues to live by herself and spends her time being helpful around the house and in the yard. She still talks about her late husband. Of their marriage, she once said, "We had our ups and downs, but we had a lot of fun. He was good to me. I still miss him."

With the recent deterioration of her vision, she has difficulty reading her Bible, but it is amazing to hear her repeat scripture and recite quotations from Shakespeare's writings. She is blessed with a remarkable memory and can recall many events that occurred decades ago. She is a woman of great faith, strength, resilience, perseverance, and a wonderful sense of humor that makes us laugh till we cry.

One thing that has followed each of us over the years is Maah's persistent prayers for us. For this, we are eternally grateful. She continues to be the glue that holds our extended family together, and we thank God for His precious gift of our mother.

Maah at 101 years

Cecil

Cecil DaCosta Howell, whom we called Daah, was one of six children born to James and Angelique Howell. He was a self-made man: a carpenter, farmer, Christian book salesman, fisherman, construction worker, and a politician. He was strong, ambitious, and hardworking with a determination to give his family the best that he could afford. Although he loved his family, he had no time for pampering; he raised us to be self-reliant. Of course, we didn't appreciate the Spartan experience at that time, but, as we matured, we understood some of the lessons he sought to instill in us.

Daah didn't attend high school, but God endowed him with a brilliant mind and sound wisdom. He was determined to do all in his power to ensure that each of his children obtained an education. I believe that this resolve was the impetus for his hard work from the crack of dawn till late in the evening. He planted sugarcane, yams, potatoes, cassava, corn, cotton, and peanuts. When times got tough, he made fish pots to catch fish that he sold to help make ends meet.

Cecil DaCosta Howell

He became a politician and vestryman (councilman) later in life and joined a coalition of five men to challenge the entrenched bureaucracy that controlled local government. On his first attempt to become a political leader, he fell short of the required votes, but his second attempt was successful. This success provided an opportunity for him to intermingle with high-ranking government officials. This experience, I believe, helped us to fit in wherever we were as we grew older, from the village environment to the company of presidents.

One of Daah's sayings was: "Early to bed, early to rise makes a man healthy, wealthy, and wise." He awakened us before the crack of dawn for five o'clock worship. I can still hear his rich tenor voice ringing in my ear as we sang, "Holy, Holy, Holy, Lord God Almighty," "Lord in the Morning," "When Morning Gilds the Skies," and "The Sun is on the Land and Sea, the day begun." None of us was fond of rising early, but, over the years, we have come to treasure those precious moments.

Daah never tolerated extravagance or wastefulness and often told us that "A penny saved is a penny gained." He counseled us, "Don't beg nor borrow from anybody. Work hard for what you want! And don't put your hat higher than you can reach it." Translated in today's vernacular, "Don't live beyond your means."

He exhibited an unwavering faith and trust in God to provide for his family. Everette shared a story that happened during World War II that made a lasting impression on his young mind. Times were tough, and the cupboards were empty. A drought had fallen on the island, which only added to the scarcity of food. He recalls following Daah as he walked all over his property in a desperate search for food. They searched for cassava, sweet potatoes, yams, anything with which to feed his starving family. They walked and prayed. When hopes of finding food vanished, right before their eyes appeared two large yams on top of the ground, where no one expected to find any. Everette never doubted that it was God who placed them there to save our family from starvation.

As mentioned earlier, Daah traveled to Trinidad in search of employment. What he saw in this new country was something greater than the little country village in Barbados where he grew up. He was young, energetic, industrious, and ambitious, and he was now adding a new dimension to his life.

His journey to Trinidad became the pivotal point around which my life moved from then on, from an obscure little village to a bigger and more complex world. During work on a small campus in Maracas Valley, he saw young men and women interacting in an academic environment. "Perhaps," he thought, "it may be too late for me, but when my children grow up, I would like them to attend this school."

Daah returned to Barbados and continued to work hard to support his family. Over the years, he tried to develop in us a sense of accountability and responsibility. I experienced this firsthand, and it significantly influenced my work ethic. Each weekday before walking to school, my brothers and I had assigned chores to complete; afterward, we had to walk a far distance to school. If a student arrived late, there was an inevitable flogging from the principal with a leather strap. I'd had a similar experience before, and I didn't want to repeat it.

One morning, it was getting late, and I was rushing to sweep the house. Hurriedly, I swept the dust behind the door, unaware that Daah was observing from behind me. Suddenly, he called out my name, and I felt his hand of correction as he uttered these unforgettable words: "Whatever your hands find to do, do it to the best of your ability" (Ecclesiastes 9:10). The pain was real, but Daah's words cut deeper and made a lasting impression on my mind. I learned the invaluable lesson of performing my tasks to the best of my ability. True character is developed most by the choices we make when no one is watching.

Another incident that stands out in my memory occurred when I was in my early teens. Daah was campaigning for the position of vestryman, and he asked me to write the letter of application for him because he said my handwriting was better than his. I was using his draft as a guide and mistakenly wrote the word "canidate" instead of "candidate." Right away, he recognized my error. I tried to squeeze in the missing "d," but it was unacceptable to him. I had to rewrite the entire letter. His correction of a seemingly insignificant letter taught me the importance of paying attention to details and helped to enhance my proofreading skills.

As children, Daah always made sure we were kept busy. He would often tell us that the devil finds work for idle hands to do, so he wanted our time to be well spent. I disliked watching our friends play and have fun while we performed our many chores; but, eventually, we all recognized the value of these early teachings. Before going to school, my brothers took care of the cows and sheep, and I did the housework, as well as wash clothes for the entire family. We also assisted in working the land, along with picking and cleaning cotton, which Daah sold to the cotton factory to augment the family income.

An activity that kept us very busy occurred during sugarcane season. We harvested sugarcane during the day and, sometimes, into the night. Daah and the boys cut the stalks down, and my sisters and I tied them on bands and carried them on our heads to the curb to be transported by truck to the factory. Our father was masterfully preparing us for the harsh demands of life, but we didn't realize it then.

Daah was a strict disciplinarian who didn't hesitate to discipline us using strong measures, and it seems that I was always being punished for one thing or another. I recall, though, a traumatic incident when he didn't administer punishment. My mother had gone a short distance away to visit her mom and had given me a piece of sugarcane to share with my siblings. I used a sickle, a sharp tool shaped like a semicircle with a handle, to cut the sugarcane. As I did that, I was watching a man walk by holding his walking stick behind his neck with his hands locked over the ends. At that instant, my brother, Edison, pointed to the piece of sugarcane he wanted. By the time my eyes returned to where I was cutting, I had accidently cut off the top joint of his index finger. I watched in shock as the piece of finger jumped around on the ground. Quickly, I ran to call Maah.

Daah was at work and returned home as soon as he got the bad news. Fearful of my fate, I hid under the bed. I heard when he entered the house but remained still in the hope that he wouldn't know I was there. He came into the bedroom and immediately looked under the bed. In an unusually calm voice, he said, "You can come out." Surprisingly, he didn't punish me. He took Edison to the doctor's office on his bicycle. The doctor inquired of the piece of finger, but we didn't have it. I recalled our neighbor picking it up but was unaware of what happened to it. The doctor sutured Edison's finger and sent him home. I don't believe that any punishment Daah would have given me could have been worse than the deep sorrow I felt at having inflicted this injury upon my brother.

On another occasion, I was sitting in my high school class and looked back to talk to a friend. In his effort to refocus my attention on what he was explaining, my teacher, a distant relative, threw a piece of chalk at me. Turning around, I asked smugly, "Am I a bird?" He looked at me sternly, but kept silent, which I thought was unusual. The following Sabbath evening, on my way home from the Missionary Volunteer Society meeting with my friends, my teacher rode by on his bicycle. I felt he was headed for my house, but pretended not to care. Deep inside, the fear of what was coming caused my stomach to churn.

On his way back, he called out, "Go home, something is waiting for you!" When I got home, Daah was sitting under the mahogany tree with the familiar whip in his hand. He told me to go to my bedroom, where he gave me a sound whipping as he uttered these words, "I sent you to school to learn, not to talk." This incident caused me to dislike my teacher, and many years passed before I forgave him. Reflecting on these experiences, horrible though they were, they had a positive impact on my character development.

On one of my visits home, I saw the concrete tub at the back of the kitchen that Daah had built in which we washed clothes. It immediately reminded me of an incident that occurred in my teens. Standing tall behind the tub was a coconut tree laden with coconuts, but we were not allowed to pick them. Nevertheless, if no one was around, I would claw my way up the tree and wring a coconut from the bunch before any unexpected witnesses showed up.

Daah observed that the coconuts were steadily decreasing, but, of course, no one admitted taking them. This particular morning, before washing the clothes, I yielded to the temptation to pick a coconut. I hastily climbed the tree, twisted one around, and dropped it to the ground. As I climbed down from the tree, I looked to see where to put my foot, and my eyes met my greatest nightmare. At the bottom of the tree stood my dad with his eyes riveted on me. I froze. Had I the wings of an eagle, I would have flown far away. His sharp voice broke the silence, "So, you're the culprit; come down!" When I reached the ground, once again, I was the recipient of one of his famous whippings. Many decades have passed since that day, but my brothers still enjoy a hearty laugh at that incident each time I visit home.

Daah was a serious, conscientious, dedicated church member, so we rarely missed church services, and he always made sure we participated in church activities. At the age of 14, Pastor W. W. Weithers, our pastor, visited our house to talk with my dad about my readiness for baptism. Daah, Pastor Weithers, and I sat in the living room for this somber occasion. Along with other topics, the pastor questioned me about the doctrines of the church. I have no idea what prompted him to do so, but, toward the end, he asked: "Have you ever eaten pork?" Ashamed, I hung my head and responded, "Yes," with a strong overtone of guilt. Daah looked at me with a stern face and blurted out: "Where did you get pork from when we don't cook pork in this house?" I had to confess that I got it from one of our non-Adventist cousins. Embarrassment covered his face as I stood guilty before him.

Pastor Weithers continued his questioning, "Have you ever eaten turtle?" I pondered if I should tell the truth and suffer the consequences or lie? They would never know, I thought to myself, but I would know, so I decided to tell the truth. I responded, "Yes," again. Daah was completely humiliated and ashamed. I confessed that I had purchased fried turtle from a little shop in the village. As Seventh-day Adventists, we adhered to the instructions in Leviticus 11 regarding the items that we should and should not eat, and I had violated those instructions. Now, my "sins" had returned to haunt me. You can "be sure your sins will find you out" (Numbers 32:23). Mine certainly did! In humility, I asked God to forgive me for my wrongdoing.

The day of my baptism arrived, and, on that beautiful Sunday morning, baptismal candidates, family, church members, and friends assembled at the beach for the baptismal ceremony. My turn came, and I waded into the water to the waiting pastor. When he attempted to immerse my body, I panicked and raised my head before he could put it under the water. Although I lived within walking distance of the sea, the fear of drowning overwhelmed me because I didn't know how to swim. Pastor Weithers tried to submerge my entire body, again, and, this time, he succeeded. Back then, if you had to be immersed a second time, some people believed that it was a sign you would eventually apostatize. I'm living proof that you can't believe everything that people say. I am grateful to God that, more than six decades later, I am still a committed Christian and church member.

In 1959, an evangelistic meeting was held in the Boscobelle community, and a new congregation was established. Some members of our family transferred from Checker Hall SDA Church to facilitate the establishment of this new group. My dad assisted with the erection of the Boscobelle SDA Church in the early '60s. For many years, he served as head elder, played the pump organ, faithfully carried out his responsibilities, and could be counted on to attend Sunday and Wednesday night prayer meetings.

In 1980 when my family returned to the U.S. from Nigeria, Daah spent time with us, along with DeLoras and her husband, Reggie, in Huntsville. He enjoyed going on early morning walks and watching the trains go by. He was happy to visit Oakwood College where three of his children had graduated. Later, seven of his grandchildren graduated also. He enjoyed his visit, and we were delighted to have him spend time with us.

Daah's visit to Huntsville

Daah was a hard worker, a devoted husband and father, and a dedicated elder who served the Lord and his church wholeheartedly. Sadly, in July 1989, he succumbed to the icy hand of death. As can be imagined, this was a horrific blow to our family. Daah, the great patriarch of our family, died at the age of 83. I was sitting in the Oakwood College Church when the shocking news came via an overseas call. He had passed without a chance for me to say goodbye or to tell him how deeply I appreciated all he had lovingly and sacrificially done for me. Dark waves of grief swept over me as I realized I would never talk to him again. It was a difficult time for our family, especially my mom; she loved him so much.

Although Daah's health had been declining, we were unprepared for his death. Everette said that the day before he passed, they had visited him at the healthcare facility, prayed with him, and left him in good spirits. Halstead and his son, James, traveled from the U.S. and visited him on their way home from the airport. They all had plans to spend time with him the following day. They were there, but he didn't know it. Life, how fragile? It is comforting to know that, when we pass through the valley of the shadow of death, we are not alone. Jesus walks beside us, upholding and strengthening us for the journey.

My dad loved the Lord and possessed high hopes and an unshakable faith that his children would become productive citizens serving God and humanity. He was blessed to see all of us become successful, and active members of the Seventh-day Adventist Church. This made him happy. His hard work had paid off, and his labor had not been in vain. Our parents handed down to their children the awesome legacy of love for God, His church, and His people; and the stamina, strength, perseverance, tenacity, and the value of hard work to accomplish all that our Heavenly Father has for us to do. To God be the glory!

Daah, a Great Father

Siblings

I am delighted to share a few snippets about my seven siblings. Everette, the oldest, was born while Maah was still a teenager. This is probably the reason that they share such a special bond that has extended throughout the years. He attended Parry School, later known as Coleridge and Parry. After completing high school, he had no plans to pursue further education. He wanted to get a job so he could earn his own money. At 18, he had one pair of trousers and one pair of shoes that he used for church, school, and everything in-between. With a job, he hoped to purchase the things he felt he needed, and, perhaps, contribute to the family, as well.

While working on the campus of Caribbean Training College in Maracas Valley, Daah caught the vision for his children to attend that institution after seeing young men and women intermingling in this spiritual environment. That vision of the future remained dormant in his heart for many years until the time was ripe. Now, the time had arrived, and he knew it.

Daah handed Everette an application form and told him to fill it out, that he was going to Caribbean Training College (CTC) in Maracas Valley—no questions asked! Being an obedient son, Everette completed the application but lacked a five-cent stamp to mail it. A week later, Daah asked Everette if he had mailed the application. Everette replied that he didn't have a stamp, so Daah gave him a stamp, and the application was mailed. Soon after, he received the letter of acceptance, which created quite a buzz of excitement in the Howell household: Everette was going to CTC!

No money was available for school fees, but God provided an opportunity for Daah to get a job in the nick of time. Maah immediately began preparation for his departure by making him two pairs of pajamas from a piece of cloth she had. Daah pulled out two more pieces he had tucked away in a drawer several months before and gave them to Everette to take to the tailors to make two suits.

At the time, Everette was unaware that the men whom he entrusted to make his suits were not professional tailors. When he returned to get them, they were not ready. He didn't get them until the evening before his departure. Unfortunately, when he tried them on, he found that one pair of pants was too long, and the jacket sleeve in one suit was stitched in with a twist. He didn't allow this to discourage him; he packed his things, said goodbye to his family and friends, and was off to CTC to pursue a two-year theology diploma.

He boarded a cargo ship that transported some passengers, and, for three days, he traveled on the deck to Trinidad via Grenada and St. Vincent. This arrangement offered the lowest fare. He landed at the Port-of-Spain harbor at night with only the equivalent of $15 in Bajan money in his pocket. The bread and fish sandwich that Maah had packed for him had spoiled, and he reluctantly threw it away. The taxi driver charged $10 to take him to Maracas, leaving him with only $5 to start college. He didn't have a pillow, blanket, nor sheets, but these luxuries were not as important as having the opportunity to be on a college campus and attend classes.

Daah told Everette that he was sending him to CTC to learn sense, and that he did. He was diligent in his studies, and, within two years, completed the requirements for graduation and was elected president of the Class of 1956. His professional career began as a ministerial intern on the island of St. Lucia. Later, he moved to Barbados where he served as assistant pastor to the late Pastor Milton Nebblett.

His service to the Seventh-day Adventist Church spans more than 60 years. He has served in various capacities, including Conference president, Union Secretary, Departmental director, missionary, pastor, counselor, teacher, lecturer, and more.

Everette is a graduate of Oakwood College and Andrews University where he received his master's degree. He is a certified Family Life Educator (AU), with a Diploma in Sociology (London). He is also a prolific writer and has published numerous articles and books, including his three latest: *Who Then is My Neighbor; Marriage and the Family—Resisting the Threats* published in 2012; and *The Transforming Power of the Holy Spirit for End Time Victories*, 2016.

Halstead, Rudolph, Neville, Everette

Halstead, the second child, received his high school education at Coleridge and Parry School and his teacher's certification from Erdiston College. He was an elementary school teacher for many years before attending Oakwood College where he graduated with a Bachelor of Science degree in Chemistry. He is grateful to the late Dr. Emerson Cooper, former chairman of the Oakwood Department of Chemistry, who provided job opportunities for him. Along with selling books in Georgia and Louisiana, working as an orderly in a hospital in N.Y. during his summer vacation, he was able to work his way through college. He's a graduate of Howard University College of Medicine, a Fellow of the American College of Surgeons (FACS), Fellow of the International College of Surgeons (FICS), and Licentiate Medical Council of Canada (LMCC). His surgery practice covered more than 30 years in the U.S., having worked in Maryland and Virginia before his retirement.

Currently, Halstead resides in Barbados and is actively involved in the Boscobelle SDA Church preaching, teaching, conducting the choir, playing the piano, and encouraging young people to read and study the Bible. He also serves as a part-time honorary Associate Lecturer to medical students, interns, and residents at the University of the West Indies.

Halstead has been a strong supporter and a financial contributor to his alma mater, Oakwood College. For many years, he contributed thousands of dollars to assist worthy students in accomplishing their dreams.

Rudolph, a certified electrical engineer, holds a bachelor's degree in electrical engineering from the Milwaukee School of Engineering. He is an entrepreneur and served as the CEO of his electrical and construction company in the U.S. before moving to Barbados. He is hardworking, kind, caring, generous, compassionate, and highly skilled in his area of expertise.

Edison, the fifth child, was a certified printer. He, too, was hardworking, kindhearted, generous, and humorous. Unfortunately, he suffered an untimely death in the U.S. in 1983. His passing brought tremendous grief to our family, especially to our parents. Daah became seriously ill as a result of this tragedy. Everette, who resided in England at the time, returned to Barbados to comfort them in their time of deep sorrow. We are thankful that God sustained them during this valley of grief.

Neville, the last son, attended Barbados Secondary School. He completed his training as a registered nurse in England and worked as a psychiatric nurse

Edison

in England and, then, at the Psychiatric Hospital in Barbados until his retirement. He followed in our dad's footsteps and became the head elder of the Boscobelle SDA Church, a position he has held for many years.

DeLoras attended Barbados SDA Secondary School and received her teacher's certification at Erdiston College. She taught elementary school before attending Oakwood College where she completed her bachelor's degree and obtained a master's degree in Early Childhood Education from Alabama A & M University. Her teaching career spanned more than 27 years in the Huntsville (Alabama) Public Schools. She's an excellent educator with an uncanny ability to tap into the minds of her students and inspire them to strive for excellence. Although retired, she continues to serve as an interventionist.

Cynthia, Shirley, DeLoras

Cynthia, the youngest sibling, attended Barbados SDA Secondary School and Caribbean Union College. By special request, she has asked that I put the following "greatly blessed, highly favored, imperfect, but forgiven child of God."

God has blessed her with an abundance of wisdom, creative, and architectural skills. She is active in her church and is a prayer warrior with a passion for witnessing. Since her retirement, she enjoys a more relaxed life spending time with her two handsome grandsons, Chase and Carter.

My parents were not privileged to complete high school, but God blessed them with wisdom and the determination to give their children the gift they didn't have. When I reflect on the wealth of blessings He has showered on our families, there is no doubt in my mind that He rewarded our parents' faithfulness, prayers, and efforts immensely. We praise and thank God for the wonderful gift of our parents.

"Behold, children are a heritage from the LORD, The fruit of the womb is a reward. Like arrows in the hand of a warrior, So are the children of one's youth" (Psalm 127:3, 4).

Chapter 2

Life in Two Caribbean Islands

*A*t an early age, I attended St. Lucy's Elementary Girls' School and, from there, the Modern High School. Later, I transitioned to the Barbados SDA Secondary School, which was the newly established Adventist high school located approximately 26 miles from my home. Christian teachers who served as positive role models profoundly influenced my journey. Among them were Lucy Kum, Ishbel Bayne, Rudolph Alleyne, B. G. O. French, Dr. Lizette Westney, Clarence Lashley, and others. During one of my visits to Barbados, I expressed my gratitude and appreciation to Ishbel Bayne and Rudolph Alleyne (now deceased) for the part they played in molding my character. More recently, I met Dr. Westney, and we were happy to see each other. I shared how what I learned from her greatly influenced my life.

It was during my final year in high school that I found myself trudging along nonchalantly without the slightest inkling that God had a plan and a purpose for my life. My dad's desire was for me to attend Caribbean Union College (CUC), formerly Caribbean Training College, but he was not impressed that I was serious about studying. To some extent, he was right. You see, back in 1958-1959, turmoil was brewing in the Middle East, and many Adventists thought that the Battle of Armageddon was on the verge of being fought with impending total destruction and that the imminent return of Jesus would follow. With such a prediction, I didn't see the need to devote much time to study. Obviously, I was proven wrong.

Daah spoke to a friend, who managed a healthcare facility, about enrolling me in a nursing class. Much to his disappointment, I didn't share his dream. The future looked bleak for me. Blindly, I arrived at a crossroad in my journey and pondered what to do and which way to turn. Unknown to me, God was charting my destiny. When it appeared that all hope of my attending CUC was beyond reach, I received an unexpected financial gift from Audrey Boyce, Everette's fiancée at the time, to cover my tuition for the first semester. Her generous act changed the course of my life and opened many doors that altered the outcome of my future. To Audrey, I say a heartfelt, "Thank You!"

Excitedly, I began to prepare for my new journey. Maah made me two dresses and gathered up a few items for me to take. Within a few weeks, I packed my few possessions in a "grip" (suitcase), said goodbye to my family and friends, and was on my way into an unknown future. Little did I know that this was the beginning of a new path which would take me to countries far across the ocean and completely change my life.

Funds were scarce, so I traveled by boat, the cheapest mode of transportation. Still vivid in my memory is holding on to the rope nervously as I walked up the shaky gangway of the boat with a prayer that I wouldn't slip and fall into the water. I was headed for the beautiful island of Trinidad, known as the land of calypso and carnival, to begin my college studies at CUC. CUC is nestled in a peaceful valley, surrounded by gorgeous mountain ranges and dense forests. The following day, I arrived safely on the campus. My dad's dream for one more of his children to attend this illustrious institution had become a reality.

Life at CUC was much different from that to which I was accustomed. I was in a strange country far away from my home environment with no mother or father overseeing me, and no big brothers to complain about me when I did something wrong. I was free at last, or so I thought. Then, reality hit me. Everything was scheduled—morning worship, breakfast in the cafeteria, work, classes, study period, room cleaning, and preparation of clothes for school and church, along with independent decision-making. Suddenly, all of the skills I had been taught at home came into play.

I had grown up in a village, but, now, I was intermingling with students from such countries as Venezuela, Guyana, Aruba, Curacao, Martinique, Antigua, Grenada, and St. Lucia. Some of my new acquaintances spoke Spanish, Dutch, French, and patois. Would I ever make it? Fortunately, a few of my friends from Barbados were now my classmates, and two of my former high school instructors had moved to Trinidad and were teaching at the college.

Living in Maracas Valley meant that a quick adjustment had to be made regarding the weather, which was somewhat colder than I was accustomed to. The nights were very cool because of the mountain ranges, and the water was extremely cold. In those days, there were no water heaters; so cold showers were the order of the day. As a result, my stay in the shower was always short and to the point. It was a lot easier adjusting to my classmates than the cold water. They were wonderful, brilliant, and talented, and we bonded beautifully from the start.

Over time, I adjusted to my new surroundings, established new friendships, attended classes, completed assignments, participated in church activities, and worked in the college cafeteria washing dishes for less than twenty cents an hour. I had arrived at a place in my journey for which my parents had been preparing me, although they were unaware of it, then.

One of the things I liked a lot was the cafeteria food. I enjoyed the new dishes and flavors. Red beans and rice and whole wheat bread were my favorites. The cafeteria was closed during Friday nights and Sabbath hours, so we were given sack lunches that consisted of a loaf of whole wheat bread along with boiled eggs, cheese, and margarine. We mashed these last three items together (mayonnaise enhanced the taste) and made sandwich filling for Friday supper and Sabbath breakfast. It was not unusual for me to eat all of my sack lunch on Friday nights with no food left for breakfast.

Peanut butter punch was one of my favorite drinks. It's delicious, but a fattening concoction made by blending peanut butter, evaporated milk, water, and sugar together with a fork or spoon. Within six months, my weight escalated from 138 lbs. to 166 lbs. My face got fat, and so did my hips. My school uniform skirt couldn't fit and had to be adjusted to accommodate my new size. Some of my classmates teased me a lot about my weight gain.

Living on the campus of CUC was different, interesting, and exciting. Before sunset on Fridays, our rooms had to be ready for inspection by the dean or residence hall monitor. Next came Vespers and, with it, a profound sense of reverence that settled all across the campus. Girls dressed up in their best attire and walked to chapel as beautifully recorded music saturated the evening breeze. It almost felt like we were being transported to the courts of heaven surrounded by holy angels. Worship services were highly spiritual and enriching.

For Sabbath service, girls dressed in all-white outfits. The guys wore black pants or suits with white shirts. During chapel, it was against the rules for young men and girls to sit next to each other, so guys sat on the right side and girls on the left.

Since I like to sing, I joined the choir. Before long, I also became involved in Sabbath School, Ingathering (door to door solicitation of money, foodstuffs, et cetera, for disaster relief), and other extracurricular activities. During breaks, no money was available to travel home to Barbados, so I stayed on campus and did housework for the family of Neville Ottley, a college administrator. Occasionally, Mrs. Lucy Kum, Chairperson of the Secretarial Science and Business Department, invited me to her home for weekend visits with her niece, Lucy, my friend and classmate. Mrs. Kum was a gourmet cook and prepared delicious, mouth-watering dishes which I enjoyed immensely. She was also a woman of class and elegance, and a great teacher who taught me many skills that remained with me throughout my professional career.

Studying was difficult, especially my accounting class, but, with God's help, I survived. In June 1961, with a heart filled with gratitude, I received my diploma along with members of my class. It was an exciting and thrilling moment, but, after the pomp and celebration had dissipated, questions began to loom in my head: Where do I go from here? Who will hire me?

I had heard a little rumor that my name was being considered for a position but had not received official word. So, following graduation, I returned to Barbados and waited anxiously for word about my employment. It was not long before an official letter arrived from CUC with a job offer. I am indebted to Mrs. Kum, who recognized my potential and recommended me for my first full-time job.

Shirley's CUC graduation

Shortly after receiving the good news, I returned to campus and took up residence in the living quarters that was labeled with the unflattering title of "Old Maids' Cottage," which housed single female employees. I began my duties as a hostess in the college cafeteria, worked with billings in the accounting office, as well as a library employee a few evenings a week. In addition to these responsibilities, I was involved in Sabbath activities as Sabbath School superintendent and Sabbath School teacher.

From CUC, my career path took me to the Adventist health clinic and, later, to Port-of-Spain Adventist Community Hospital; there I served in various capacities: receptionist, cashier, secretary, and medical secretary/records librarian. I also was privileged to work as secretary to William Shea, M.D., when he was medical director at the hospital. He was a kind, caring, and compassionate Christian physician with a friendly attitude. Other missionary doctors with whom I served included Victor Solonick, Trygve Opsahl, Cuthbert Arthur, and James Miyashiro. I was deeply impressed by their dedication, commitment, hard work, and willingness to sacrifice the comforts of their homes and lifestyles in the U.S. to bring health and healing to the sick and suffering on the island of Trinidad.

Working in the outpatient department of the hospital, I met patients from all walks of life. This experience taught me to be kind and helpful to everyone; you never know under what circumstance or situation you might meet them again. Here's an example: One of my responsibilities as a receptionist was to handle the registration of outpatients, some of whom traveled long distances in search of medical attention. Over the years, the hospital had gained the reputation of excellent patient care. Frequently, there were more patients than the doctors could attend to, and it was my responsibility to tell them they would have to return another day. I disliked this part of my job because it was sad to listen to their heartfelt pleas for help and even more sad to watch them walk away without receiving medical treatment.

Among the patients who visited the doctor was an elderly man whose son brought him to the clinic. Occasionally, I assisted him with a wheelchair as his son parked the car. It never occurred to me that my kindness would pay off one day.

In preparation for travel to the U.S. to pursue further study, I submitted my application for a new passport to the passport office and was given a specific date to return. When I went back, the clerk informed me that my passport was not ready and that I would have to come back. Needless to say, I was unhappy. I had used my lunch break and paid the taxi fare to get to the passport office. Now, I would have to return to work empty-handed. Frustrated, I walked away without even thinking to pray about the situation.

Hurrying down the street to get a taxi, I saw a man, who looked familiar, walking toward me. As we approached each other, I recognized him as Mr. Boydkin who used to bring his father to the hospital for treatment. After our greetings, he asked, "Nurse, what brings you to this side of town?" I didn't hesitate to complain about my experience at the passport office, and that I would have to take more time off from work to return. He said he was sorry and invited me to come with him. I obeyed without questioning why, which was out of character for me. I followed him as he walked into the passport office. He invited me to sit down and said that he would be right back. Within a few minutes, he returned, handed me my passport, and wished me success with my plans. When I opened the passport, I was surprised to see Mr. Boydkin's signature as the passport officer. Until that moment, I had no idea where he worked. I thanked him for his kindness and left his office praising God for this unexpected miracle.

While sitting in the taxi on my way back to work, a verse of scripture popped into my head that my father often repeated in my childhood. This experience caused its real significance to hit me: "Cast your bread upon the waters for you shall find it after many days" (Eccl. 11:1). More than 50 years have passed since that unforgettable day and my passport has long since expired, but I've kept it as a reminder of God's faithfulness, Mr. Boydkin's kindness, and that scripture.

During my service at Port-of-Spain Community Adventist Hospital, I lived in the homes of Carmen Lynch and Alecia Maitland. Their devotion and love for God and the wonderful Christian atmosphere in their homes impressed me deeply. Worships were inspiring, and the environment was nurturing. Both families exhibited the essence of Christianity through their kindness and generosity. They indeed possessed the fruit of the Spirit. I believe God placed these dear ones in my life at that particular point to help me in my spiritual growth. We have remained dear friends over the years.

"I will instruct you and teach you in the way you should go; I will counsel you with my loving eyes on you" (Psa. 32:8, NIV).

Chapter 3

Higher Education in the USA

*P*eriodically, we all have to perform a little self-analysis to determine what our next steps will be. "Who am I?" "What am I doing?" "Where am I going?" "How do I plan to get there?" I had reached the point in my journey where the answers to those questions would shape my future. Although my work at the hospital was fascinating, it was hard to ignore the nagging desire to improve myself academically. After answering these questions for myself, I began more intentionally to set aside a portion of my meager income each month toward my education.

It took approximately four years to save $1,000 U.S., the deposit required of international students. I applied to two schools in the U.S.: Oakwood College and Andrews University (AU). Having friends at both institutions, I decided to attend the first one that responded to my application. With my acceptance letter from Andrews University in hand, I submitted a letter to the hospital administrator requesting study leave.

In August 1965, I traveled home to Barbados where I spent some time with my family before departing for the U.S. A week later, I arrived in Philadelphia and spent several days with my great aunt, Aunt Dora, whom I had never met, but I'd worn beautiful clothes that she had shipped to Barbados. I was delighted to spend time with her. It was at her home that I got my first exposure to living in America. What a difference life was from life in

Barbados and Trinidad. Before leaving for AU, Aunt Dora took me shopping to purchase a winter coat and a few items in preparation for the cold weather.

Soon, I was on the road again. I traveled by car with Everette and his family to AU, where he was enrolled in the graduate program. The car was old, and the distance was more than 600 miles, very far for me. I had never traveled such a long distance by car before, and I thought we would never reach our destination. On the highways, I saw strange signs all along the way. The one I couldn't make sense of was "Do Not Pass." How did they expect us to get where we were going without passing? It was later that I learned that "Do Not Pass" meant not to overtake another vehicle at that point in the road.

It was exciting to finally reach the campus. I was about to embark on a new chapter in my journey. My three West Indian roommates, Joy Nembhard Peters, Thelda Van Lange Greaves, and Sherri Smith, were instrumental in helping me adjust to my new home-away-from-home. Thelda and I were friends from Trinidad, so that was a plus. Four of us shared a room, known as Room 10, in the basement of Lamson Hall. Fortunately for us, our dispositions blended well.

Soon, though, my euphoria wore off, and reality set in. I had been out of school for four years and experienced difficulty getting back into "study mode." After registration and the beginning of classes, it was not long before cold weather set in, which called for a significant physical adjustment on my part. Coming from the Caribbean where it's warm all year, I came face to face with bitter cold weather and snow. Wearing boots and thick winter coats didn't help much, either; it was a difficult time for me.

I can still remember my first introduction to snow. It happened one Friday night while I was sound asleep. It seemed as if the sky opened up and blanketed rooftops, trees, cars, and the earth with a very thick layer of lily-white, fluffy snow. Upon awakening the next morning, we were surprised to see that the campus had been transformed from the darkness of the night to a winter wonderland. It was breathtakingly beautiful.

Shirley's First Snow

Something that I had little understanding of and considered crazy was that business continued as usual, with or without snow. I was amazed that workmen continued with construction, as usual. And, even worse, we still had to attend classes! My English teacher told us that, even if a tornado blew away our assignment, we were still expected to submit it in class. I felt it was heartless of our teachers to expect us to attend classes or to go to work with this thick, cold, white stuff pasted on every area of the ground.

In addition to carrying a full academic load, I worked in the cafeteria collecting dirty dishes from the window and preparing them for the giant machine where they were washed. I also cleaned tables. I had now become a professional dish room worker. Work began at 6:00 a.m., rain, sun, or snow. Many mornings, I didn't want to get out of bed to face the cold weather, but, somehow, I always made it on time. Mr. Craig, my elderly dish room supervisor, was kind and friendly. He made us laugh with his funny jokes, which helped to lessen the dullness of the work and made the time go by faster.

Life at AU wasn't too bad. Everette was a graduate student in the Theological Seminary during my first year there, and he and his wife, Audrey, occasionally invited me to their apartment for Sabbath lunch where I got to spend time with their little daughter, Richelle. Also, Thelda's uncle, Ivan Van Lange, my former health science teacher at CUC, lived in Chicago, and he took us to spend a weekend with his family. His wife, Grace, and I had lived a few miles from each other in Barbados, and had attended the same church and graduated from CUC in the same class. I looked forward to those opportunities to get away from campus.

My roommates and I were fortunate to have two West Indian families living in the community who were caring and hospitable. From time to time, they invited students to their homes for Sabbath lunch and fellowship. I still cherish fond memories of delicious meals at the homes of Dr. Ken and Lynette Riley and the late Pastor and Mrs. Zadok Reid.

As time progressed, I found myself adjusting to my new way of life. Before long, my first year had come to an end, and I was pleased with my GPA of 2.75 on a 3.00 scale. With this significant step behind me, my search for summer employment began. As an international student, I didn't know much about life in the U.S. and was unsure how I would obtain money for my tuition for the upcoming semester, but God already had a plan in place. Glyne, my classmate and a fellow "Bajan," invited me to spend the summer vacation at her home in Hartford, Connecticut.

I travelled by car with friends to New York, then on to Hartford. The following day, my job search began. It was a daunting and scary experience, checking advertisements in the newspaper for jobs and walking the streets of a strange city going from one employment agency or one business to another, day after day until I almost walked the soles off of my shoes. My job situation looked bleak. Feelings of doubt and anxiety began to invade my head. The thought that I had made the wrong decision to come to Hartford plagued me. Just as I was about to give up my search, God opened wide the door of employment at Circuit Court 14 in Hartford and kept it open until my graduation. This job lasted for two summers, enabling me to obtain the necessary funds for tuition.

It was an extraordinary as well as an interesting privilege which proved to be educationally and financially rewarding. I prepared court documents, did secretarial work, served as cashier, and filled in for staffers on vacation. Monday was my least favorite day because the court was usually filled with alcoholics who had been arrested over the weekend and for whom court papers had to be processed. Also, the stench that remained in the courtroom after their departure often traveled into the office.

My work area was located in the central office, and I sat behind a gorgeous Black woman named Lois, who befriended me. In those days, very few people of color worked at the circuit court, so I was happy to meet her. On one occasion, she whispered, "You make me look good; these people are impressed with your work and want you to stay." Some weeks later, Ms. Alma Dibella, the chief administrator, called me to her office and expressed appreciation for my work and invited me to become a full-time employee.

In addition to my circuit court job, I worked in the evenings for a telemarketing company. During my four-hour shift, I made phone calls to people at their homes to persuade them to purchase popular magazines. It was stressful because no one wanted to be bothered and often hung up the phone without giving me the chance to explain the purpose of my call. Anyone who didn't make their quota for the week was released. God blessed, and I was able to maintain my quota and keep my job for two summers.

Occasionally, on Sundays, I did secretarial work for a sheriff. When I received my paychecks, to avoid the temptation to go shopping, I purchased a money order immediately and mailed it to the business office at AU to be put toward my fall tuition.

Before long, the summer ended. Because of limited funds, I traveled by bus back to campus. Some passengers changed buses in Detroit and had to wait for several hours for a bus to Benton Harbor. I was afraid that someone would try to steal my luggage, so I slept with one eye closed and the other on my suitcase. The journey was long and tiring, but I made it back safely to campus. My roommates and I were happy to see each other.

During my second year at AU, I had a new roommate, Gloria Brown, a Jamaican. Also, I graduated from the dish room to the bindery, a further distance from my residence hall. One morning, I was hurrying to get to work when I slipped and fell in the snow. I got up quickly, looked around to see if anyone was watching, and started walking hurriedly. I hadn't gone too far when I fell, again. I never got used to the snow.

Singing was one of my hobbies and an extracurricular activity that brought much satisfaction. I became a member of both the University Choir and the Women's Chorale which was conducted by Marianne Sjoren. My roommates, Joy, and Thelda, were gifted pianists, and, occasionally, we provided special music for churches in surrounding communities.

Pioneer Memorial Church was where I attended most worship services. Dorm worships were fine, but, on those mornings when I didn't have to work, it was hard to get out of bed and dressed for the 6:00 a.m. worship service, especially if I had stayed up late the night before to study. It was compulsory to attend a certain number of worship sessions per week or face a penalty.

One morning, the first bell, signaling the warning before the start of worship, had rung. Without enough time to change, I grabbed my winter coat, covered my red pajamas, and ran upstairs to the chapel. The door was still open when I reached the chapel, but the residence hall monitor pulled back my coat exposing my pajamas and refused to let me enter. This caught me off-guard, but I politely informed her that I was private property and that she had no right to do that. Reluctantly, she allowed me to enter.

This monitor was often stricter than the deans. I recall an incident that took place during my final year when my roommate, Beulah, concocted a plan to scare her. One night, Beulah made up her bed so it looked like someone was sleeping in it; then, she hid in the closet before the monitor entered. As usual, the monitor walked in, checked the room, and, on her way out, Beulah dashed out of the closet and frightened her. It was hilarious to hear our stern monitor scream to the top of her voice. Beulah and I had a good laugh, but, of course, the monitor was furious.

Studying continued to be a challenge. A challenging course I had to take was Anatomy and Physiology, taught by Mr. Heidkte. He was known as a very tough professor. We had to dissect a cat and memorize the names of its muscles. I didn't particularly like living cats; now, I had to handle a dead one to get a grade. What further added to my dislike of the class was the smell of formaldehyde that remained on my fingers no matter how diligently I scrubbed them.

For the final exam, my roommates and I stayed up most of the night trying to memorize muscles and a slew of other overwhelming details. The next morning, I ran hurriedly to take the test. It was very hard. The only thing I could recall without difficulty was how to spell my name. Anyhow, God had compassion on me, and, gradually, I regained some of my memory and was able to pass the test.

Among my many memories of life at Andrews was the time I took a Home Economics class from Martha Lorenz. One of the class requirements was to make a dress. After taking my measurements, she remarked, "You have a perfect figure; you should become a model." Such a thought never crossed my mind. I was unaware of anything unusual about my figure. It was certainly nice of her to make that comment.

Another memorable moment occurred when Dr. George Akers, a highly respected and loved faculty member, called out my name among the top ten best-dressed female students at AU. He had conducted a "Facets of Femininity Week" in Lamson Hall Chapel, and, at its conclusion, he read the results of a survey he had sent to faculty members. I was surprised that the faculty knew I existed, and even more taken aback when my name was called in this context.

Time rolled by quickly, and I completed my second year successfully and again headed to Circuit Court 14 for my summer employment. Upon my return to campus, I got a new job working in the Catalog Department of James White Library, a new room (5333) in the new addition to Lamson Hall, and a new roommate, Beulah Andrews, a friend whom I knew from Trinidad. By the end of the Fall Semester 1967, I had completed the course requirements for graduation; however, International students had to be enrolled in school to remain in the U.S., so I registered for two classes and increased my work hours in the library for the winter semester. God blessed tremendously, and I completed my studies.

My graduation was June 2, 1968, an extraordinarily high day for me. With inexpressible joy, I happily walked across the stage of the Pioneer Memorial Church and received my bachelor's degree in Secretarial Science with a minor in Home Economics. I am eternally grateful to God, Dr. Glyne Thorington, her mother, Mrs. Enid Thorington (now deceased), and other family members

Shirley's AU graduation

who allowed me to stay in their home for two summers. Their generosity enabled me to acquire the money for my tuition, and their kind act was the beginning of a beautiful friendship that has lasted more than 50 years.

God had my future all planned long before I was born. The Psalmist David put it succinctly:

"Your eyes saw my unformed body. All the days ordained for me were written in your book before one of them came to be" (Psalm 139:16, NIV).

Chapter 4

Love, Courtship, and Marriage

Before sharing with you how my relationship with Morris Iheanacho got started, I want to give you a few snippets about his background. "Dè Morris," as anyone of the Igbo tribe of Nigeria younger than he respectfully calls him, was born in the little vil-

lage of Mgboko Obete, about ten miles from Aba, in eastern Nigeria. As an only child, he was very attached to his mother and still recalls being breastfed until the age of four years old. His mother loved him dearly and nicknamed him, "Nna." His grandmother called him "Nwokoma." He recalls that, whenever he visited his grandmother's house, she always prepared delicious soup for him. Some of his male cousins told me that he was a well-behaved youngster and that their parents often admonished them to be like him.

His mother, Florence Sophia Iheanacho, was the only Seventh-day Adventist among her siblings, so Morris attended the Seventh-day Adventist church from birth. He was four years old when his dad passed, leaving his mother a single parent. Morris and his mother shared a

Mrs. Florence Sophia Iheanacho

special bond. He was her pride and joy, and she was willing to make any sacrifice necessary for her beloved son. He shared an incident that happened when he was attending an elementary school that demonstrated how deeply she loved him.

He was studying for an exam and asked his mother to prepare a special breakfast for him the following morning. It was dark when she went outside to get the yams and was unaware that a poisonous snake lurked in the darkness. It bit her ankle and caused it to swell. Morris was distraught. Fortunately, the local herbalist came to her aid, drained the poison, and applied a special remedy to soothe the pain and relieve the swelling. She was confined to bed for several days but recovered completely.

Morris recalls how he had to walk without shoes seven miles to and from elementary school every day. With no husband to assist her, his mom struggled to keep him in school. One morning, he was crying on his way to school when a relative stopped him and asked him what was wrong. Morris told him that his mother didn't have money for his school fees and he didn't want to go to school because the teacher would whip him for not having his school fees. His kind relative gave him the money and told him that his mother could repay him when she got the money, which she did.

Morris worked hard on the family farm where he assisted his mother in planting and harvesting produce. He then had to walk several miles to the market in Aba to sell them. From an early age, he was trained to work hard.

Following completion of elementary school, Morris was unable to attend high school because of his mother's inability to pay his tuition. As a result, he enrolled in a preparatory evangelism school where he received training as an evangelist. He successfully completed the course requirements and was assigned to pastor several churches.

Working as a pastor in that period was tough; the salary was meager, with barely enough to manage one's bills. Morris' mom, also a seamstress like my mom, sold her sewing machine to purchase an old bike so that he could cover the 20 miles that constituted his

Morris A. Iheanacho

territory to visit his churches and parishioners. Back in the 1960s, bicycles were the popular mode of transportation; many pastors used them because it was all they could afford.

Morris had a thirst for knowledge and tried to improve himself at every opportunity. While carrying out his pastoral responsibilities, he took correspondence courses in preparation for the General Certificate of Education (high school equivalent). In 1961, he was selected by the East Nigerian Conference to attend the Adventist College of West Africa (now Babcock University). He and two male students were members of the second class to enter ACWA. They worked on the college farm to help defray their tuition expenses.

On a recent visit to the home of our friends, Fyneboy and Margaret Obiocha in Hartford, Connecticut, Morris and Fyneboy chatted about the days spent at ACWA and recalled how they complained about the vegetarian meals the missionary cook prepared. The students wanted their traditional soup with fish and meat. As they have matured, they have regretted complaining because they realized that she was just trying to teach them to eat healthily.

As Morris neared the end of his studies, graduation seemed impossible, because, once again, he lacked the money to pay his tuition. He shared his predicament with Dr. Roger Coon, an American missionary who served in Nigeria for several years. Dr. Coon was impressed to help him and contacted friends in the U.S. who provided the money Morris needed to graduate. He deeply appreciated Dr. Coon's kindness and generosity.

He continued his pastoral responsibilities but later enrolled at Newbold College in England where he received his diploma in theology and history, while simultaneously earning his bachelor's degree from Columbia Union College in Takoma Park, Maryland, now Washington Adventist University. At the time, Newbold College had an affiliation with Columbia Union College. After graduation, Morris returned home and continued his pastoral ministry.

Among the cities he pastored were Aba, Port Harcourt, and Calaba, located in eastern Nigeria. He also served as an interpreter for the late Pastor C. Dunbar Henri, a missionary/evangelist, who conducted evangelistic meetings in eastern Nigeria. Morris was also privileged to assist the late Dr. E. E. Cleveland, a world-renowned evangelist, with evangelistic meetings held in Accra, Ghana.

With a deep interest in pursuing graduate studies, Morris began to prepare himself to take advantage of the opportunity when it became available. From Nigeria, he traveled to Sweden where he worked as a book salesman for two summers selling Christian books to raise his tuition to attend Andrews University (AU). Selling books in Sweden without being able to speak nor understand the language was difficult. He tried to learn as much of the language as he could to communicate with potential customers; however, if the prospective buyer didn't understand or speak English, neither Morris nor his fellow salesperson, James Kio, could converse with them.

On one occasion, Morris and James made a presentation, but their prospective customer only understood Swedish. Unfortunately, neither Morris nor James could understand what he was saying. In their effort to try to explain the details of purchasing books, Morris spoke in his Igbo language and Kio in Yoruba. None of them could understand what the other was saying. Morris said it sounded like they were speaking in tongues. This must have been a hilarious sight, and they all laughed at each other good-naturedly. In spite of the language barrier, God blessed them with a sale.

During his time in Sweden, Morris made tremendous sacrifices to save as much money as possible. He ate peanut butter, cheese, cucumber, and honey sandwiches for breakfast and supper and looked forward eagerly to Sabbaths when Swedish families at the church he attended invited them for lunch. The kindness and hospitality of these strangers deeply impressed him. Also, he and his teammate offered to mow the landlord's lawn, and, in return, he permitted them to stay at his home rent-free. With perseverance, hard work, and God's blessings, he saved the necessary funds to pursue graduate studies at AU.

My first recollection of Morris was during the Fall of 1967. He was a graduate student but had to take an undergraduate class in American History, a prerequisite for his graduate coursework. I was an undergraduate taking the same class. The school had already been in session for several days when this handsome gentleman walked into the classroom carrying his briefcase and walking with an air of sophistication and the self-confidence of a professor. Right away, my curiosity was piqued; very few Black students were in my class and certainly none of his stature. His profile still stands out in my memory. He was wearing a nicely tailored suit, which he told me later, he had purchased in Sweden. His cheeks were round, and his hair was cut short. My eyes followed him to his seat as I thought to myself, "He sure thinks he's hot stuff." I was reluctant to admit that I thought so too.

We had no communication between us until spring of the following year. I was exiting the James White Library, where I worked when I heard footsteps behind me. When I looked back, my eyes met Morris' as he walked hurriedly to catch up with me. I knew his name because I had seen his picture in the *Cast*, a book which contained the pictures of students enrolled at the university, along with information regarding their place of origin, classification, etc. We greeted each other and talked briefly. I was reticent to entertain a conversation with him, so I hastened on to shorten our time together.

Soon after arriving in my dorm room, I received a message that I had a phone call. Cautiously, I picked up the phone, wondering who could be calling me. Lo, and behold, to my surprise, it was Morris. We didn't talk for a very long time because, as far as I was concerned, he had two major strikes against him: He was from Africa, and, over the years, we had bought into many of the negative stereotypes perpetuated by the media and hearsay. Needless to say, many of the stories were not very complimentary to Africa or its people. To make matters worse, one of the stereotypes was that African men had more than one wife. Secondly, I am five feet, ten inches tall, and his height is five feet, eight inches. I had no interest in marrying someone shorter than me.

My nonchalant attitude didn't deter him in the least; he continued to call me. After some time, I began to look forward to his calls, which caused me to ponder what was going on inside my heart. One Saturday night, he invited me to a Lyceum program. As we walked across the campus to the building where the Lyceum was being held, I felt his hand reach for mine. Having been raised in the West Indian culture, holding hands on a first date was unacceptable. I kept my hand in my coat pocket while silently asking myself, "Why is this man trying to hold my hand when he doesn't even know me?"

As time passed, our friendship grew and deepened as we continued to interact and learn more about each other. Later, I met some of his Igbo friends when he invited me along with them to his apartment for Sabbath lunch. We enjoyed good fellowship; and, of course, the food was finger-lickin' good. He's a great cook!

By this time, I was beginning to sense the concern of some of my friends who felt that Morris might be married or have other women in Nigeria and that he would probably take me to his country, and they'd never see me again. I didn't share their concern because of some of his Nigerian friends, who knew him, assured me that he was a gentleman and was not married. So, we continued to share each other's company.

Before graduation, I had been asked to continue my work in the Catalog Department of the AU library but declined the offer to give myself time away from the influence of my friends to decide if I wanted my relationship with Morris to proceed. I had also received an offer of employment from the Chief Administrator at Circuit Court 14 in Hartford; however, I decided to go to Washington, D.C., where my brother, Halstead, was attending medical school at Howard University. I planned to live with him and his wife, Margaret until I found my bearings.

Following graduation, I said goodbye to Morris and my friends and boarded the bus for the U.S. Capitol. It was a long and tiring journey, but I finally arrived safely. Shortly after, the country was plunged into deep sadness by the assassination of Robert Kennedy, brother of John F. Kennedy. The day following my arrival, the interview process began; this proved quite tedious. After a few unsuccessful interviews, I was offered a job with the Organization of American States but accepted the position of secretary to Dr. Roland Scott, Professor and Chairman of the Department of Pediatrics at Howard University School of Medicine. Dr. Scott was highly recognized for his extensive research in sickle cell anemia. I was privileged to work and interact with many notable medical professionals and researchers from around the world.

One of the blessings of working at Howard University was that my job was within walking distance of where I resided, and, since I didn't know how to drive and funds were limited, I didn't have to worry about transportation. Halstead rented the upstairs portion of a house, and the landlady lived downstairs. Occasionally, I walked home for lunch.

One day, as I walked up the stairs, it was evident that our place had been burglarized. Clothes and papers were scattered on the floor, and the room was in disarray. Cautiously, I entered the bedroom, fearful that the thief might still be around. Upon noticing that the drawer where I kept my tithes and offerings was open, I checked it immediately. To my surprise, the money was still in the envelope, untouched, although most of the contents of the drawer were on the floor; proof to me that my Master Protector had kept it safe from the eyes of the thief. The intruder was never caught.

Morris and I continued to talk on the phone regularly, resulting in a rapidly increased long distance telephone bill. One hot summer day, he drove from Benton Harbor, where he was employed at a tire factory, to Washington, D.C. Since some of his relatives lived in the D.C. area, it worked out well when he visited. He later confessed that the trip seemed shorter when he was coming to see me, but on his return, time appeared to drag on.

By now, our friendship was becoming very serious so Morris wrote a letter to my dad, who lived in Barbados, requesting my hand in marriage. I learned from DeLoras, some years later, that, when the letter arrived, my family was curious about this unknown young man from an unknown country they had never heard of before. They wondered where in the world Biafra was. They searched the map to find its location and any other pertinent information. My dad was amenable to what they found and granted permission for Morris to marry his daughter. I was happy to receive the good news.

During the holiday season, December 1968, Morris popped the question, "Will you marry me?" Without hesitation, I accepted his offer, and we were engaged during this festive season. I must admit that my positive response to his question altered my life significantly. Immediately, I began to plan our wedding with the help of Margaret and my friend, Claire Hosten.

My biggest concern was finding shoes to fit my long feet. For those inquiring minds, I wear a size 12; women with large feet will understand. Mrs. Lynch, my former landlord in Trinidad, had immigrated to New York, and she invited me to spend a weekend with her. We walked from one store to the next in search of shoes and my wedding gown. It was exhausting and discouraging, but we finally found beautiful selections that fit well.

It was rough, at times, trying to juggle the demands of work and make wedding plans, but, with God's help, I managed. Before long, our wedding day arrived. On a beautiful sunny Sunday afternoon, August 17, 1969, to be exact, at the First Seventh-day Adventist Church in Washington, D.C., my family, loved ones, and friends gathered from near and far to witness this celebratory moment. Beaming with joy, I walked down the aisle holding Halstead's arm with my heart beating rapidly as enchanting wedding music filled the sanctuary.

From a distance, I could see sparkles in Morris' eyes as he stood at the altar. The moment that we had waited for had come; to share our lives together, to have and to hold, in sickness and health, in joy and sorrow, for richer or poorer, till death separated us. I can hardly believe that more than 47 years have gone by since that unforgettable day. The memory is still vivid in my mind.

The ceremony was beautiful. My friend, Yvonne Roberts, sang "Entreat Me Not to Leave Thee," accompanied by Nevilla Ottley Adjahoe on the organ. Nevilla's dad, whom I called Daddy Ottley, sang the "Wedding Prayer." His rich and melodious tenor voice wafted through the air with sweet music. With great delight, in the presence of my family and friends, like Ruth, the Moabite, I vowed: "Whither you go, I will go;... your people shall be my people, and your God my God" (Ruth 1:16). It was a thrilling and incredibly breathtaking experience. Surprisingly, something happened during the ceremony that created concern and anxiety among some of our guests that, many years later, still evokes laughter from my friends when we meet.

Morris' & Shirley's Wedding

Pastor Lionel Arthur, the officiating minister, had difficulty pronouncing Morris' surname, although he had practiced it several times before our wedding day. I was amused when he asked me to repeat the name after him. The way he pronounced it (I-hen-e-ah-nah-ko instead of E-han-ah-cho) caused me to laugh. Try as I may, I couldn't stop laughing. I beckoned for him to continue, but, instead, he said, "No, you have to repeat after me, 'I, Shirley Cyrene Howell, do take Morris Achor I-hen-e-ah-nah-ko as my lawfully wedded husband.'" Hearing this hilarious mispronunciation again, caused me to shake with laughter even more.

By now, a serious expression covered Morris' face, but I just couldn't stop laughing. Finally, after a long pause, I muttered the words and Pastor Arthur completed the ceremony. Some guests, unaware of what was happening, thought that I had changed my mind about marrying Morris. His Igbo friends were unhappy with me, too. Sorry, but I just couldn't help it. Later when I listened to the tape, there was an extremely long pause, and I found myself laughing again. It became evident to me, then, why people were so concerned. My friend, Dr. Iola Brown, visited us recently, and she said that every time she recalls our wedding she still laughs, 47 years later.

Mr. & Mrs. Morris Iheanacho

Years before, when I made the decision to attend Andrews University, it never occurred to me that I would marry someone from Africa. Now, I had been transformed from a single country girl to Mrs. Shirley Iheanacho. And to think that God had this precious gift handsomely wrapped waiting for me to open it. One of my favorite texts comes to mind, "For I know the plans I have for you," says the Lord, "plans to prosper you and not to harm you, plans to give you hope and a future" (Jeremiah 29:11). Yes, God had a plan for my life, and, like a mosaic, piece by piece, He was putting it together to form a gorgeous picture. And, so began my journey as Mrs. Iheanacho.

"And now abide faith, hope, love, these three; but the greatest of these is love"
(1 Cor. 13:13, NKJV).

Chapter 5

New Beginnings

F ollowing an exciting honeymoon at Aunt Dora's home in Philadelphia and my resignation from Howard University, we drove to Kalamazoo, Michigan. Morris had transferred from AU to Western Michigan University to pursue his master's degree in Library Science. We settled in our apartment, and I began the tedious task of finding employment.

We had only one car, and I didn't know how to drive, so we prayed earnestly that I would find a job near the university. After a few unsuccessful job interviews, I accepted the position as secretary to the administrator of the Kalamazoo County Board of Supervisors. My first day on the job, I encountered an embarrassing situation. My boss asked for a cup of coffee. A glass pot was sitting on the percolator with dark liquid in it, and I assumed that was what he wanted, so I filled the cup and gave it to him. He took a sip, and his eyes opened wide as he looked at me and blurted out, "This coffee is stale; you need to make a fresh pot!" I didn't know how to prepare coffee, so I got my first coffee-making lesson from my boss. Thankfully, he didn't fire me.

Working in the office of the officials who ran the county government was informative and educational. I had the opportunity to meet and interact with government officials, administrators, judges, and attorneys. One observation that stuck out was that they were just a few Black employees in the county building. Fortunately, I was accepted by the Board of

Supervisors and didn't experience any problems. My boss was friendly, and so were his charming wife and children.

While studying, Morris worked as a student library assistant in the university library to obtain extra income; he also took care of dog kennels owned by a government official. Needless to say, working in the dog kennel was his least favorite job for several reasons, but he was confident that, with God's help, it would only be temporary. In addition to my new job, I sold AVON products in surrounding apartment complexes to help supplement our income.

Gradually, I grew accustomed to married life and learned to write and pronounce my new name with ease. I also learned a lot about my husband, his country, and his culture. It was during this period that the Biafran War was raging between eastern Nigeria (Biafra) and the rest of Nigeria. Every evening when he arrived home from school, Morris painstakingly kept his ears glued to the BBC radio listening for news about the conditions in his country.

This period was a very stressful time for him, not only because he knew nothing of the whereabouts of his family, but also because he didn't know what was happening in his village. Relief came when the war ended, and he received word of his family's safety. The good news brought him joy and peace of mind knowing that God had sheltered his family during this dreadful time.

Life in Kalamazoo was somewhat lonely, at first, because I was not familiar with anyone outside of my work environment. We attended the little Black Adventist Church in the community, and, as time progressed, we made friends with some of the church members and participated in the worship activities. Sometimes, I provided special music for Sabbath School and divine worship. Occasionally, we were blessed to have two ministerial interns from the AU Theological Seminary in Berrien Springs come and preach at our church. We looked forward to their visits to our apartment, after the service, for Sabbath lunch and fellowship.

From time to time, we traveled to Chicago to visit our Igbo friends, Josiah and Rachel Nwaogwugwu. It was during one of these visits that we experienced an embarrassing situation while returning to Kalamazoo. Since I didn't know how to drive, Morris did all the driving, and I tried (unsuccessfully) to be his navigator. Not being too familiar with road signs, I was unsure of how to get to the Kalamazoo exit. Several times, I told Morris that we were on the wrong exit, and he would turn around. Each time, we had to pay the toll. Later, it became apparent that we were to follow the Chicago exit until it branched off to the Kalamazoo exit.

We finally found it, but, by this time, we had depleted our cash on tolls. Morris observed that the gas gauge was on empty, so he stopped at the nearest gas station, and pumped gas into our car. There was not enough cash to pay the attendant, so I wrote a check. Unfortunately, he refused to take it and insisted that we pay with cash or credit card; we had neither. We were both dumbfounded when he walked to the car with a plastic container, inserted a long tube into the gas tank, and siphoned out the gas. Humiliated and embarrassed, we drove away, concerned that not enough gas remained in the tank to get us to our apartment. Here, again, God had already worked it out, and we made it home safely.

Over time, we adjusted to our new life and, after several months, I became pregnant, with the attendant morning sickness. My boss' wife, Marge, created a special box, labeled "Shirley's Survival Kit" in which she placed all kinds of goodies to help ease my stomach discomfort. I was deeply appreciative of her thoughtfulness.

Morris worked hard to complete his graduate studies and, in August 1970, he walked across the stage, with a deep sense of satisfaction and accomplishment, to receive his Master of Science degree in Librarianship from Western Michigan University. It was an exciting moment to witness the culmination of his hard work. We thanked God for making Morris' dream become a reality.

With graduation behind him, his search for full-time employment began. He traveled to distant locations for job interviews but without success. Prospective employers were excited and interested in his credentials when they talked with him on the phone; but, when he appeared in person, for obvious reasons, he was rejected. In late September, he accepted an invitation to travel to Washington, D.C., for an interview. He was strongly impressed that he would be hired and that we would move to D.C. Unfortunately, when he arrived for the interview, he was told that the position was no longer available. We were both extremely disappointed and frustrated.

By now, I was six months pregnant. During my prenatal checkup, my doctor commented that I had gained more weight in the sixth month than the previous months combined, but that I was still within the normal weight limit. For some reason, which I don't recall, I managed to convince myself that I should go on a diet. Since Morris would be away for several days on job interviews, I decided to bake a chicken, which I expected to last the entire week. I also baked a cake. I'm not sure who should be blamed, my unborn baby who seemed to be playing soccer inside me, or I, but, when I began to eat a piece of the chicken, it tasted so good I couldn't stop. I continued eating it, piece by piece until I had eaten the whole thing, along with some cake and punch. Well, that was my first and last excursion into dieting for weight loss. I knew, then, that dieting wasn't for me.

Time continued to tick away, and anxious thoughts about Morris' job situation took center stage in our lives. Having no offer of employment hampered our desire to be settled before our baby's due date. By now, I had resigned from my job thinking that Morris would be hired, so we had no income coming in. We tried not to worry, and we prayed that God would help Morris find a job soon.

Approximately one month before my delivery date, Morris received a job offer to head the library at Michigan Training Unit located in Ionia, Michigan. It was located about 83 miles from Kalamazoo. Needless to say, we were excited and overjoyed. Looking back, I can see how God was positioning us for the future plans He had for us.

Since it was nearing my delivery date, Morris commuted from Kalamazoo to Ionia as we awaited the birth of our first child. Early on the morning of November 16, contractions began. Morris called the doctor, who told him to take me to Borgess Hospital, which was less than a mile from our apartment. After examining me, he said that I had not dilated sufficiently, so he advised Morris to go on to work.

During the day, nursing students worked untiringly to teach me deep breathing techniques. When Morris returned from work that evening, I still had not given birth. The following morning, November 17, was my due date, but Morris had to leave early for work. Around six

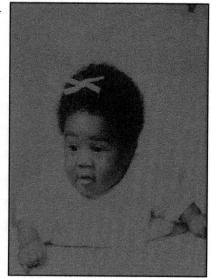

Ngozi, "Blessing"

54

a.m., our 6 lb. 10 oz. bouncing baby daughter heralded her arrival with a loud cry. The delivery process was long and arduous, but it was worth it to look into the face of our beautiful bundle of joy.

Morris had chosen the name "Ngozi" ("Blessing"), and I, the name "Bonita." However, I convinced myself that with two difficult names, Ngozi Iheanacho, to learn to spell and pronounce, there was no need to burden her with another. This is a decision I've regretted since then. Ngozi is the only family member without a middle name.

The week following our discharge from the hospital, we moved to the city of Ionia. Funds were low, so Morris had to make two trips in our car to transport our few belongings. Snow drifts on the streets made the journey treacherous, but with God's help, we made it safely to our new residence.

After some adjustments to new motherhood, a new apartment, new community, new church, new everything, we settled in quite well. Morris' work hours were unusual—from twelve noon to nine p.m., which gave him more time to be with us during the day.

Following several weeks at home, I began to search for employment. Unfortunately, I was mentally unprepared for what would follow. I applied for a position at the local hospital, and although I had the necessary experience and academic preparation for the position, I was not hired. Dr. Darrel Opicka, a Caucasian, my new family physician, and a fellow church member, asked the medical records director why I was rejected. She told him bluntly that she didn't want a Black person working in medical records. Morris and I were deeply disappointed but decided to put my job search on hold. I continued to be a stay-at-home mom.

We attended the Ionia Seventh-day Adventist Church and were welcomed warmly by the members, especially the few Black families who attended that church. I became involved with children's Sabbath School and provided special music for Sabbath School or divine worship when requested.

One of the things my family had to get accustomed to right away was the strange stares from people. Ionia is a predominantly Caucasian city with a small Black population, so we often aroused much curiosity. I recall taking Ngozi for a ride in her stroller when I heard the loud screeching of brakes. A driver, who had been staring at us, swerved to avoid hitting an electric pole.

One of the families at church with whom we became acquainted was the Hatcher family who lived in the neighboring city of Palo. They extended a warm welcome to us and frequently invited us to their home and treated us like we were family. A year later, Mrs. Hatcher taught me how to drive a car. At first, I thought I would never learn, but, before long, I mastered the art and passed the driving test. It was a happy day for me!

God blessed us and approximately 16 months after arriving in Ionia, we purchased a house and moved in before the birth of our second daughter, Chioma ("God is Good"). Three months following her birth, I accepted a position at the same hospital where I had been denied earlier. I worked in the medical laboratory for approximately three years.

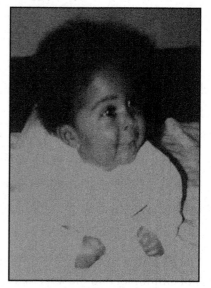

"You will show me the path of life; In Your presence is fullness of joy; At Your right hand are pleasures forevermore" (Psalm 16:11, NKJV).

Chioma, "God is Good"

Chapter 6

Call to Service

*I*n your journey through life, there may be certain scriptures that have encouraged or impacted you significantly, and you have adopted them as your own. I have treasured several. However, the one that has had the most profound influence in my life is Jeremiah 29:11 — "For I know the plans I have for you," declares the LORD, "plans to prosper you and not to harm you, plans to give you hope and a future" (NIV). This powerful verse will be my primary focus throughout my story.

The Call

Taking a reflective look back on my journey, I am drawn to a beautiful, warm day in the fall of 1975 when the direction of my life took an unforeseen turn. It all began when Morris received a phone call from Andrews University's president, Dr. Richard Hammill, inviting him to serve as the librarian at the Adventist Seminary of West Africa (ASWA, formerly ACWA; now, Babcock University) located in Nigeria. The college was seeking affiliation with AU and desperately needed a professional librarian. For various reasons, Morris was not excited about returning to Nigeria. He had a family, a great job with the State of Michigan, a house that he would have to sell, and Ngozi had just started kindergarten. Also, having worked as a pastor in Nigeria for many years, he was familiar with the disparity between the salary of national workers and that of missionaries, and he didn't want to deal with church policies that were unfavorable to nationals returning.

Dr. Joseph Smoot, Vice President for Academic Affairs at AU at the time, personally persuaded Morris to accept the call. He visited our home and, after several telephone conversations, and many prayers, my husband, reluctantly, accepted the invitation to return to Nigeria. He began the process of listing our house in the local newspaper. For several months, some houses in our neighborhood had displayed "For Sale" sign but were not sold, so we believed that our prospects of selling our home were nil.

Much to Morris' delight, weeks went by without a buyer. In his heart, he didn't want the property to sell. Dr. Smoot was not easily discouraged, though, and arranged for Dr. Wilson Trickett, a business professor at AU and a realtor, to come to Ionia to market our house. He came, looked it over, expressed that it was a lovely house in a beautiful neighborhood, and we shouldn't have difficulty finding a buyer. Before returning to Berrien Springs, he listed it in the newspaper with a prayer that God would bless our family and provide a buyer.

Within a few days, the Lord answered Dr. Trickett's prayer. Thursday afternoon, we received an offer from a young couple. We were surprised by this quick sale. It was evident that the Lord's hand was moving in our circumstances and guiding us to Nigeria. Morris could no longer use the sale of the house as an excuse to believe that he was not to go to Nigeria. The call of God was upon us; He had declared Himself, loud and clear, "For I know the plans I have for you, plans to prosper you and not to harm you; plans to give you hope and a future." I was excited about Morris' decision to return to his homeland and looked forward to meeting his mother and to her meeting her grandchildren.

For the previous five years, we had lived quite comfortably in Ionia, but, everything was about to change. We mentioned to our church family and friends that we had accepted a call to serve at the Adventist college in Nigeria, and they were excited about our new venture. Since I frequently sang solos at the Ionia SDA Church and in a few churches in the community, Anna Jean Opicka, my friend and the church organist, suggested that I give a concert before traveling overseas.

The announcement was published in the local newspaper, and preparations were begun. Dr. Richard Campbell, one of the surgeons with whom I worked at the hospital; Anna Jean and Deborah May, a friend and choir director from another church, were excellent accompanists. Some of the songs I sang were: "Fill My Cup, Lord"; "The Holy City"; "Let Us Break Bread Together"; "Thanks Be To God"; "Because He Lives"; and "Sweet, Sweet Spirit." Ngozi and Chioma joined me on this song, which brought smiles to the faces of the congregation as they listened to their sweet little voices.

With the sale of the house completed, everything began to move forward rapidly. Letters of resignation were submitted to our bosses, and we began the arduous task of preparing to move thousands of miles across the ocean. I was unaware of what the future held for me, but I was willing to keep the portion of my marriage vows made six years earlier: "Wherever you go, I will go."

Several months before receiving the call to Nigeria, Morris and I had applied for U.S. citizenship and were scheduled to be sworn in as citizens in the spring of 1976. We considered it wise for one of us to remain in Ionia to obtain citizenship before traveling to Nigeria, but we were discouraged from doing so by General Conference officials, who preferred that our family travel together, so we forfeited the opportunity to obtain citizenship at that time. However, we knew that God was working out the details of our lives and that He would direct and guide us on this unknown journey upon which we were about to embark.

Morris accepted an invitation from Dr. Smoot for us to visit the AU campus before traveling overseas. I had the privilege to see one of my former professors, Ms. Hannah, again. She was happy to hear of our mission to Nigeria and gladly shared educational nuggets and a supply of books to enhance my teaching skills. I was grateful for her generosity. During that visit, I met my former boss from Port-of-Spain Community Adventist Hospital in Trinidad, Dr. William Shea. He had given up practicing medicine to become a seminary professor. He and his wife invited us to their beautiful home for dinner, where we reminisced about our service years in Trinidad.

Our family returned to Ionia and completed the details for travel and prepared for departure. Most of our belongings were packed and shipped to Nigeria at the expense of the General Conference of Seventh-day Adventists. We said goodbye to our friends and drove to Washington, D.C., from where our car was shipped to Nigeria at our expense. Before departing for England, we visited with family residing in the D.C. area. We spent Christmas holiday with Neville and his family in Chester, England. While there we visited many interesting sites and places, including Wales.

Following an enjoyable Christmas celebration, we traveled by train to London Heathrow Airport. The day was long and tiresome, but we finally boarded the plane and were on our way to Nigeria. We had begun our journey of faith, unaware of the far-reaching and life-changing impact Morris' decision to return to his country would have on our family and future. However, we knew that God had a plan and a purpose for our lives, and we were confident that He would lead us to the right path.

Dense fog in Nigeria made it difficult to land, so our plane was diverted to the Accra Airport in Ghana, causing a delay. We finally arrived at the Lagos Airport, and I still remember the sea of people dressed in intricate and elaborate native attire and others in all-white apparel. I learned that many were returning from their journey to Mecca. Since our flight arrived later than scheduled, no one was at the airport to pick us up, so I had an opportunity to observe some things about my new country. One thing that shocked me was people prostrating themselves before other people. I thought this was unusual, so I asked Morris if I was expected to do the same. He assured me that I wasn't. In those days, it was customary in western Nigeria for people to greet their seniors that way as a sign of respect.

Our transportation arrived, and we traveled to the Union headquarters located in Ikeja, a short distance from the airport. The roads were under construction and jammed with heavy traffic and drivers recklessly trying to overtake each other, so it took longer for us to reach Ikeja. After a rather scary ride, we arrived safely. We waited at the home of the Nigerian Union president, Pastor Gustafson, for someone to take us to the ASWA campus about 45 miles away.

At last, we reached the campus. By now, I was overcome by exhaustion and dehydration, given the more than 24-hour journey from Chester to Nigeria. The school nurse thought I might have contracted malaria and administered a chloroquine shot. Within a few minutes, I fainted. You can imagine my embarrassment at arriving in a new place and becoming ill on the first day. We found out later, after another fainting episode, that I was allergic to chloroquine injections.

The house to which our family was assigned was not ready for occupancy, and our household goods had not arrived. For several days, we stayed with Morris' cousin, Philemon Onwere, and his family. Philemon was the business manager at ASWA, and his wife, Christiana, served as the charge nurse for the village clinic. We were very appreciative of their hospitality. Later, we moved into a furnished, one-bedroom duplex on campus as we awaited the arrival of our goods. Although our housing situation was still not ideal, we did have a little more privacy and room to spread out.

As newcomers to the community, there were a few things we had to become accustomed to right away. Among them was the loud noise that blared from the public address system in the village nearby. We had never heard anything like it. The first few times, we huddled together, afraid that something terrible was happening outside our window. We later learned that this sound signaled the early morning call to prayer for the large Muslim community that resided in the village. Wherever they were, they knew it was prayer time. I was impressed by their dedication.

Clearing our household goods and car through customs was frustratingly difficult and time-consuming. Morris and Philemon often traveled to Lagos starting at around 4:00 a.m. to avoid the rush-hour traffic. Negotiating with uncaring customs officials seemed to drain every ounce of energy and patience from Morris. Every time he thought our goods would be released, another unexpected delay cropped up, which created more exasperation and disappointment.

After weeks of anxious waiting, the truck arrived with our goods. There was an explosion of excitement and joy in our household! We were delighted to move into our brand new house with a huge yard in which five-year-old Ngozi and three-year-old Chioma could run and play. We busily unpacked and arranged furniture here and there. It was a a wonderful feeling to settle in our home finally.

The girls adjusted remarkably well to their new environment, and everything progressed quite nicely. We enrolled Ngozi in a private school in the village of Ikene, a few miles from our campus where Philemon's children also attended. Several months later, she transferred to the school on campus provided for the children of missionaries, which was within walking distance of our house.

Chioma was too young to attend elementary school and had to stay at home with Chibuzo, our new housekeeper, whom Christiana had recommended to assist us with housework and

the yard. Although Chibuzo was very nice, Chioma was not used to her and wanted to follow me to my classes. She would often cry if she saw me leaving. On many occasions, I had to sneak out of the house without her knowledge. One day, while I was teaching, Chioma showed up outside my classroom door without Chibuzo's knowledge. I happened to turn around, and there she was with her shy face and little hand waving at me as she called out, "Hi, Mwaahmee!" I was embarrassed, but the students were happy to see her. I quickly took her to the library to wait until my class ended.

Morris in library at ASWA

In addition to his responsibilities as the librarian, Morris taught college classes and, later, served as church treasurer. I taught secretarial science courses, assisted with children's Sabbath School, and provided special music for church services and other occasions from time to time. I also sang with the Advent Heralds, a choral group comprised of college students and faculty.

Shirley's Typing Class

62

When we arrived on the campus, we had no idea what to expect, but we quickly adjusted to our new life. Much to our joy, God richly blessed us. We were fortunate to live on a campus where some amenities were available that helped to make our stay comfortable.

One of the things I missed was the telephone; none of the residences had them. To make overseas calls, we had to travel to Lagos early in the morning, so our calls were limited. Although we missed some of the luxuries we had grown accustomed to in the U.S., life was good.

Friday evenings were special; it seemed as if a quiet reverence hovered over the campus, and, with it came an overwhelming feeling of nostalgia. During the week, we were busy with school, so we welcomed these evenings of quiet reflection. It was during those times that I often played my favorite record with a particular song written by Mosie Lister titled, "His Hand in Mine." The words were like a soothing balm to my soul; sometimes tears rolled down my cheeks as I was overcome by precious memories of years spent in Ionia.

"You may ask me how I know my Lord is near;
You may doubt the things I say and doubt the way I feel,
But I know He's real today, He'll always be.
I can feel His hand in mine, and that's enough for me.
I will never walk alone; He holds my hand;
He will guide each step I take, and if I fall,
I know that He'll understand.
Till the day He tells me why He loves me so,
I can feel His hand in mine; that's all I need to know."

Whenever I hear this song, it brings back fond memories of yesteryears.

Our First Village Trip

By now, six months had passed, and our family had adjusted considerably well to our new environment. With great anticipation, we looked forward to meeting Morris' mother along with relatives who lived in eastern Nigeria, approximately 500 miles from campus.

Our first visit was delayed until summer vacation when we could stay longer. As soon as the college was dismissed for the summer, we packed up our car and departed for Mgboko Obete, located in Abia State, approximately 10 miles from Aba. Before going to the village, we spent Friday night and Saturday in Umuahia at the home of the late Dr. Godfrey Onwere, and his wife, Vivian. Dr. Onwere was Philemon's brother, we both were students at Andrews University during the 60s.

Saturday night was very stressful for me because Vivian tried to teach me the Igbo language before I went to the village, and I had difficulty remembering all of this information in such a short time. She taught me special greetings to use with elders and repeated the words frequently to ensure I pronounced them correctly. However, I was still unsure about what to say and when. It seemed like I was cramming for a major exam and was not doing well at all. A few of the words I learned that night were: "Kedu," "Hello"; "Ndewo," "Hi, how are you?"; "Mazi Kanka," used to greet older people. "Ka nka," "Live long" or "Long life"; "Ndo","Sorry"; "Ka chi bo," "Good night"; "Bia" "Come." My new learning experience created some anxiety, but I was determined to succeed.

Late Sunday morning, we arrived in Mgboko Obete. There was a frenzy of excitement! We were finally in Morris' village. Since the house he was building for his mother wasn't ready, we stayed at the home of John Onwere, brother of Godfrey and Philemon, and his wife, Patricia, whose compound was nearby. They gladly opened their home to our family, and we enjoyed their company and hospitality.

As this was my first visit to the village, I didn't know what to expect. Not surprisingly, I was both nervous and curious. Morris is not talkative like me; therefore, I could not depend on him to offer much assistance in this area. My anticipation was high, but the one question foremost in my mind was, "How would his family accept me, a foreign woman?" Of course, I kept my thoughts to myself and tried not to give any indication of the nervousness I was feeling deep inside.

At last, we were face-to-face with my mother-in-law! I was happy that my dream had become a reality. She was delighted to see her only son, as well as her grandchildren and daughter-in-law. The expression on her face revealed tremendous joy and excitement to have us so near. What a fulfilling experience to see her! She was beautiful and somewhat shy. I looked at her and thought of how much Ngozi resembled her. She neither spoke nor understood English, and, after using all the Igbo greetings Vivian had taught me, the only thing I had left with which to communicate was my smile.

An elaborate welcome party had been planned for us by Morris' family. The purpose was twofold: to congratulate him on his academic accomplishments and to welcome him home with his family. It was indeed a joyous occasion, and villagers were happy that their "lost son" had returned home.

The celebration was held in the yard under a huge mango tree with branches spread out like an umbrella, which provided shade from the sweltering heat. Women danced, sang, and expressed declarations of joy as they surrounded and looked me over from head to toe. They spoke in Igbo and, of course, I couldn't understand a word, so I just smiled until my face felt like it was permanently frozen in that position. Several times, I attempted to speak a few of the Igbo words Vivian had taught me, but I became confused and began greeting everyone, young and old, with the special greeting reserved for seniors.

Morris was delighted to see his mother and listened as she told him of the many nights she placed his picture on her bosom and cried herself to sleep. Some women used to taunt her that she would never see her son again because he had married a foreign woman. Now, here we were, right before her eyes! She was filled with delight and gave each of us an Igbo name. Mine is "Ogbodiya" which means "friend of my husband." Her name for Ngozi was "Nwanganga," "the child of my pride." Sadly, I don't recall her name for Chioma, but remember that it was beautiful.

It was evident how much my mother-in-law loved her son; she was very proud of him, his family, and achievements. I was thrilled that she had the opportunity to see him again and to become acquainted with her extended family. She accepted us with open arms. Ngozi and Chioma fell in love with her at first sight, and the three of them bonded immediately. Wherever she went, both girls held her hands and went with her. Their ready acceptance made her happy, and I was pleased to see how quickly they had adjusted to their new surroundings.

Morris was glad to be home again and made himself comfortable visiting family and friends. The girls were with their grandmother or playing with children in the village. I was glad to be there, and it was good to see Morris and the children so happy. Strangely, an intense loneliness engulfed me even though I was in the presence of dozens of people. I was in a new country, in unfamiliar territory, among strangers who spoke a strange language I could neither understand nor speak.

I'm grateful that my Heavenly Father, who knows all things and has promised never to leave us nor forsake us (Hebrews 13:5.), is always with me. In my deepest moments of loneliness, He provided someone to ease my anxiety in the person of Mrs. Alice Onwere, Philemon's mother. She greeted me in English: "Hello, how are you?" Those words sounded like sweet music to my ears. I hugged her and held her arm tightly as tears trickled down my cheeks. At last, there was someone with whom I could communicate. I followed her wherever she went and refused to let her out of my sight. I was embarrassed for her to see my tears, but she understood. I will always cherish fond memories of the love and kindness she extended to me on the loneliest day of my life.

The celebration was impressive, and it was evident that much planning and preparation had gone into the festivities. Women were decked out in matching colorful Igbo wrappers (fabric used in place of a skirt), beautiful blouses, and head scarves of varying colors and creative styles. Dozens of bicycles were lined up in the yard. Never had I seen so many bicycles, all parked in perfect alignment.

A variety of delicious native foods were served: Igbo soups, joloff rice, similar to Spanish rice; akara, made from black-eyed peas soaked in water to remove the skin, then ground and mixed with a variety of seasonings and deep-fried in oil. "Moi-moi," also made from grounded black-eyed peas, onions, tomato paste, pepper, salt and other ingredients wrapped in pieces of banana leaves or foil and cooked in a large pot; fried plantains, fish, chicken, malt, drinks, and a host of other delicacies. We all enjoyed a grand celebration.

We were in the village for a few days when I experienced something that made me real happy. I was standing outside my mother-in law's house when she exited and began to walk through the bushes. Ngozi and Chioma were nearby and ran to catch up with her. I was curious as to where they were headed and decided to join this small procession. To my amazement, we ended up at the village market. I looked on as my mother-in-law, with a notable spring in her steps and a heart overflowing with joyful pride, navigated throughout the marketplace, selecting items, bargaining, and purchasing the best of everything she could find. It was clear to me that she was sending a nonverbal message to the women who had cruelly taunted her that she would never see her son again.

We enjoyed a memorable time, adapted quite readily to village life, and experienced great fellowship and camaraderie. Morris' family, friends, and the villagers readily accepted us and treated us superbly, although I was unable to understand nor speak the Igbo language. I regretted not encouraging Morris more persistently to teach us his native language so we would have been able to communicate with his family.

Time does not stand still, so, before long, we had to say goodbye. It was a sad moment, but we had to return to our work responsibilities. I will always remember my first visit to my husband's village fondly. I am convinced that if Morris had not received and accepted the call from President Hammill at that time, many more years would have passed before our visit to Nigeria. Through God's divine providence, our children had the wonderful opportunity to meet their paternal grandmother and to experience first-hand the rich heritage of their father.

My mother-in-law had done an excellent job in raising her son. He is meticulous and well organized; his undergarments, socks, and ties are always neatly folded and perfectly arranged in his dresser drawers. When he takes off his clothes, he puts them on a hanger. Every morning, he folds his pajamas neatly before putting them away. He has a place for everything, and everything is in its place. He's so much unlike his wife!

With a house full of females, it was mandatory that he have his own bathroom. I must admit, though, that, sometimes, I sneak into his bathroom to use an item. I dare not forget to put it back in the exact spot from which I took it or try not to leave any telltale evidence behind. On those occasions when I fall short of this, he invariably finds me out.

At income tax time, he knows where to find every receipt. When it comes to breakfast, the table must be set with knife, fork, spoon, and a variety of chopped fruits creatively arranged on his plate. Breakfast is incomplete without his toast spread with crunchy peanut, lots of honey along with circular slices of banana neatly arranged on each piece of toast. He would rather not eat than to rush through a meal.

One thing that has stood out through the course of our marriage is Morris' faith and commitment to God. He never neglects his daily personal devotion and study of the Bible, and consistently kneels by his bed every morning and evening to pray. I reap the benefits of my mother-in-law's parenting to this very day.

Morris is highly respected and loved by his family, classmates, friends, and former parishioners. His friends always boast about his heroic qualities and how fortunate I am to be married to him. I tell them he is fortunate to be married to me, too.

"Make a joyful shout to God, all the earth! Sing out the honor of His name; Make His praise glorious" (Psalm 66:1, 2, NKJV).

Chapter 7

A Grandmother's Prayer

Several months following our visit to the village, Morris' mother came to spend time with us on campus. Since my knowledge of the Igbo language was extremely limited, we communicated with her through Morris or my Igbo students. During this visit, she mentioned to Ekele, one of my students, that I treated her better than some Nigerian women treated their family members. Later, she said to tell me to "bring more kids." Morris and I had no plans for more children, so I told Ekele to tell her "no more kids!" My mother-in-law responded that she was going to pray to her God that I bring more kids. Not to be outdone, I replied, "I will pray to my God not to have anymore." Well, several months after she returned to the village, my abdominal walls began to expand. A visit to the doctor confirmed that I was pregnant.

Two faculty members on campus became pregnant a few months ahead of me. Fortunately, we were blessed to have a doctor on campus, Dr. Aline Clemonds, who served as director of the village clinic and from whom we received excellent prenatal care. Later in our pregnancies, we were referred to another doctor for delivery in the Shagamu Hospital.

My pregnancy went well, so we didn't anticipate anything unusual. Little did we know that I was about to come face to face with a life-threatening experience. The afternoon before our baby was born, I had feasted on a lot of boiled ugu seeds. The ugu leaf is similar to spinach and, in Nigeria, it is used to make ugu soup or used as an ordinary vegetable much like other greens. The seeds were delicious, and my husband cautioned me not to eat too many. That night, I went to bed feeling fine, but around midnight I was suddenly awakened by sharp pains. The frequency and intensity of the contractions signaled our baby's imminent arrival.

According to the doctor's calculation, our baby was due January 13, 1978; but it was only December 19, 1977. Dr. Clemonds was away visiting in another state, so I decided to gather up my delivery gown, toiletries, and the other items I was instructed to bring. We left the girls with one of Morris' cousins. Morris, not wanting to take any chances, drove me to the hospital about five miles away. The roads were filled with huge potholes and every time the car sank into one of them, I cried out in excruciating pain. I felt like the baby would arrive at any moment. We reached the hospital after what seemed like an eternity and were surprised to see several women waiting to deliver their babies; some were lying on cots while others groaned in pain on the floor. We observed only one nurse on duty. It didn't take long to realize that this experience was going to be far different from my previous deliveries in the U.S.

We informed the nurse of the doctor's instructions to call him as soon as we arrived, but she ignored us. The delivery proceeded well, but the placenta refused to come out. The nurse pulled and pulled in her effort to remove it manually, but it wouldn't budge. Morris was in the delivery room the entire time. Sensing my deteriorating condition, he spoke angrily, "Call the doctor, my wife is bleeding to death." My face was drenched in sweat, and my pelvic region ached with searing pain. My gown was soaked in blood all the way up my back.

Akunna, "Father's Treasure"

Finally, the nurse relented and called the doctor. He came speedily and immediately instructed her to take my blood pressure and my pulse as he rattled off other instructions. I sensed that my condition was grave because his face became very red as he gave the orders. A short time later, he removed the placenta, and the nurse told me to go back to my room; however, when I stood up, I was weak and dizzy, so the doctor told her to get me a wheelchair. Arriving in my room, I stretched out in bed completely exhausted. When the morning nurse came on duty, I overheard my nurse tell her that I'd lost a lot of blood and was weak. I must admit that I missed the pampering I received in Kalamazoo and Ionia where our other two daughters were born. I thanked God for being with me and sparing me from what could have been a tragic situation.

My baby and I stayed at the hospital for approximately eight hours. As soon as I stood up without feeling dizzy, I told Morris I wanted to go home. I hadn't eaten anything and knew I would receive better care at home.

We arrived in our driveway, and I got out of the car. Dr. Andre Stijnman, my Dutch neighbor, waved to me; when I raised my hand to wave back, I was so weak that I collapsed on the car. He immediately rushed over to help me. Fortunately, Morris was carrying Akunna, our little bundle of joy. As we entered the house, Ngozi and Chioma welcomed us enthusiastically. Their faces lit up with excitement to see their baby sister. I was happy to be home, again. After a few days of eating my favorite ugu soup, I quickly regained my energy.

Morris' mom was delighted to learn of the newest addition to our family. Akunna ("Father's Treasure") was the name Morris gave her, but his Mom named her "Akunne" ("Mother's Treasure"). I gave her the middle name of Moreen.

God timed Akunna's birth date perfectly. Had she been born on the date scheduled, I would have had to take time off from my teaching responsibility that semester. As it turned out, she was born three weeks ahead of the due date, making it possible for me to resume teaching at the beginning of the second semester.

Several days after arriving home, Igbo women, who lived in the village not far from our campus, came to our house to welcome our baby. It was a lovely occasion. They were happy that I had given birth to another child, and they made joyful sounds as they patted their lips and danced. They showered me with talcum powder, which is an expression of happiness and joy. They taught me how to carry Akunna on my back, held securely by a large piece of fabric. I was reluctant to use this method, fearing she would slip out and fall.

A few weeks after Akunna's birth, the wives of expatriates had a baby shower for her. Mrs. Stijnman also shared some of her daughter's clothes with Akunna, which helped a lot. Annette, Dr. Clemonds' daughter, loved Akunna very much and acted like her second mother.

Life was moving along smoothly, and we were enjoying our new addition when suddenly, at around six months old, Akunna began to cry for no discernible reason. She was a very happy baby, so this was unusual for her. At first, we thought she was hungry or needed to be changed, but after taking care of her discomforts, she still continued to cry.

News of Akunna's illness reached Mrs. Ekase, the girls' dorm dean. She came with what she considered to be the remedy for Akunna's distress. Helpless, we looked on as she rubbed an ointment called ori (shea butter) all over Akunna's body, pulling her limbs in the process. I didn't understand what she was doing but was willing to give it a try—anything to provide relief. At one point, she held Akunna by both legs with her head dangling as she shook her. I couldn't bear to see her in such an unnatural position, so I told Mrs. Ekase to stop. Unfortunately, Akunna's condition didn't improve.

We shared our concern with Christiana, and she arranged for us to bring Akunna to the private hospital in Ikeja where she was employed as a nurse. The doctor diagnosed the condition as "a strangulated hernia," and surgery was performed the next morning. Soon, Akunna was smiling again, and so were we. We were thankful that, providentially, the surgeon was available to correct the problem. Akunna continued to grow rapidly and surprised us when she began to walk without assistance at the age of eight months. She also learned to talk very early. This new addition to our family brought us much joy.

"The Lord is my strength and my shield; My heart trusted in Him, and I am helped;
Therefore my heart greatly rejoices, And with my song I will praise Him"
(Psalm 28:7, NKJV).

Chapter 8

Life in Nigeria

A few years passed, and we had become seasoned dwellers in Nigeria. During our visits to Morris' home, I learned a lot about life in the village, as well as how to prepare different kinds of native foods.

An interesting aspect of life in Nigeria was the harvesting of palm nuts. It was fascinating to watch village men climb tall trees to harvest them. Afterward, they pounded the palm nuts to extract the rich red oil used in various African dishes. Some of this oil is marketed in the nearby city of Aba as well as overseas.

Our family enjoyed eating many delicious tropical fruits such as guavas, mangoes, pineapples, and udaras, a yellowish-brown round fruit with a meaty substance inside that turns gummy after a lot of chewing. Ngozi and Chioma liked udara alot. A large udara tree was in our backyard, and we were often awakened early in the morning by the chatter of village children who came with flashlights in search of udaras that had fallen during the night.

Although our girls loved living in Nigeria, they didn't care for some of the native foods as much as I did. It was unbelievable how quickly their appetites vanished if they smelled ugu soup as they walked home from school. As they entered the door, they would immediately announce, "I am not hungry." Like their Dad, Ngozi and Chioma preferred the native brown beans with rice, gravy, fish, ugu vegetables, and macaroni and cheese. My favorite dish was ugu soup; it is made of ground egusi (melon seeds), chopped okra, fish or chicken, ugu leaves, onions, seasonings, etc. I enjoyed it so much that I didn't mind eating it several days a week, unlike my husband, who would only eat it once or twice a week. He disliked the smell of the stockfish (dried fish imported from Norway) that was used to prepare the soup. I must admit that it does have a distinctive odor, but it didn't diminish my love for it.

Kola Nuts

The kola nut is brown in color and holds special significance for Igbos. It is considered the highest symbol of Igbo hospitality. When important guests visit the community or one's home, kola nuts are brought out and handed to the oldest man. Kola nuts are used for a variety of events, but the main reason is to welcome guests to a home or village. This ritual has three steps, and the village elders could penalize anyone who failed to follow them. The first step is the presentation of the kola nuts, the second is breaking them into pieces, and the third is distribution. The presentation of kola nuts is a privilege reserved exclusively for the men. After they are presented to the senior man, they are passed around the room until they come back to the host. The elder person holds a kola nut up and says a prayer for good health and peace for the people.

The kola nut also plays a critical role when a man is seeking the hand of an Igbo girl in marriage. This ceremony is serious and entails many steps before the prospective husband is permitted to marry the woman. The two families come together before plans for the wedding are made. Each family tries to find out as much as they can about their prospective family: background, health, illnesses, divorces, etc. I witnessed one of these ceremonies, and it was very impressive. I believe that, as a result of this tradition, marriages are strengthened, and familial bonding is encouraged.

Bargaining

An interesting aspect of living in Nigeria was learning how to bargain. I had to learn the art quickly or risk paying more for an item than its actual value. Bargaining takes a lot of practice and patience and can be tiring, frustrating, and time-consuming. Vendors in the marketplace are known to sell items at inflated prices to foreigners or anyone who doesn't speak their language. When they offer an item at a certain price, experience teaches that you keep bargaining until a happy medium is reached. To avoid bargaining, one would have to shop at supermarkets in the main cities like Lagos and Ibadan.

After several visits to the local village market, I developed a friendship with one of the vendors and learned how to greet her in Yoruba: "E'karo," "Good Morning" and "S'alafia ni," "How are you?" She was pleasant and always greeted me with a smile. I depended on her assistance in selecting the best fish, as well as other items. On one of my market visits, I learned that she and her unborn baby had been tragically killed in an automobile accident. I was deeply saddened.

From time to time, Morris took us to the supermarket in Ibadan as a special treat. It was somewhat like supermarkets in America. There was no bargaining; we simply paid the price as marked. Although the items were costlier than in the village markets, we had a wider variety from which to choose. Our girls and I liked to shop in Ibadan because we got to purchase our favorite desserts: ice cream and large doughnuts filled with red jelly.

Harmattan

The weather in Nigeria is sweltering, but, during Harmattan season, between November and January, it is marked by dry, parching winds with a lot of white dust that blows toward the western coast of Africa from the Sahara Desert. The dry wind lowers the humidity, which can lead to hot days and cool nights. When the dust in the wind gets too thick, it can create problems for air travel and can interrupt commerce and flight schedules. Nights and early mornings were cold and required the use of sweaters or jackets until about mid-morning when the sun got hot. I disliked this season because of the white dust that settled everywhere—on houses, furniture, cars, etc. No matter how well I cleaned, the dust always seemed to remain.

Malaria

Malaria is a debilitating tropical disease that is accompanied by high fever, chills, muscle weakness, loss of appetite, and dehydration. Malaria is spread by mosquitoes and causes the death of thousands of African children and adults yearly. From time to time, my family and I suffered debilitating bouts of this dreaded disease. Morris always knew when I'd contracted malaria because I would become weak with no desire to eat, which is unlike me.

Snakes

I feared several African creatures, and one of them was the snake. There was no getting away from them. They often hid in nearby bushes or trees. Occasionally, walking home from teaching my classes, I would see a huge black snake gliding across the street a distance away, and I would cringe every time. A close-up experience with a snake occurred when Akunna was playing outside in her sandbox. I looked out to check on her and saw a green mamba wriggling its way hurriedly down the driveway not far from where she was playing. The green mamba is in the same family as the black mamba but is shy and non-aggressive. However, if provoked, the green mamba will bite. Although its venom is only one/tenth as toxic as that of the black mamba, it can still be deadly. I quickly grabbed Akunna as I let out a loud scream and ran into the house. I watched from the window as it slithered away into the ugu field nearby.

On one occasion, we were having dinner at the home of the Craig family when someone shouted out that a black snake was in the toilet bowl. Apparently, it had entered through the air vent outside the house and had gotten stuck. We all were afraid. Fortunately, a brave student killed it. Another time, my family and guests were dining at our house when a green mamba appeared between the air-conditioning unit and the window. Morris tried desperately to reach it, but its location made it difficult. After many unsuccessful attempts, he doused it with gasoline, and we watched as it fell to the ground.

Sand Flies

During one of our visits to the east, we stayed in a guest room operated by the Seventh-day Adventist Conference office nearby. In the night, we encountered sand flies which had invaded the guest room and kept me awake most of the night as I tried to prevent them from having a field day on our arms and legs. Blood stains were on the wall where I had killed many of them. A few days after we returned to the campus, both Ngozi and Chioma became seriously ill with sand fly fever. It was heart-wrenching to watch their limp bodies stretched out on the floor without energy to raise their heads and no appetite. High fever, accompanied by vomiting, had left them awfully weak.

Dr. Clemonds was not on campus, so we were in a quandary as to what to do. We prayed for God's healing. Then, good news came that Dr. David Kelln, a missionary doctor serving in another state, was on campus. He came and administered treatment, and within a few days, the girls gradually regained their energy and were back to normal. We knew without a doubt that it was God who had guided Dr. Kelln to be on campus at that time to come to our rescue.

Uninvited Intruder

Occasionally, we traveled with other missionary families to the Lagos beach or the warm springs. The kids enjoyed going to new and fun places. One Sabbath, we attended a church near Ibadan for Sabbath worship at the invitation of Dr. and Mrs. Inanga. Dr. Inanga was a university professor, whose wife was from the Caribbean, and he was from eastern Nigeria, so we had some things in common. After the service, I was standing outside the church chatting with church goers when, suddenly, I felt something crawling up my leg. I was wearing a long skirt, so I shook it vigorously to get rid of this intruder. To our amazement, a lizard crawled out at high speed as I let out a loud scream! People standing nearby looked on amused.

My Secret Trip to Lagos

Our campus community was comprised of individuals from diverse cultures and countries, and I was blessed to have a close friend and neighbor, Florence Quarcoo, a Ghanaian, to live nearby. Occasionally, when Morris was at work, she would prepare delicious Ghanaian food and bring it to me. She was always concerned that "Brother Iheanacho" might be upset with her for giving me spicy Ghanaian food. I enjoyed her cooking.

Florence, a professional seamstress, specialized in making children's clothes, which she sold to department stores in Lagos. She invited me to travel with her to find a market for some dresses I had made. Morris was attending a meeting in Benin, in mid-west Nigeria, and it seemed an ideal opportunity to go to Lagos and return home without his knowledge. I felt he would not have allowed me to go because of the hazardous driving conditions that were often encountered on the roads.

The following day, Florence and I traveled on the college bus that transported college students to Lagos to sell religious books and to take bread and granola, made at the college bakery, to markets in the city. We arrived at Yaba from where we would travel by another bus into Lagos. Florence cautioned me that the crowd waiting for the bus was often large, and there was usually a lot of pushing and shoving to get on the bus and that I should be prepared to push also. I felt up to the task because I had experienced similar scenes when I attended high school in Barbados.

We reached the bus stop early, but, surprisingly, there was already a crowd waiting. I tried to stay as close as possible to Florence; I didn't know where I was or where I was going, and I didn't speak the language. Anxiety was beginning to overcome me. Worse yet, Morris was unaware of my trip.

The bus arrived, and the pushing and shoving became more intense than I anticipated. I tried to push and shove as hard as the other passengers, but it was difficult because everyone seemed to be pushing much harder. Florence succeeded in getting on the bus, but I was still outside struggling with other women to get on. At last, the major portion of my body was on the bus, but my left leg was trapped outside between a few large women sandwiched around me, and my shoe was dangling, threatening to fall off. Florence kept calling, "Shirley, are you on, are you all right?" "No!" I shouted as the crowd continued to press hard on me.

The shoving and pushing intensified, and I became fearful that something would happen to me. I began to pray: "Lord, have mercy on me. Please help me get my other leg on the bus and get back to the campus safely. I will never do this again." Our Heavenly Father, Who is never too busy to listen to our cry for help, didn't say, "It serves you right, Shirley. Why are you calling on Me to help you when you decided to sneak away to Lagos without your husband's knowledge?" In His compassion, He allowed someone to move aside slightly, creating enough space to loosen my leg with my shoe still on my foot. At that moment, it felt like a huge burden had been lifted. I heaved a sigh of relief and silently thanked God for His deliverance. We traveled to and from Lagos safely without Morris' knowledge. I finally revealed my secret a few years ago, and he laughed heartily, although I doubt that he would have found it funny had I told him at the time.

A Thief in the Night

There was a time when the safety and security of our peaceful campus were threatened by the intrusion of a thief. Somehow, the thief devised a way to enter the homes of overseas missionaries late at night and steal electronic equipment and other valuable items without being detected. Residents were unaware that their homes were being burglarized until the following morning when they discovered that items were missing. Many of us were gripped with fear and anxiety as we considered whose house might be next.

Then, late one night, something happened that heightened my fear. Customarily, I would check on Ngozi and Chioma before I went to sleep. This particular night, on my way back to my bedroom, I happened to look out through their bedroom window and saw a man standing at the front door trying to remove some of the louvers. I was stunned. The thief was at our house! As quietly as possible, I hurried to my bedroom. In hushed tones, I said, "Morris, wake up; the thief is on our front porch."

With the absence of telephones on campus, it was hard to get the word out to our neighbors. Hurriedly, Morris got dressed, but, by then, the thief had disappeared. Morris jumped into the car and honked the car horn as he drove up and down the street alerting the residents and students to the fact that the thief had tried to strike again. Male students from the dormitory converged on the surrounding areas to catch the thief, but their efforts proved fruitless; he had disappeared into the thick bushes. Checking around our house the next day, we saw visible signs that the thief had tried to enter our home through the bedroom window on the opposite side of the house. Had he succeeded, we might not have known when he entered. We narrowly escaped being his victims. Here again, we saw evidence of God's protection over our family.

The memory of that incident remained with me for a long time. It was hard to fall asleep at night because of the concern that the thief might be lurking outside. Also, when the night watchman made his rounds, he flashed his bright light into our bedroom. This was probably his way of alerting us that he was on duty. Some individuals had questioned whether or not he had been asleep when the thief was burglarizing people's homes. We are thankful that the angel of the Lord encamped around us and delivered us from the hands of the thief (Psalm 34:7).

Living in Nigeria, I was able to learn so much more about my husband's culture. An aspect that I found out about too late was the dowry—a significant monetary gift, or something of great value, given to the parents of a prospective bride—the more beautiful and educated the young woman, the more lavish the dowry. I often joke that Morris got off the hook because my parents were unaware of this cultural tradition.

At the time we lived in Nigeria, women were expected to have many children. If they were girls, cultural mores dictated that the woman would keep trying for a male child. Since I had three girls, I was expected to do likewise. Morris is an only child with three daughters and having no son meant that he had no one to carry on his name. Fortunately for me, at no time did I feel pressured by him or members of his family to have a male child. If they had concerns, they never expressed or revealed them to me, neither in their attitudes nor in conversation.

Some of Morris' friends consider him unusual in his response to cultural expectations. He's a mild-mannered man, not seeking to enrich himself in any way, even in his non-perusal of the property which he inherited after the death of his father. That is quite unusual, especially for an only male child. To his credit, he prefers a quiet life, unencumbered by excess and the acquisition of material possessions.

Although we are from different cultural backgrounds, with God's help, our marriage is still thriving after more than four decades. It was not always easy, and it took some time to adjust and to understand his culture. Like most marriages, we have the same strengths and weaknesses, ups and downs, and we face challenges that come with marriages between two people from the same cultural background. We also had the additional challenge of the two of us, with our two different cultures, residing in the United States. As Christians who love the Lord and each other, we consistently strive to find ways to resolve challenges that occur from time to time and to keep our focus on the positive. Our commitment to God, each other, and our family form a firm basis from which to resolve whatever differences we might have, and the Lord has blessed tremendously through the years. For this, we are truly grateful.

I must mention that there are culturally mixed marriages that work well and others that don't, as in all marriages. While living in Nigeria, I was aware of women who became uncomfortable or disenchanted with the culture and their spouses and returned to the U.S. or Canada with the children without the husband's knowledge. As you can imagine, this created hostilities and family conflicts.

Shirley and Girls at Home

"Above all, love each other deeply, because love covers over a multitude of sins"
(I Peter 4:8, NIV).

Chapter 9

Family Returns to the U.S.A.

*W*e had lived more than three years in Nigeria, so, in the summer of 1979, Morris paid the expenses for our girls and me to return to the States for a vacation. Also, my U.S. permanent resident document was about to expire, so we used the opportunity to renew my residency papers. An added bonus was that we were able to attend the wedding of my sister, DeLoras. We were delighted to be back in the U.S. to see family and friends.

It was during my absence that Dr. Calvin Rock, the president of Oakwood College at the time, and his wife, Mrs. Clara Rock, visited some West African countries, including Nigeria. Customarily, the college president or the business manager escorted overseas officials around the campus. However, on this occasion, both gentlemen were away attending school-related meetings in another part of the country, so Morris was chosen to escort the Rocks on their tour.

Toward the end of their visit, Morris mentioned that he was planning to return to the U.S. to work for the State of Michigan. Dr. Rock responded that, if he wanted to work for Caesar, it was fine to work for the State of Michigan, but if he wanted to work for the Lord, he should consider coming to Oakwood College. Morris smiled; Oakwood College was not part of his plan. Before his departure, Dr. Rock invited Morris to call him when he arrived in the U.S. Morris responded politely, but his heart was set on Michigan.

The Rocks returned to the U.S., and Morris didn't expect to speak with them again. When my children and I returned from our overseas vacation, he shared the news of their visit and the ensuing conversation. We both continued our various responsibilities without giving further thought to Dr. Rock's offer. We finalized plans to return to the U.S., and our family visited the village one last time to say goodbye to Morris' mother and relatives. We hugged and embraced not knowing when we would see each other again. We were all sad to leave his mom behind; she had taken good care of us and made us feel loved and welcomed each time we visited. Now, we were about to travel overseas, a very long way from ASWA and the village. I will always cherish fond memories of the times we spent with her and how she lovingly accepted me into her family. Before our departure, we shipped a truckload of our household goods to the village for her use.

By mid-December 1979, I had administered final exams, grades had been submitted to the registrar's office, and we had begun our packing. A major problem that lingered on our minds as the day for our departure approached was our American car. It is hard to obtain parts for repairs in Nigeria, so finding a buyer was a major challenge. We prayed that God would provide someone soon. Thursday afternoon, the day before our departure from the campus, we still had no buyer, and our anxiety intensified.

As a last resort, Morris planned to leave the car with a friend to sell and transfer the money to the U.S. Providentially, late Friday morning, just a few hours from our departure, a wealthy man from the village offered to pay cash for the car. We were elated to be the beneficiaries of God's miracle-working power. This was one of many instances wherein it seemed as if God was testing our faith, but we tried to remain strong, and He never failed us.

Our four memorable years of service at ASWA had come to an end, and we were about to embark on a new and unknown journey. We thanked God for the opportunity to touch the lives of our students and to make a difference during our period of service in Nigeria. Early Friday afternoon, we said our last goodbyes and departed for Ikeja, where we spent the night with Philemon's family. The next day, we attended Sabbath service at the church's headquarters nearby. Saturday evening arrived quickly and, before long, we were on our way to the airport.

Standing at the check-in counter, we came face to face with a major problem: my Nigerian visa had expired in November, and the attendant declared loudly, "You're in the country illegally; you can't leave without a valid visa." We stood in shock and disbelief. Since it was our plan to return to the U.S. in December, we didn't think that it was necessary to renew my visa; now here we were in a serious dilemma.

This was not good news! It meant that I would have to remain in Nigeria until a new visa could be issued, and the process could take several weeks or even longer, judging from how long it took to process official documents. This revelation caught us unaware, but we were determined not to panic. I told the officer that, since I was in the country illegally, he should allow me to leave. That didn't work. His tone grew increasingly aggressive, and he kept repeating that I was in the country illegally and insisted that I couldn't leave without a valid visa. Other passengers looked at us curiously, and our girls looked on in fear.

There were tense moments as we waited with baited breath to hear what my fate would be. It seemed as if all our perfectly laid plans were about to disintegrate. We looked at each other wondering what next. Silently, I prayed that God would help us get out of this dilemma. We pled with the officer again, but he refused to budge. Then suddenly something happened; we saw Philemon go to the side of the counter and hand the officer a sum of cash. He quickly accepted it, stamped my documents, and allowed me to leave. Inwardly, I breathed a sigh of relief and a prayer of thanksgiving.

Once again, our Heavenly Father had performed a miracle for our family at just the right time. His promises never fail. He says, "I will answer them before they even call to me. While they are still talking to me about their needs, I will go ahead and answer their prayers!" (Isaiah 65:24, NLT). With a sense of relief and overflowing gratitude in our hearts, we happily boarded the plane bound for the U.S.

After approximately 17 hours in the air, the plane landed safely at the Washington National Airport. Papa Anyatonwu picked us up and took us to his home. It was late December, and the city was snow-covered. What a difference from the warm, sunny weather we'd left behind. We had lived in sunny Nigeria for four years, and our clothes were inappropriate for this cold weather. Ngozi and Chioma had outgrown their winter coats and clothes, so we had to purchase coats and warm clothing immediately. Both Ngozi and Chioma had almost forgotten what snow looked like, and Akunna, who had never seen it, enjoyed playing in it.

We stayed with Morris' relatives while awaiting the letter of employment from the State of Michigan. Over the years, Papa had been like a father to Morris. His caring wife and lovely children accepted us into their family, fed us lavishly, treated us royally, and went above and beyond our expectations to accommodate us and help us navigate our new transition. At no time did any family member cause us to feel uncomfortable. That was a blessing!

Philemon Onwere, Mama & Papa Anyatonwu

The girls missed their friends, the warm weather, and the large open areas for playing. We had to adjust to all five of us sharing one bedroom after having lived in a big bungalow with lots of space and a huge yard. But, these minor inconveniences paled in light of the loving care extended to us by the Anyatonwu's.

Two weeks passed, and there was still no word about a job. I knew in my heart that I didn't want to return to Michigan to deal with so much snow; I wanted a fresh start. Secretly, I prayed that the letter of employment wouldn't come. Morris was confident that it would. One day, while sitting on the bed contemplating what we should do next, I was impressed to remind him of Dr. Rock's job offer and his request that Morris should call him when he arrived in the U.S. Reluctantly, he called, and Dr. Rock invited him to come to Oakwood for an interview. A few days later, Morris was on the plane to Huntsville to meet with Dr. Rock. At the end of the interview, Dr. Rock, in the presence of Dr. Mervyn A. Warren, the Academic Dean, offered Morris the position of catalog librarian, which he readily accepted. Before he returned to D.C., DeLoras and her husband, Reggie, who lived in Huntsville, assisted Morris in securing an apartment.

The day following his return to D.C., Morris received the official letter from the State of Michigan offering him the job for which he had been waiting. God, in His divine wisdom and providence, delayed the letter and led Morris away from the direction in which his plans would have taken him. Only God knew the wonderful plans He was working out for our family. Late January 1980, we expressed our profound thanks to the Anyatonwu family, said goodbye, and boarded the plane for Huntsville, Alabama, and Oakwood College where we would establish our new home. Recently, Ihuoma, one of Papa's sons, told us that on the day we left to go to Huntsville, they felt a void in their home, and they missed us very much.

There is no doubt in my mind that God opened the door of opportunity for Morris to return to his country of birth, render service to his alma mater at a critical phase in the history of the college, and, then, positioned him for Dr. Rock to offer him a job. It was never Morris' dream to serve at Oakwood, but it was part of God's master plan, and He worked out every detail to make it a reality. Isn't God awesome!

Oakwood Elementary School was already in session when we arrived on campus, so Morris quickly enrolled our two eldest daughters. Ngozi, who was 9, started in the fifth grade, and Chioma, at age 7, began the third grade. Several months later, both girls took the national exam and, in some subjects, scored higher than the grades they were currently in. This was unequivocal proof that their educational experience in Nigeria had been academically sound and then some.

Looking back, I wish I had been more alert and sensitive to their needs as it related to their new school and their sometimes, unfriendly environment. More than three decades have passed since January 1980, and they still recall the mean way some of their classmates treated them because of their unusual names and having come from Africa.

Our first visit to the Oakwood College Church was a memorable experience. As we entered the hallway of the church, we met Elder Eric C. Ward (former Oakwood College

Church pastor, now deceased). He reached out and greeted us warmly. Chioma held his hand as if she knew him. Although this was our first visit to his church, he made us feel welcome and comfortable. His warm and friendly attitude made a profound impact on our girls; they still consider him their favorite pastor.

About a week after settling in, I began my search for employment, but it yielded nothing. It was very hard for us financially with two children in church school, a two-year-old, and only one check to take care of all of our needs. Major items such as a car, winter clothes, school fees, etc., had almost depleted our limited funds. We continued to pray that I would find full-time employment soon. Although I received high scores on the secretarial exam administered by Oakwood Personnel Office, my efforts to find full-time work on campus proved futile. It was the same in the community.

Approximately three months after our arrival, there was still no sign of employment for me. One day, as I opened one of the few books we brought back from Nigeria, I found two $20 bills tucked away between the pages. It was a welcomed sight! It was only $40, but, to me, it might as well have been a hundred. God provided those funds in a time of great need. This little incident convinced me that He hadn't forgotten us. I continued to trust Him to provide for our needs.

One day, while Morris was at work and Ngozi and Chioma were at school, I was sitting in the apartment with Akunna wallowing in self-pity when the phone rang. It was DeLoras; she invited me to go with her to Alabama A&M University to visit her friend. Initially, we entered the wrong building by mistake, or so we thought. As we were about to leave, DeLoras saw another friend, Diane, sitting in her office. We turned back, and DeLoras introduced me to her and mentioned that I had recently returned from Nigeria and was seeking employment. Diane smiled and announced, "You are in the right place; we have a position available in my department. I can set up an interview for your sister right now!" WOW, an interview! Yes! I was ecstatic! Everything was happening so quickly.

I wasn't appropriately dressed for an interview, so I hurried home, changed clothes, and returned. The interview went well, and Dr. Wendell Thompson, Director of the Reading Program in the School of Education, offered me a job as his secretary. I gladly accepted his offer and began work the following week.

I was privileged to work with Dr. Thompson, a kind, gracious, and compassionate Christian gentleman, who pastored a local Baptist church. I also worked with three excellent professors in the Department: Ms. Sallie Mosley, Dr. Carol Piper, and Ms. Connie Cunningham. We got along very well together, and, because I was, now, working for professors, I occasionally proctored exams. It still amazes me how God worked out this job opportunity. Unknown to my sister and me, He had impressed her to go to the right building, at the right time, to meet the right person while it had seemed, to us, to be the wrong building. "And we know that in all things God works for the good of those who love him, who have been called according to his purpose" (Romans 8:28, NIV).

Our family worked hard to adjust to our new environment, the people, our jobs, school, and the seasonal weather changes. It was a hectic and challenging time for us; just as one situation was resolved, another one became evident. I settled into my new job at Alabama A&M University while Morris continued his work at Oakwood, and the girls made new friends. Amid our busy schedules, we continued to have daily family worship in order not to neglect family communion with our Heavenly Father.

Our morning commute was an involved process. Our first stop was to take Ngozi and Chioma to Oakwood Elementary School and Akunna to the babysitter. Akunna had gotten used to me being at home, and, now, I was leaving her with a total stranger. It was emotionally draining for both of us. Every time I attempted to leave, she would hold on to me crying loudly. While at work, I often received calls from Mrs. Osborne, Akunna's babysitter, to come and get her because she would not stop crying. As time passed, she gradually settled in.

The next stop was my job, about five miles from Huntsville, in Normal, Alabama. From there, Morris traveled back to Oakwood. When school was dismissed, Ngozi and Chioma walked to the library to wait for their dad to take them home. Many years have passed since that time, but Ngozi and Chioma continue to recall the mischief they got into at the library, which we were unaware of at the time.

Our needs continued to grow, so we had to create new and innovative ways to make ends meet. During my spare time on weekends, I typed term papers for international students at the university and made dresses for the girls and myself. It was a blessing when their school transitioned from regular clothes to uniforms.

Life was challenging, but, no matter how bleak the future appeared, we never went hungry nor had to ask anyone for assistance. God took care of our needs. We are the recipients of His faithfulness and beautiful promise to "supply all our need according to His riches in glory by Jesus Christ" (Philippians 4:19, NKJV).

Chapter 10

From the Valley of Grief Comes Joy

*I*t seemed that no sooner had we gotten into the rhythm of our daily routine than we received the painfully shocking news of the passing of Morris' mom, Florence. It was a severe blow. Deep sorrow engulfed our family as we pondered what had happened because she had been in good health when we left her eight months earlier. We found ourselves questioning why God had permitted this to happen at such a critical point in our lives, and especially so soon after we had returned to the U.S. Questions filled our minds. Had we made the right decision to return when we did? Should we have stayed in Nigeria for a longer period of time to be closer to her in what would become her last days? Could we have done anything to prolong her life? This was an exceptionally sad and emotionally overwhelming time, especially for Morris, her only child.

Morris made flight arrangements to return home. Because of our limited finances, the girls and I were unable to accompany him. In September 1980, grief-stricken and heartbroken, Morris made the long journey home to bury his beloved mother. The visit was emotionally draining and financially taxing for him as an only child. Because he resided in the U.S., family members and villagers had very high expectations of him. He had to provide a large sum of money to purchase the necessary items customary for burial and the other expenses associated with it.

With God's help, he survived this traumatic experience and returned to Huntsville safely. Shortly after his arrival, he became seriously ill. The physical exhaustion and emotional strain of losing his beloved mother had taken their toll on him. He was weak and powerless; it was so sad to see him in such a state. Once again, God showed us His favor and touched and restored Morris' health, enabling him to regain his strength so that he could return to work.

Within a few months, circumstances began to improve for our family. We started 1981 with a measure of happiness following deep sadness. We purchased a four-bedroom house! How that happened was another of God's miraculous doings. We had left the money from the sale of our car in Nigeria, and we were praying for a way to obtain it for the down payment on a house. Unfortunately, the usual courtesy extended to missionaries for the transfer of their money through the General Conference headquarters was not extended to our family, so our money remained in the Nigerian Union Conference treasury for some time.

During Morris' trip home for his mom's burial, he visited the Adventist headquarters located in Ikeja where, providentially, he met the church's division auditor who had traveled from England to Nigeria to audit the books. In their conversation, he asked Morris why his money was still on the books, and Morris explained the reason. Immediately, he authorized the transfer of the money and requested the Treasury personnel to process it to the U.S. These funds were used as the down payment for our much-needed and long-awaited house.

After a year living in an apartment, we had grown weary of cramped quarters and were eager to move to a larger place. We were all excited as we began our search for a new house. We wanted a four-bedroom house so that each of our daughters could have her own bedroom; we also wanted a den or a large family room. We secured the services of James Walker, a Christian realtor and family friend, and our search of properties in various neighborhoods began in earnest.

We checked several houses until we found one we liked, but it had only three bedrooms and no den. A three-bedroom house was far better than the two-bedroom apartment we were living in. We made an offer, but another bidder had submitted theirs before we did, and the house was no longer available. Disappointed, but not daunted by this setback, we continued our search, and God led us to the right house at the right price, and in the right location that same day.

The house we finally purchased was larger and nicer than the one we had selected previously. In addition to four bedrooms, it had a combination dining/living room, a den, a large backyard, and was located about a mile from Oakwood. It was perfect. We were pleased with the purchase, and we thanked God for helping us secure our new home. The girls were ecstatic. Akunna, three years old at the time, didn't want to return to the apartment. Whenever we got in our car, her countenance became sad as she pointed in the direction of the apartment and said, "Don't go that way; don't go that way."

Looking back on this miracle experience, we saw that, even in the delay in getting our money from Nigeria, God was working everything out in our favor. Had the money been transferred earlier, it might have been spent on pressing need, thus, making it harder to provide the down payment for our new home. Sometimes, what we consider a roadblock or a setback that is impeding our progress is indeed our Heavenly Father turning it into an "Aha!" moment. I am very grateful to God, Who, in the midst of our valley of grief, filled our cup with joy and gladness. He works in mysterious ways His wonders to perform.

Morris and I still live in that same house more than 36 years later, and God has blessed us with wonderful neighbors like Carl and Debra Smith, and Savonia McClellan, for whom we are very grateful. Our girls are adults and live in other cities, but, when they come to visit, they boldly claim their rooms and complain about my stuff cluttering their closets. I am thankful that even when we couldn't see the future, God was always ahead of us, guiding, directing, and working out His incredible plan for the Iheanacho family. He never forsook nor abandoned us, and our hearts rejoice.

"Blessed be the name of the Lord now and forever. Everywhere—from east to west— praise the name of the Lord" (Psalm 113:2, 3, NLT).

Chapter 11

My Oakwood Journey

*B*y December 1981, our finances had begun to improve, so we, along with our niece, Richelle, traveled to California to spend the Christmas holidays with my brothers, Rudolph and Edison, whom I had not seen for many years. On our way, we visited the Hoover Dam and other interesting places. We had a great time visiting family and friends while also enjoying various popular amusement sites, which the kids enjoyed immensely. We treasure fond memories of our visit out west.

Soon after our return home, I received a phone call from Dr. Rock offering me a position in the President's office. It was raining and thundering that night, and I doubted that I'd heard him correctly. Also, I didn't know him well and thought that he must have made a mistake. The next day, I contacted him at his office and asked, "Dr. Rock, do you know you called me last night and offered me a job in your office?" His quick and unexpected response stunned me: "Yes, I was of sound mind!" The door of opportunity had finally opened for me to work at Oakwood. There is no doubt it was God's doing. On January 20, 1982, I joined my husband as an Oakwood employee, and thus began my 26-year-journey at this God-ordained institution of higher learning.

As a young girl, and even as an adult, it never occurred to me that my career path would one day take me to this prestigious college. Now, here I was, the new kid on the block, in the President's office, surrounded by strange and unfamiliar faces. Not long after assuming my responsibilities, a junior administrator entered the president's office and was surprised to see me seated at my desk. "How did you get here?" she asked. "The President hired me," I responded nervously.

Life is a potpourri—a mixture of positives and negatives. While working in the President's office, as in any other office, I experienced good times and some not so good. Other times, obstacles threatened to dampen my spirit, but, I tried to keep my focus and perform my duties to the best of my ability, with the Lord's help and guidance, and He blessed.

Although computer literacy was not my forte, I was blessed with many of the other skills that were necessary to manage and represent the President's office in a reputable, effective, and efficient manner. God was always with me. My life was in His hands, and He knew how to turn obstacles into stepping stones. With His ever-present help, my excellent secretarial training and background, and my people skills, I was able to survive more than 20 memorable years—the longest period for a secretary/administrative assistant in the history of the President's office at Oakwood. God is faithful, and He kept His promise found in Isaiah 40:31, NLT: "But those who wait on the LORD will find new strength. They will fly high on wings like eagles. They will run and not grow weary. They will walk and not faint." It is true that in His time, He makes all things beautiful (Ecclesiastes 3:11).

Among the privileges I treasured while working in the office of the president was the opportunity to meet high-ranking church officials like Dr. Charles E. Bradford, retired President of the North American Division of SDA and Chairman of the Oakwood Board of Trustees, along with G. Ralph Thompson, retired Secretary of the General Conference of SDA. Other individuals I met included Hollywood celebrities and notable government representatives, like Colin Powell, former Secretary of State; Jonathan Bush, brother of former President George H. W. Bush; Mae Jemison, the first Black female astronaut; and the late Florence Joyner Griffin (Flo Jo), one of the world's fastest track stars in the eighties, and many more.

In 2002, the Board of Trustees created a new office—Provost and Senior Vice President—to assist the president, Dr. Delbert W. Baker, with some of his many responsibilities. Dr. Mervyn Warren, the person elected by the Board to direct this new office, invited me to be his assistant. My work in that office spanned six years until my retirement in July 2007.

No matter the difficulties that we've encountered along the way, I am still convinced that God, in His providence, placed us where He willed to accomplish specific goals that He set for us. He enlarged our territory of service, witnessing, and sharing His love and blessings with hundreds of students and people worldwide and in all walks of life. He also provided many opportunities for us to reach out and help others along the way, and to contribute to the furtherance of His work in the various capacities in which we served. Our lives have been tremendously blessed and enriched through these experiences.

I recall a beautiful, sunny afternoon when a young man whom I had helped with a President's Scholarship when he was a freshman, walked into my office with a sad countenance. "What's going on in your life?" I inquired. "My professor told me that I cannot graduate in May, that I would have to wait until next year," he responded sadly. I asked him if he wanted to graduate and what he would have to do to make it a reality. He said that he wanted to graduate, but would need to CLEP (College Level Examination Program) two courses to test out of them without having actually to take them, and he didn't have the money to purchase the study guides. I gave him the money and encouraged him to do his best. He returned a few weeks later with a big smile on his face and the good news that he had passed the tests and fulfilled the requirements for graduation.

His mother was delighted to hear this, but there was yet another significant hurdle to overcome! When she called the accounting office to ascertain the amount of her son's final bill, she was told that his balance was $1,404.50. Students are not allowed to graduate with outstanding bills, so, right away, she began to make plans to secure a loan. She was a faithful supporter of Oakwood College. For several years, she had served as a chaperone for prospective students attending College Days, when Oakwood hosts high school seniors over a long weekend to give them a snapshot view of life at Oakwood. Therefore, I felt that something should be done to assist her in her time of need, so I advised her not to secure a loan until she heard from me. In the meantime, I contacted a few supportive friends and faithful contributors like Dr. Cooper, Dr. Hodges, Dr. Warren, Attorney Murrain, including Morris, and was able to raise $1,150. A friend of Jonathan's family contributed $250.00. We wanted Jonathan to be a part of this process so that he would have some ownership in it, so he paid the remaining balance of $4.50.

It was exciting to watch God move in the hearts of these benefactors to accomplish His plan for this young man. Best of all, a few weeks later, Jonathan's mother watched with joy and pride as her son walked across the stage to receive his college diploma. We were all very happy and thanked God that Jonathan didn't have to wait an additional year to see his dreams of a degree fulfilled. He obtained a job teaching in an inner-city school and made a remarkable difference in the lives of his students. Approximately one year later, I received a copy of the official announcement that Jonathan had been named "Teacher of the Year." All praise to God Almighty! Not long ago, I came across a beautiful thank-you card he had sent me during his freshman year.

David, another student, whom I called my campus grandson, was lacking one course to graduate. It was too late to register for the class so he would have to CLEP out of it; but, as with Jonathan, he lacked the funds to pay for it. I gave him the money for the test and admonished him to be serious about the exam and not to disappoint me.

He passed the exam, but I was disappointed when he said that he wasn't planning to march at graduation. Because he's an only child and this would be his mother's only opportunity to see her child achieve this milestone, I had a serious "motherly" talk with him and counseled him not to deny her the honor and privilege of seeing him graduate. I had never met his mother, but we had occasionally spoken on the telephone. I called her and invited her to stay at our home for commencement weekend. She was happy that her son was graduating and gladly accepted the offer.

A few days later, she called, "Sister 'I,'" she said, "I don't think I can come to David's graduation. I had some dental work done, and the dentist said my new teeth would not be ready in time for me to travel." I was disappointed and told her that, teeth or no teeth, she was coming. I knew that she didn't want to miss this moment. She came and was thrilled to witness her son receive his diploma. Years have passed since this incident, but David's mother never fails to express her gratitude for the assistance her son received.

David currently lives in Spain, but we have kept in touch. Some time ago, he called to inform me of a freshman student who was attending Oakwood. He wanted me to extend to this young man an invitation for Sabbath lunch as I had done for him when he was an

Oakwood student. I was delighted to honor his request. The young man and his friends enjoyed a great meal and fellowship.

A few years ago, I met a former student who returned to the campus for the thirtieth-anniversary celebration of Dr. Eurydice Osterman's Oakwood College Choir. She was happy to see me and introduced me to her husband and son. She looked familiar, and I was a little embarrassed that I couldn't recall her name. She said her name was Donna and asked if I remembered her. She continued, "When I was a student at Oakwood, I didn't have enough money to register, and I came to the President's office in search of a scholarship. You told me to wait a minute, and you made a few phone calls. I was able to get into school. You helped me on more than one occasion. I appreciate all you did for me. Thank you very much!" That's what life is all about—making a difference and helping others. When we follow this principle, as the song says, our living shall not be in vain. Paul reiterates this idea in Hebrews 13:16 when he says: "But do not forget to do good and to share, for with such sacrifices God is well pleased" (NJKV).

God performed many wonderful blessings for my family on a regular basis. Another miracle that He put in place was for my daughter, Akunna. She had completed her master's degree in chemistry at the University of Virginia and was scheduled to begin work at Johns Hopkins University. Unfortunately, she was unable to secure an apartment at an affordable price near the university and became increasingly concerned as the time to move rapidly approached. I received an email from her asking if I knew Dr. Lois Peters and that someone had mentioned that she had rental properties. Akunna requested that I contact her and ascertain if this was true.

I had known Lois for many years; she had served as a member of the Oakwood University Board of Trustees. I immediately called her and, after our usual warm greeting, I asked if she had rental property available that my daughter could rent. I can still hear the excitement in her voice as she responded, "Tell your daughter that she is welcomed to stay at my house for a year until she gets settled, and she doesn't have to worry about paying rent." Dr. Peters' generous response surprised me. "But Lois, you don't know my daughter," I said. "No, I don't, but I know you. You have been helpful to me over the years. Every time I've called Oakwood with a problem or inquiry, you either took care of it or connected me with someone who could. I am happy for the opportunity to return the favor," was her welcomed response.

Akunna was a guest at the Peters home for a year. As she was preparing to move to an apartment, Lois, in her generous and kind-hearted manner, extended the courtesy for another year. Thank you, Lois. "Out of the fullness of his grace he has blessed us all, giving us one blessing after another" (John 1:16, Good News Translation).

This experience reiterated the importance of being helpful, kind, and courteous to fellow travelers you meet on the road of life. You never know under what circumstance or situation you may meet them again. Mahatma Gandhi, an Anti-War Activist, born in 1869, puts it succinctly in these powerful words, "I shall pass through this world but once. Any good therefore that I can do or any kindness that I can show to any human being, let me do it now. Let me not defer it or neglect it, for I shall not pass this way again."

God continued to provide evidence to assure me that He was looking out for me. Without His divine intervention, the incident I am about to share could have been an embarrassment for the university administrators, and more so for me. Jessica, my student assistant, was working on an assignment that I had asked her to save on a disk. I was about to hand it to her when I felt impressed to check it. To my astonishment and disbelief, it contained the beginning draft of a letter I had started a few months earlier. I became concerned right away. Back in June, before leaving on vacation, I had prepared the draft for my boss and had copied the address information on a disk for my assistant to process when it was completed. Apparently, it was overlooked, and, when I returned many days later, I forgot to follow through.

The draft, dated June 2006, was addressed to a gentleman, General Olshefski, who was scheduled to speak for the Faculty-Staff Colloquium the following morning, August 6. Frantically, I searched everywhere for any indication that the letter had been completed and mailed—my computer, Jessica's computer, the file cabinet—but my search only confirmed my dreaded fear.

Since the Provost's and President's offices often collaborated on the colloquium speakers, I contacted the President's office and inquired as to whether or not an official letter had been sent to the general. The negative response further deepened my anguish. The situation was getting worse; I was in big trouble. It was after 5:00 p.m. and no one was in the general's office. I could only leave voicemails with every source I checked; there were no live people I could talk to at this late time. Nervously, I petitioned God for help, "Lord, please help me! It will be a huge embarrassment if I don't reach the general. He's scheduled to speak at 9:30 tomorrow morning. Please help me find a way to contact him soon. Thank You, in Jesus' name, Amen."

As my mother would often say, "Time waits for no man!" And time seemed to be moving double-time. I opted not to inform my boss until I had checked out every possible source. I told Jeannie, the President's administrative assistant, not to mention anything to the President; I would handle it myself. She shared the general's home telephone number with me, and I dialed it. On the other end was a very pleasant female voice. I asked if I had reached the general's residence and if he was at home. She responded that I had reached the right residence, but that he was not at home.

I explained that I had a serious dilemma and needed her assistance and explained the situation to her and that, from all indications, he had never received the official invitation. I asked if she could give him a message. She started to laugh. I told her not to laugh that I was in deep trouble. She assured me that if he could, he would be willing to come. She gave me the direct phone number to his office. Before dialing it, I prayed again, "Lord, You've got to help me out, please, please!"

I dialed the number, and General Olshefski answered right away. He started to laugh. He said that his wife had told him to expect my call. I apologized for my oversight, and he asked what time he was scheduled to speak. I told him, and he checked his calendar and said he was available. Joy and extreme relief flooded my heart. I wanted to shout. I informed him of the specific topic President Baker wanted him to cover, and he said he'd be happy to do it. I breathed a deep sigh of relief and offered up a HUGE prayer of gratitude to God for working this one out and saving me from what could have been a horribly bad situation.

The next day, I met General Olshefski in the parking lot; he greeted me with a big smile, and remarked, "You must be Shirley!" "Good morning, Sir, I hate to admit it, but I am," I humbly responded. I apologized once more for the oversight, and we chatted as I escorted him to the auditorium where the president introduced him to the audience. His remarks were positive, informative, interesting, and well-received. Everyone was impressed with his humor, personality, and humility. And you know what else? He never mentioned a word about having just received the invitation the evening before, and I never told the president or the provost. If they read this book, I believe it will be their first knowledge of it.

Can you imagine what would have happened if God had not impressed me to check the disk? What an awful mess I would have been in? "Great is the LORD, and greatly to be praised. And His greatness is unsearchable" (Psa. 145:3, (NKJV).

At the end of the two-day colloquium, my boss honored me with a dozen beautiful red roses for my work. He referred to me as the Queen of Colloquium. I had worked with Colloquia for more than 25 years, and was unaware, at the time, that this one would prove to be my last as an employee of Oakwood University because I retired the following year. It was certainly nice to end on a positive note, especially when one considers how it could have ended. The Lord repeatedly declared these life-giving words to me: "For I know the plans I have for you, plans to prosper you and not to harm you, plans to give you hope and a future." Lord, I thank You for Your faithfulness and for doing exceeding abundantly more than I could ask or think!

Presidents with Whom I've Served

This book would be incomplete if I failed to recognize the four distinguished presidents with whom I had the honor to serve for the major portion of my professional life. They were: Dr. Calvin B. Rock, Dr. Emerson A. Cooper (interim), Dr. Benjamin F. Reaves, and Dr. Delbert W. Baker. Each president exhibited a profound love for God, family, students, and work. It was a delight to work with these committed and dedicated leaders. As time passed, I learned to understand their expectations and unique ways of doing things. I have great respect for them and the wisdom they exhibited in strategizing and positioning Oakwood University as a leading historically Black university.

These men were gifted visionaries, and anyone working with them had to possess the stamina, personality, diplomacy, and skills necessary to assist them in their various roles. Physical, mental, emotional, and spiritual acumen were an essential part of handling the various complexities and demanding challenges that developed from time to time. One of the many lessons I learned was that you must be careful what you say or do; you never know who is listening, watching, or taking notes.

It became evident many years ago, when, as an elder at the Oakwood University Church, a fellow elder and I visited the home of the late Mrs. Ruth Stafford, retired chairperson of the Oakwood College Nursing Department, who had been confined to her home because of illness. One of her relatives introduced me as the president's secretary. I was surprised by her quick response, "Yes, I know her. In all the years I've lived in this community, I've never heard anyone say a bad word about her or that she brought information out of the President's office." That was quite an observation coming from someone who didn't know me personally.

Comments of Four Presidents

Dr. Calvin Bovell Rock—1971 to 1985.

Dr. Rock was the first president with whom I served. His comments are as follows: "Shirley Cyrene Iheanacho served in the president's office the last several years of my tenure at Oakwood College. By her organizational skills, her affable personality, her editorial abilities, and overall secretarial talents, she not only 'ran a good ship,' but 'fought a good fight' and deserves even now an emphatic 'well done' for her part in the progress then attained. She had the task of sending out notices, transcribing letters, keeping up with board minutes, scheduling appointments, responding to requests for information, comforting parents, interfacing with visitors (dignitaries and otherwise), typing sermons, not to mention answering phones. Doing this while rearing three lively daughters was all daunting, but she did it with class and efficiency for which I am eternally grateful, and Oakwood richly blessed."

Dr. Emerson A. Cooper, Interim President— (deceased)
August 1985 to December 1985.

Dr. Cooper helped to sharpen my editorial skills by requesting that I proofread his books and other publications. He writes: "I would also like to take this opportunity to commend

Mrs. Shirley Iheanacho for her excellent contribution to the operation of the office of the presidency during my administration. I know of no other person who could have served Oakwood College in that office with such an ideal blend of personality, competence, and dedication in carrying out all the operations of that office."

Dr. Benjamin F. Reaves—1985 to 1996.

Dr. Reaves is the president with whom I had the longest tenure. He states: "During my tenure as President of Oakwood College, it was my major blessing to have as my executive secretary Shirley I. She was not only energetic and efficient, but she was also experienced. I can say she was the epitome of what an executive secretary should be. Her positive, upbeat personality and willingness to do whatever was needed to serve the College was an incredible asset. As I reflect on those years together, I marvel at her perceptive ability to identify with my way of thinking and speaking that she could flesh out the barest skeletal outline I might provide in a manner that accurately reflected what I meant to communicate. Her masterful ability to deal with the various publics often calmed the spirits of concerned parents who called on various issues. Whatever the matter, they found her calm, courteous, and concerned about what mattered to them.

From the day I took on those enormous responsibilities, Shirley, with her experience of four years serving in the President's office accelerated my journey up the learning curve of challenges and activities that filled the agenda of my new office. As a consequence of our teamwork, we were able to engage the pressing issues that confronted us rapidly. With Shirley's office expertise at home, externally, I was able to advance the College's national identity.

Dr. Delbert W. Baker—1996 to 2010.

Dr. Baker's comments are as follows: "The Fall of 1996 brought me to Oakwood College as its 10th president. Having come to the helm to join an outstanding list of presidential predecessors, I would continue the institution's progress toward advancement and achievement. I came at a pivotal time in the history of the school which was celebrating its Centennial. The Millennium was approaching, and Oakwood was soon to begin its information technology era officially. It was a momentous time regarding historicity, movement, fluctuation and transition, and a time of change.

The Office of the President needed a steady, calm, and professional presence. Shirley Iheanacho filled that role. I say that for some reasons: She had a vast experience, having worked with three presidents previously: Calvin Rock, Emerson Cooper, and Benjamin Reaves. Her background and personal philosophy had given her a real commitment to living up to the full responsibility that an academic setting required — everything from the appropriate professional image to an efficiency and quality in all correspondence and institution documents.

Shirley maintained a spiritual mentorship, not simply with the office, but with students, faculty, and staff. As a woman of integrity and high personal goals, her influence was a blessing to the presidents she served as well. All of this helped to form the core essentials of the office of the presidency during that time of transition.

A distinctly personable element, which, while not highly touted in a public sense, found her seeking to meet the needs of students with whom she came in contact. Every semester she raised what now amounts to many thousands of dollars by making contacts with willing contributors. She was successfully able to use this quality in her role of Administrative Assistant to the President. People were aware she knew the needs of the school and under-stood challenges facing the students.

Through her standing via her role in the President's Office, she was able to leverage the assistance needed to help others. It was the concept of the story of Esther who 'came to the kingdom for such a time as this.' In fact, many students made this very statement. Letters she received were very laudatory of how she went beyond the call of duty to assist them with needed finances, as well as giving counsel and praying with them. This counsel extended to other employees who would stop in to share their burdens and receive in return, helpful, often therapeutic advice.

She was willing to give frank and honest suggestions and insights to me in my role. As an administrator, this was invaluable. She was often able to identify land mines, potential personnel problems, and efficiencies for the office. She was always one to stress a balanced life. She was able to give good advice on the presidential level. She would share from her vast store of information on how presidents dealt with situations in the past, although never presenting in such a way as to be awkward or to suggest that I follow the same. She had a good sense of delineating her opinion while respecting your personal authority. Further, Shirley was highly respected by the Board of Trustees who knew her as a point of stability.

A spiritual woman of prayer and Bible study, Shirley had a strong commitment to family. She and Morris have been good friends to Susan and me, and to our three sons, David, Benjamin, and Jonathan. She could also be found praying with others by phone and was a Bible student and scholar in her own right. One of the elders at the Oakwood Church, she was highly respected in her role. Shirley carried herself with class and dignity among the leaders of the school while having the common touch in relating to others not a part of the leadership structure.

Shirley exercised an initiative in producing writings during the time her husband was ill that became a blessing to other wives also experiencing similar crises. At times when called upon to speak or write for various publications, she juggled responsibilities of home, family, and office with grace. It was a wonderful compliment to her. She maintained strong family ties with her siblings and often spoke of her mother and her life in Barbados. Shirley and Morris have presented a fine image of a couple who are consistent, converted Christians, totally committed to Oakwood University. As a community-minded person, she was often brimming with suggestions on how to best network with the public.

Shirley was consistent in her initiation of ideas that she felt would strengthen the office, a very important concept for me. She would often contribute lists of helpful suggestions: people to talk with, calls I needed to make, community contacts to follow-through on, or things for which to watch out. She was committed to looking out for the president and his office, a valuable quality in assisting me. Shirley was composed in the midst of crisis. When legal and weighty issues would surface, I could always count on her to be calm, consecrated, and committed.

When all is said and done, Shirley Iheanacho will go down in the history of Oakwood University as one of our leading administrative assistants who left a rich legacy. I will always appreciate the years I spent working with her in the Office of the President. From the Bible, two traits are highlighted: "Whatsoever thy hand findeth to do, do it with thy might" (Ecclesiastes 9:10, KJV), and "Moreover it is required in stewards that a man be found faithful" (1 Corinthians 4:2). Shirley Iheanacho personifies both of these qualities."

Before I transitioned from the President's office to the Office of the Provost and Senior Vice President, President Baker requested a description of my responsibilities in the President's office. He expressed astonishment at the number of things I did behind the scenes outside of my portfolio of which he was unaware.

Dr. Cooper, Dr. Reaves, Shirley, Dr. Baker, Dr. Rock

Oakwood's First Ladies

I count it an honor to give special tribute to three distinguished "First Ladies" with whom I served during my 20-year tenure in the office of the president at Oakwood: Mrs. Clara Rock, Mrs. Jean Reaves, and Dr. Susan Baker. These phenomenal women were Christ-like, dignified, caring, loving, humble, kind, generous, professional, brilliant, and exceedingly supportive of their spouses. Each, in her unique way, contributed immeasurably to her husband's outstanding successes and accomplishments. They loved the Lord, their families, the students, and Oakwood. We thank God for these amazing ladies and their distinguished service. A special salute to Mrs. Rock who influenced Dr. Rock to offer my husband a job. It opened the door for me to serve this great university.

Dr. Mervyn A. Warren, Provost and Senior Vice President

During my last six years at Oakwood University, I had the honor to serve as the administrative assistant to Dr. Mervyn A. Warren, Provost and Senior Vice President from 2002 to 2007. Dr. Warren's distinguished career has spanned more than five decades at Oakwood University. Here are his comments:

"Standing before the freshman class at Oakwood University, the educator gives the self-same formula for success which is repeated every year for the ensuing school term: 'Start strong; Start strong!' I have heard it over and over again for the students, but, in 2002, it was my turn for such a formula as I began my new tenure as Provost. When Shirley Cyrene Howell Iheanacho accepted the invitation to work with me as Administrative Assistant, I instantly assumed confidence and a sense of advantage derived from her well-known efficiency and experience from her having worked recently with four successive presidents at the same institution, Oakwood. That she remained in the Office of the Provost for five consecutive years until her retirement speaks

Shirley and Dr. Warren

well, I like to think, on behalf of her desire and freedom to contribute to dedicated efforts of institutional leadership, relationships, and professional fellowship.

To the table of service, she brought strengths from her two decades of office administrative management. Furthermore, she performed her duties with dignity and efficiency along with her altruism and financial assistance for students, the worth of which only heaven knows. Whatever Provost Initiatives her hands were a part of, hers was the 'Midas touch.'

In my functioning consociately with the school President and providing some measure of coordination of the Vice Presidents, I was exceptionally blessed to have Shirley right there by my side, a professional already familiar with the dynamics and playing field of major administration. She was key to our efforts to 'start strong' and strive to go from strength to strength. And above everything, that which soars above all that we could ever think, say, or write is: She practices her Christian commitment to God and lives to bring cheer to her family, friends, and fellow human beings."

Other individuals who had a profound impact on my Oakwood journey were: Dr. Roy E. Malcolm, Dr. Rosa T. Banks, and Dr. Bernard Benn. Dr. Malcolm served in various professional areas at the university, and we had the opportunity to serve on various committees and to work together on several special projects. I also proofread many of his books, college bulletins, etc. Dr. Banks was the first and only female on the President's Cabinet at that time. She was intelligent, professional, competent, and knowledgeable about the affairs of the college. She opened the door for other females to serve on the President's Council. The late Dr. Bernard Benn, who served as professor and chairperson of the English department at OU for many years, was my unpaid and unofficial consultant who readily responded when I called with questions regarding correct grammar, etc., as well contributed to scholarship requests.

My island friend, Shirley Bailey, worked as a secretary in the office of Academic Affairs and Public Relations. She and I were privileged to work together on ad hoc committees and various projects.

I must mention my classmate, Attorney Bill Murrain. We both graduated from Andrews University in the Class of 1968. He served as a member of the Oakwood Board of Trustees with distinction for 23 years. He was a faithful contributor of scholarships to assist needy students whenever I called on him. I thank God for these individuals and countless others whom He placed in my path and who enriched and profoundly impacted my Oakwood journey.

"Praise the LORD! For it is good to sing praises to our God; For it is pleasant, and praise is beautiful" (Psalm 147:1, NKJV).

Chapter 12

Children and Grandchildren

"Children are a gift from the LORD; they are a reward from him" (Psalms 127:3, NLT). God blessed my husband and me to be the proud parents of three brilliant and beautiful daughters who have been a major part of the success God enabled us to achieve over the years. I am pleased to share a few highlights about them and our two grandsons.

During elementary school, high school, and college, the girls were active in church programs and many service-oriented community activities. In addition to their regular studies, music was an integral part of their curriculum. They became involved, to some degree, with piano, violin, guitar, and/or clarinet lessons. All three were blessed with brilliant minds and were the recipients of numerous academic honors and service awards. Upon completion of high school, they received four-year scholarships to prestigious colleges and universities, including Oakwood University.

During one of my spring cleaning days, I came across my old autograph book and was amused to read a note that Ngozi wrote on December 31, 1981, at the age of 11: "To Mom, From Dr. Ngozi, Love always, Ngozi. P.S. You can get ten free injections and one heart transplant, all the rest would have to be payed for with cash. Just joking, Ngozi." I also read a letter from Chioma dated March 14, 1984, when she was 11. She titled it: "Things I did today" 1. Cleaned the den two times. 2. Vacuumed the kitchen twice. 3. Emptied the garbage (kitchen). 4. Cleaned Akunna's bedroom. 5. Emptied upper trash cans. 6. Watched Akunna and Titia playing. 7. Scrubbed the table real good. 8. Swept the kitchen. 9. Went to sleep; 10. Woke up to Titia crying. 11. Solved arguments; 12. Washed many dishes; 13. Made breakfast. By the end of the day, I was ". . ." Here she drew a picture of herself stretched out on a bed, with her hands dropped to the sides of the bed, and a note coming from her lips that said, "Thank you, Jesus." I had a good laugh as I reminisced.

Akunna wrote the following when she was in elementary school: "Mother, You're pretty, sweet and loving. As mothers should be; and best of all Mother, You gave the world Me!!! I love you! Akunna Iheanacho." May 7, 1987, she penned these words: "Dear Mom, I know I don't always show that I love you. But I do and don't have enough words to tell you I love you. Love, Akunna. The best Mom in the world." I thank God for these precious gifts of my beautiful daughters who have blessed my heart with profound joy.

Ngozi is astute, hardworking, kindhearted, generous, always caring and helpful. She played the clarinet and piano in elementary and high school and sang in the academy and college choirs. She was an excellent swimmer and ran track. All throughout her academic career, she received academic honors and awards. In her freshman year at Oakwood, she was crowned debutante queen. In addition to her studies, she was involved in extracurricular activities, including tutoring elementary and high school students.

In 1991, she obtained her B.S. degree in Biology, cum laude, from Oakwood University and was accepted at Yale University to pursue graduate studies. Instead, she attended Case Western Reserve University where she completed her master's degree in anesthesiology in 1993. She is a board-certified anesthetist and works at a children's hospital.

Ngozi Master's degree graduation

Wedding bells rang out for Ngozi and Timothy Bolton at the Oakwood University Church on Sunday, May 24, 1998. The occasion was like a mini-reunion of my friends and former roommates. Florence Scobie, Anne Winbush, Beulah Andrews, Anne Marie Francis, and others worked untiringly to transform the church into a place of spring beauty and elegance. It was a beautiful experience as Morris and I escorted our first-born daughter down the aisle to meet her husband-to-be. We listened attentively as they pledged their lives to each other. I can hardly believe that more than 18 years have gone by since that memorable occasion. Ngozi and Tim have blessed us with one grandson, Timothy Darryl Iheanacho Bolton. Together, they are involved in activities and outreach ministries at their church, including feeding the homeless.

Tim's & Ngozi's wedding

Chioma, our second daughter, is gifted and talented in numerous ways. She is brilliant, generous, with a kind, caring, warm heart, and an infectious smile. She attended Oakwood University, majored in Computer Information Systems, and is a Certified IT Asset Manager, Certified Software Asset Manager, Certified Software Manager, and a Certified Negotiator. She is employed as a Program Manager at one of the world's leading computer companies.

In elementary and high school, she was the winner of many awards for her feats in track and field. She loves to sing and has sung in many choirs. She took piano, guitar, and violin lessons and excelled in playing the piano and violin during high school. At the end of one of her lessons, her violin teacher commented that she had gifted fingers. A further demonstration of this occurred during her freshman year at Oakwood University when she performed "Perpetual Mobile" at a Talent Show and was awarded the first prize. After her performance, a thunderous applause erupted from the audience as they stood to their feet. Chioma looked on in shock at this unexpected outpouring of appreciation for her talent and proficiency. In

September 1999, she married David Trofort in a private ceremony, and, in July 2000, Morris and I became the proud grandparents of our first grandson, Nikolas Adjua Malachi Trofort.

Akunna, though at times reserved, lights up any room in which she is present. She is thoughtful and has always demonstrated a tenacious faith in God. She makes careful observations and truly has a gift with words. She received countless honors and awards from elementary school through college for her scholastic achievements.

Akunna took violin, piano, and clarinet lessons in elementary school, and was a member of the marching band in middle school. She was also a member of the woodwind section of the Huntsville Metropolitan Youth Orchestra during middle and high school. She was an excellent sprinter and, like Chioma won awards for track and field. She loves to sing. As a high school senior, she sang "What about the Children" for the Honors Award Program at Huntsville High School. Following the program, one of her teachers commented that Akunna's song brought tears to her eyes. During her time at Oakwood, she sang with the Aeolians, the Oakwood College Choir, Dynamic Praise, and the Madison Mission SDA Church Mass Choir. She continues to sing with several ensembles and choirs. She also serves as a member of the praise team at her local church and is an active participant in community involvement and outreach activities.

She graduated cum laude with a B.S. from Oakwood University and completed her master's degree in Chemistry at the University of Virginia. "God is not a man, that he should lie, or a son of man, that he should change his mind. Has he said, and will he not do it? Or has he spoken, and will he not fulfill it?" (Numbers 23:19, ESV). And Isaiah 41:13: "For I, the LORD your God, will hold your right hand, Saying to you, "Fear not, I will help you.""

God fulfilled these scriptures for Akunna and much more in profound and magnificent ways during her journey at Johns Hopkins University School of Medicine in pursuit of her Ph.D. in Cellular and Molecular Physiology. Her journey was grueling, with many sleepless nights and stressful days filled with disappointments, doubt, and uncertainty. At one point, after she had completed all the coursework long in advance, finishing her scientific research project proved to be an uphill battle. Sometimes, her dream of attaining her Ph.D. seemed unattainable, and I was tempted to tell her to pursue something else, but she continued to place her trust and faith in God. She petitioned Him daily to help her and to work things out to His glory. Loved ones and friends prayed; her family and prayer warriors prayed and fasted, yet God seemed silent. Even so, she never gave up; she persevered amidst severe odds and sometimes seemingly insurmountable obstacles. She would often say that without a test there is no testimony.

Often, in my prayer time, I struggled, "Lord, why are You standing by and letting all of this happen when Akunna is trying so hard, spending many long days and nights in the research lab, trying this technique and that without success?" During our telephone conversations, she always displayed a cheerful and optimistic attitude. She would often say, "Without a test, there is no testimony. I don't believe that God would have allowed me to be admitted to the program only to allow me to fail."

Morris and I set aside one day a week to fast and pray for her, and she would call us so that we could pray together. I admired her determination and her persistent and relentless spirit. One morning, during our telephone prayer time, I heard her agonizing plea to God: "Lord, I am tired; I don't know what else to do. Please show me." My heart was pained, and I could not hold back the tears. I prayed for God to have mercy and help her.

In our desperation, we sometimes try to tell God what to do and how and when to do it. We may even question His wisdom or timing or why He didn't answer when we wanted Him to or why He answered in the way He did. We would do well to remember that He is God, the Master Controller of the universe, as well as the minutest details of our lives. He knows what He's doing. He doesn't need our help. Sometimes He brings us to the end of our rope where we find ourselves totally helpless without His intervention. Then, in our helplessness and approaching hopelessness, we give it over to Him.

Sometimes God may delay fulfillment of His promise to test our faith and the genuineness of our prayers. This was the case with Akunna's journey to her Ph.D., and, I must admit, that, as my faith was tested through her experience, I sometimes failed God's tests. In my defense, I'm sure that most mothers would attest to the fact that it's much easier to maintain our faith through our own personal struggles than when we see our "babies," even after they're grown, going through struggles with, seemingly, no answer in sight.

Thankfully, God answered our prayers, and Akunna completed her research and dissertation. Friday, January 3, 2014, 1:30 p.m., was the appointed day and time for her thesis seminar and the defense of her Ph.D. Morris and I were jubilant. We flew to Baltimore to witness this long-awaited moment. As we exited the airport terminal, icy winds slapped our faces, and snow flurries accompanied us to Akunna's apartment. Before going to bed, we thanked God for safe travel and for blessing Akunna to reach this significant milestone. We also prayed that He would work everything out well for her.

During the night, a snowstorm raged, and we awoke to a snow-covered winter wonderland. I could hardly believe my eyes. It was breathtakingly beautiful, but, to me, unwelcome. Early that morning, Akunna received a call from a university administrator informing her that the university was closed due to the inclement weather and that she would have to reschedule her defense. Upon hearing this unwanted news, waves of disappointment swept over me. Honestly, my spirit was broken, and I silently questioned God as to why He had allowed this to happen after all the challenges and obstacles Akunna had overcome to reach this goal.

Although this was a very stressful time for all of us, I was amazed by Akunna's calm and unruffled attitude. She told the administrator that she didn't want to reschedule her defense because she was scheduled to begin full-time employment the following Monday. Akunna saw the concern on our faces and said, "God is in control, and He knows what to do." She continued to review her presentation.

Dr. Sandra Gabelli, Akunna's advisor, called and assured her that she would try to get the building opened for her defense. We prayed for God to intervene in this seemingly impossible situation. Several hours later, Dr. Gabelli called with the good news that the building would be opened for Akunna's presentation. We all rejoiced at this great news. We humbly thanked God for the marvelous thing He had done. Mark 10:27 (ESV) tells us, "With men it is impossible, but not with God; for with God all things are possible." Only God can turn impossible situations into possibilities (see Luke 1:37). "If God is for us, who can be against us?" (Romans 8:31). Sometimes, I wonder why we puny human beings try to limit our great and all-knowing God; but, of course, I just answered my own question. We're puny human beings.

Since the streets and Akunna's car were covered with snow and ice, Dr. Gabelli offered to take us to the university in her four-wheel drive vehicle. On our way, she mentioned that, if at least seven people attended the presentation, including members of Akunna's dissertation committee, it would fulfill the necessary legal requirements. We continued to pray for God's mercy and intervention. At the appointed time, Dr. Gabelli proudly introduced Akunna and spoke glowingly of her research findings, dedication, tireless efforts, and positive attitude. We prayed silently, again, that God would bless her presentation.

Shortly before her defense, Akunna had shared an email with her dad and me that she had received from one of her dissertation committee members. He wrote: "I read through your thesis. . . must say I am EXTREMELY impressed! You can write beautifully and with great clarity. It was a joy to read!!! You did a fabulous job putting this thesis together. I have no issue with it at all." So, it was with this show of support and the calm confidence of God's presence with her that Akunna stood up to make her presentation. I listened with great interest as she began. Although I didn't understand the scientific terminology (some of the words seemed a mile long), it was exciting to hear her present her research findings, as well as to view the beautiful slide presentation. Later, I turned around and was surprised to see that the room was full. Colleagues from her department and other departments, friends, and supporters had braved the awful weather to be present. Only one committee member was absent because of an overseas commitment. God worked out everything perfectly. Yes, we can count on our Heavenly Father to come through for us, right on time. He's always faithful.

During the reception Dr. Gabelli held in Akunna's honor, we were privileged to meet her colleagues and members of her dissertation committee. They commented that they were impressed with her excellent presentation and that it had been a pleasure to work with her. As her parents, Morris and I were very gratified to know that Akunna's faith, determination, and superior work ethic were so evident in her interaction with her supervisors, colleagues, and peers.

After the reception, Dr. Gabelli commented, "Whatever Akunna is involved with, I have come to expect a miracle." What a beautiful testimony! God came through for Akunna. On January 6, 2014, she began her career as a full-time biomedical staff scientist. We give all the praise, honor, and glory to our Heavenly Father. He showed Himself strong, once again. He kept His word to help, uphold, strengthen, and to be with her to the end.

I believe that the Lord allowed her to go through this experience to teach her that it is not by her might or power, but by His spirit that she had been able to achieve such significant milestones. That way, there would be no mistaking that it was He Who had done this for her. He also used her as a living testimony of His awesomeness to the people in her department.

Akunna's graduation was scheduled for Thursday, May 22, 2014. We traveled to Maryland for this celebratory moment and stayed at the beautiful home of our long-time friends, Dr. Myron and Cheryl Ottley. The forecast was for thunderclouds and rain. During the night, the weather broke loose with a vengeance. The thunder rolled, roared, and exploded; torrential rains poured down non-stop; blinding lightning flashed, and ominous clouds filled the sky. At times, the crack of thunder was so loud, it felt like the roof would collapse.

Early the next morning, during worship, I prayed that the rain would stop so that we could get to graduation on time. The university had announced earlier that, rain or shine, the graduation ceremony would proceed as planned. My mind raced as I tried to think of how we could get to the graduation venue in all of the rain. Arming ourselves with large umbrellas, we waited anxiously for the rain to subside, but there was no letting up. We decided to brave the weather and go outside to the car. As we stepped out of the house, the rain stopped, and the sun shone brilliantly. Though we had some trepidation that the rain would resume, to our joy and amazement, it didn't. Our God had come through for us, again, and we were filled with gratitude to Him for what He had done.

At 8:20 a.m., the processional began for the university-wide graduation. Excitement was in the air everywhere. Thousands of family members and friends of the graduates filled the stadium. Special guests, faculty, and graduates, decked out in colorful academic regalia, marched to their seats with faces glowing with pride and joy. It was a spectacular sight! Fluffy white clouds floated majestically across the azure skies, and the sun continued to outdo itself with warmth and dazzling splendor. There was no sign of rain, not even one drop, and the skies remained amazingly clear. The setting was perfect for the auspicious occasion that we were about to witness.

Akunna's Ph.D. graduation

The ceremony for the School of Medicine, at which Akunna would be hooded, and her degree conferred, occurred at 2:30 in the afternoon. Throughout the day, we walked around with umbrellas in our hands, a testament to the fickleness of the human condition when our God had shown us clearly that there was no need for them. His grace and faithfulness know no bounds, and He loves us so much that He shows us favor even in our disbelief and anxiety. We all enjoyed an unforgettably perfect day.

The following Sabbath, we worshiped at Akunna's church and later attended a sumptuous dinner in her honor hosted by Gerald and Ruby Anderson at their home. Before dinner was served, Akunna presented us with a beautiful Certificate of Appreciation. For Sabbath vespers, guests and family were invited to share tributes. Akunna shared her testimony of God's goodness and blessings and thanked Him for being with her throughout her incredible journey. She was thankful, too, for friends who prayed for and encouraged her along the journey. She concluded with these profound words: "I have mountains of evidence of God's faithfulness; I couldn't have done it without Him. It isn't that I'm so brilliant; it was God who enabled me to achieve this accomplishment. I thank Him for the stumbling blocks in my life that He turned into stepping stones." What a powerful testimony! We thanked

God for rewarding her hard work, tenacity, and determination a hundredfold. Our God is an awesome God!

Akunna's experience has been a real lesson for me. It has strengthened my faith and trust in God and my understanding that He will work things out for our good, no matter how unattainable our goals may appear to us. I am learning not to limit His ability to do the impossible. Yes, God is faithful; He fulfills His promises: "When you go through deep waters, He will be with you. When you go through rivers of difficulty, you will not drown. When you walk through the fire of oppression, you will not be burned up; the flames shall not consume you" (Isaiah 43:2, NLT). "Behold, I have graven you on the palms of my hands; your walls are continually before me" (Isaiah 49:16, AKJV). "Do not be afraid or discouraged, for the LORD will personally go ahead of you. He will be with you; he will neither fail you nor abandon you" (Deuteronomy 31:8, NLT). "For I the LORD your God will hold your right hand, Saying to you, "Fear not, I will help you" (Isaiah 41:13.). And Hebrews 13:5, "I will never leave you nor forsake you." And last but not least is Jeremiah 29:11, "For I know the plans I have for you," declares the LORD, "plans to prosper you and not to harm you, plans to give you hope and a future" (NIV).

I thank God for answering so many prayers and for working out, for Akunna's good, the many difficult and trying experiences she encountered. "The Lord is good, a refuge in time of trouble. He cares for those who trust in Him" (Nahum 1:7, NIV). Amen!

At family gatherings, Morris and I listen silently as the girls frequently recall childhood experiences. Their stories are not only interesting but entertaining as they reminisce about life in Nigeria and Huntsville. They recall attending school in Huntsville, going to the public library during their summer vacations, having to write book reports at my request, the chores they had to complete, the many places to which our family traveled around the country and overseas during their vacation, and the spankings they got growing up as kids.

My profound gratitude goes to our Heavenly Father for the gift of our daughters. For the joyful pride we have experienced as parents, for their loving, kind, caring ways, and lavished generosity, we are forever grateful. Any successes they have achieved can be attributed to the loving kindness of a merciful and compassionate God.

Iheanacho & Bolton families

Dedication of Our Grandsons

A remarkable year of blessings occurred for the Iheanacho family in 2000. Morris and I became proud grandparents for the first time! We stood in awe as we witnessed Nikolas, Chioma's son, come into the world. Then, six weeks later, we watched Ngozi's Timothy let out his first audible sounds. Words are inadequate to capture the joy we felt. We sent up heartfelt prayers of thanksgiving to God for the safe deliveries of both of our precious grandsons.

Nikolas & Timothy

I remember that years before, my friends spoke glowingly and displayed many photographs of their grandchildren. I didn't think too much of it, at the time, but, now, I find myself doing the same, exact thing. On the day of the dedication of both Nikolas and Timothy, several friends of our daughters traveled from around the country to attend this special ceremony conducted by Dr. John Nixon at the Oakwood University Church. Duawne Starling, Nikolas's godfather, as well as a close family friend, sang "Take My Life and Let It Be Consecrated, Lord, to Thee" (Frances R. Havergal). As sweet music floated down the aisles of the church, a hushed silence fell over the sanctuary. It seemed as if we were being ushered into the presence of God. As I pondered the lyrics of this lovely hymn, I quietly rededicated my life to God and prayed for our two innocent grandsons, asleep in the arms of the officiating elders. It was and is my strong desire that God would protect them from the dangers that lurk everywhere. I petitioned Him to bless their parents with wisdom, patience, and understanding to train them in the right way, to raise their sons and to keep them safe from the evils of this world.

Nikolas & Timothy with Dads

More than 16 years have sped by since that special moment of dedication to God. Nikolas and Timothy bonded with each other from an early age and have shared a lot of fun together. We are so grateful that God has spared our lives to watch them grow and begin their passage into youth. They have enhanced our lives with an abundance of love, laughter, wisdom, and spiritual blessings. It never occurred to me that being a grandparent could bring so much joy and excitement into our lives. We praise God for them. Over the years, we've learned that we have to be careful of what we do and say in their presence. They listen intently, storing everything in their memory bank. Sometimes, we are amazed to hear them repeat what they've heard. It's reassuring to know that our words of love and guidance to them have not been in vain.

Grandsons' Stories

Nikolas was 18 months old when I went to Chicago to visit with him and Chioma. One morning, around 2:00, I was awakened by his tiny hands shaking my body and calling out, "Gamma, wake up; weed (read) Bible!" "It's two o'clock in the morning, Nikolas," I mumbled. "It's time to sleep, not read. Go back to bed." He, of course, persisted, "Gamma, wake up; weed Bible!" The room was somewhat dark when he opened the Bible and gave it to me. I pretended to read, but he was not satisfied. "Light, Gamma, light," he continued. He reached out and turned on the light. Reluctantly, I read a story, after which he happily went back to sleep.

A few years later, when Nikolas was four, while we were visiting him, he walked into the bedroom and announced excitedly: "Gramma, I have a secret weapon!" Somewhat concerned that he might be referring to a gun, I inquired, "A secret weapon?" He raised his right hand to the sky and exclaimed, "Yes, Gramma, when Satan tempts me and tries to get me to do bad things, I say, 'Satan, in the name of Jesus, leave me alone,' and, then, I say, 'Thank you, Jesus, for saving me.'"

During that same visit, Nikolas had finished playing with his toys and left them scattered across his bedroom floor. I told him to put them away neatly. Pleadingly, he said, "Gramma, can you please help me?" "But Nikolas, you are the one who put them there, you know how to pick them up," I told him. He looked up at me and said, "Gramma, Jesus said, 'Be ye kind one to another.'" Overcome by a feeling of guilt and happy amazement at the wisdom of this child, I reached down and helped him. A grateful smile brightened his face.

One morning, after worship at his house, seven-year-old Nikolas showed me a blue notebook. On the cover was written, "Nikolas' Prayer List for People Who Need Help." He opened it and showed me more than 20 names of his classmates, teachers, family, and friends. He commented that he prays for them daily. I noticed that my name was missing, and I asked why. He said, "Gramma, I didn't know you needed help; I thought you had everything under control." After assuring him that I didn't, he added my name. When he visited us at Thanksgiving, he told me that he had forgotten his prayer book, but that he had memorized the 40 names he now had and repeated them in my hearing. Over time, his list grew to more than 100.

Nikolas has a remarkable sense of humor. On another occasion, when my husband and I were visiting, he blurted out, "I wish I still had those good old days like Gramma and Grampa." Surprised by his comments, I asked: "What good old days are you talking about, Nikolas; you are only ten years old?" "I had good old days, too, like you old people, Gramma. I wish I could go back in time when I didn't have any homework, like when I was in daycare and preschool. I always liked lunchtime. That was fun! Grampa has good old days every day now he's retired, and he doesn't have to work. I want to retire, too, but I have to help some people first." Since Nikolas was seven years old, he has wanted to retire. This may be the result of keeping too close company with his grandparents!

One evening during our worship, Morris asked Nikolas to read a few verses from the book of Proverbs. At the end of one of the readings, Morris asked him if he knew who wrote the book of Proverbs and hinted that it was written by the wisest man who ever lived. Nikolas responded, "Solomon." Then, he added, "I can't figure out how come if Solomon was so wise, why did he marry so many women? How could he stand so many women? Maybe he put each of them in a room by themselves, or maybe he put three in a room. Women like to bicker a lot, and they must have said to each other, 'Solomon likes you better than he likes me, or he spends more time with you than with me.' How could he stand all that bickering and whining?" I asked him how he knew that women liked to bicker. He responded, "Girls in my class like to bicker and whine a lot; that's a female thing!"

On a recent visit to see Chioma and Nikolas, Morris and I were having worship when Nikolas joined us and asked if he could read the devotional. We were only too happy to give our consent. He also offered to pray because he said that we prayed too long. After reading the devotional, he began to pray. He started out by thanking God for his parents and grandparents and spoke of how he loved Morris and me so much. He asked God to bless his mom and dad and all his cousins and to help them to be good. His prayer became longer and longer, and I couldn't resist the temptation to open my eyes to look at him. Just then, he said, "Lord, if it seems like I am repeating myself, I am. I love Grampa and Gramma very much, and I am going to miss them. Please help them to come back so we can see each other." His heartfelt prayer touched my inner soul deeply, but I couldn't help but smile at the length of his prayer. He seemed to be completely unaware that he had done the very thing that he didn't want us to do.

Timmy, Ngozi's son, was spending a portion of his vacation at our home in Huntsville. After playing with his toys, he said, "Gramma, can you please make some French fries for me?" Unwilling to grant his request, I told him I didn't think I could make them. He responded, "Gramma, the Bible says, 'I can do all things through Christ who strengthens me.' You can do it!" Well, I got busy and made the French fries. After eating, he said, "I like them Gramma; they were nice, only a little yellow. I knew you could do it."

One day, I was talking on the phone to four-year-old Timmy when he called out, "Hi, Gramma, how you doing? Do you know who I'm voting for?" "No, I don't," I answered. "I'm voting for President Bush," he replied. "President Bush! How come you're voting for President Bush?" I asked. "I like him. President Bush is a good President; me and my partner and best friend, Shelby, are voting for President Bush, but my other friend is voting for Senator Kerry," he replied. He later changed his mind because, after the election, when I asked him whom he had voted for, his response surprised me, "I voted for Senator Kerry because, with four more years of Bush, there will be more homeless people walking on the street for no reason, and young people will have to sign up to fight the war for no reason. That is why I voted for Senator Kerry." I laughed out loud.

At the age of five years, Timmy shared with me his Sabbath School lesson about the lost sheep. He said, "Gramma, the little sheep got lost, and the shepherd went looking for him and found him in the bush with thorns all over him. The shepherd had to clean him up and put a band-aid on his leg. The little lamb got into trouble because he didn't listen. Some little boys don't listen; some big boys don't listen, like me. So, sometimes I mess up when I don't listen or pay attention."

During one of our later telephone conversations, I mentioned to him that my prayer partner and I had committed to memorizing Bible verses, but I was having difficulty remembering them, and I wanted him to pray for me. He said, "Gramma, I have an idea; in your free time, you can write down the words on a piece of paper. Put all the words and all the dots, too. Then, you cut the paper in pieces, and then try to do a puzzle; remember to put in all the dots. You have to mix up the words first. Then try to remember the words when you put the puzzle pieces together. Another thing you can do is to get Grampa to hold the Bible when you are trying to learn the verses. If you miss a word, he can help you until you learn the whole thing." What incredible wisdom from the lips of a six-year-old!

At seven, Timmy informed me that he was running for President of his elementary school. He proceeded to show me his portfolio and to explain his campaign strategy. One of his campaign promises was to get more books for his school and help tutor kids who needed assistance with science and math. He said, "My opponents are offering fun and games, but I am offering academics in addition to fun and games." I watched him work feverishly preparing his posters:

VOTE FOR TIMMY — SUCCESS AND FUN! After the election, he called to say that he had won. I congratulated him and asked when he planned to have his victory party. His response caused me to laugh out loud, "I used up all my allowance on my campaign, so I don't have any money left. My mom said that I would have to work to get more money."

My husband and I were visiting Nikolas when Timothy called and asked Nikolas, "Why do we have to read the Bible?" Nikolas responded, "That's a good question, Timmy, that's a good question!" He continued, "We read the Bible to learn more about God than what we learn when we go to church. We can find out more about God when we read the Bible."

We enjoy our grandsons immensely and are grateful to God for these precious gifts to our family. What a serious and solemn responsibility rests on grandparents to help guide, train, and nurture their grandchildren in the path of godliness and right-living and to teach them how to make wise choices. We encourage Nikolas and Timothy to read the Bible and pray; to be obedient, kind, and respectful. The Lord has truly blessed them and their parents. We pray for His continued blessings and guidance in their lives.

Grampa with Timothy and Nikolas

"OH, sing to the LORD a new song! For He has done marvelous things"
(Psalm 98:1, NKJV).

125

Chapter 13

Life-Threatening Health Challenges

"God has not promised skies always blue, Flower-strewn pathways all our lives through; God has not promised sun without rain, joy without sorrow, peace without pain. But God has promised: Strength for the day, rest for the labor, Light for the way, Grace for the trials, help from above, Unfailing kindness, undying love" (Annie Johnson Flint).

Sometimes, life has given us some hard knocks that have caused me to buckle under and question why. However, with the passing of time, I have learned that, no matter what comes my way, good times or bad, if I put my faith and trust in God, He will turn terrible situations around and work everything out for my good. From our perspective, we may not consider our troubles good at the time, but when the dust settles, and we take the time to reflect, we will see that God has gently led us each step of the way. Life would certainly be less stressful and worrisome if we had the faith to believe that trying times are temporary, for our ultimate good, and will eventually pass.

This situation hit home rather seriously in 1999. Morris and I were busy with our responsibilities as Oakwood employees, unaware that danger lurked around the bend. He had gotten his annual physical examination, and preliminary results indicated everything was within normal limits, except his Prostate Specific Antigen (PSA) levels. A biopsy confirmed that he had prostate cancer. The news struck us like a severe blow to the head because Morris had had no prior symptoms or indications that anything was wrong. I was terrified.

126

The word *cancer* is only a six-letter word, but it has the power to strike fear and despair into a person's heart.

The night after we received the news, I recall lying in bed next to my husband. I looked at him sleeping so peacefully, like a baby, with a smile on his face and his arms folded across his chest, as if he was ready for translation. I must admit that he remained calm. His faith in God was firmly grounded, and he never complained. God gave Morris sweet peace as he trusted Him to handle the situation.

On the other hand, I must confess that my response to the situation was the opposite. When I tried to sleep, anxious thoughts bombarded my mind. Frightening questions collided at high speeds in my head. What if the treatment doesn't work and cancer spreads to other parts of his body? What if he loses his hair? What if he is sick for a long time? How will our children handle this unexpected crisis? Unfortunately, so often, when adversity strikes, we have a tendency to worry and quickly succumb to fear and disbelief instead of praying and claiming God's precious promises.

Well, when I awakened the next morning, as you can imagine, I was exhausted. I had wasted my night worrying, but the problem was still there. Nothing had changed as a result of my worrying. As the hymn says, "O what peace we often forfeit, O what needless pain we bear, all because we do not carry everything to God in prayer" (Joseph M. Scriven). Worrying doesn't help one iota! It's like a rocking chair; you can sit and rock all day and night, but it remains in the same spot. So, take my advice, don't waste time worrying and complaining; it will get you nowhere. Choose to pray instead. Prayer is one of the most powerful gifts God has given to each of us; unfortunately, we seldom take advantage of it.

After sharing the news with our family, we prayed that God would go before us, direct our path, and give us courage and strength for the journey. I am still amazed at how He did it. A scripture that brought some solace to my heart during this valley experience was Isaiah 43:1-3. I like the way the *Message* Bible puts it: "But now, God's Message, the God who made you in the first place, Jacob, the One who got you started, Israel: 'Don't be afraid, I've redeemed you. I've called your name. You're mine. When you're in over your head, I'll be there with you. When you're in rough waters, you will not go down. When you're between a rock and a hard place, it won't be a dead end—Because I am God, your personal God, The

Holy One of Israel, your Savior. I paid a huge price for you... that's how much you mean to me! That's how much I love you! I'd sell off the whole world to get you back, trade the creation just for you.'" Well, that's how deeply God loves and cares for us.

Contrary to the recommendation of his urologist, instead of surgery, Morris opted to undergo proton therapy treatment at Loma Linda University Medical Center in California. Within a few weeks, we departed from Huntsville on our journey of faith into the unknown. Before leaving Huntsville, we tried to secure a reasonably-priced apartment within walking distance of the medical center but were unsuccessful. With time against us, we settled into a one-room apartment across the street from the hospital. The rent was considerably higher than we anticipated, but it was the only place available close to the hospital.

Sitting next to Morris in the plane, anxious thoughts again invaded my mind, and I tried hard to conceal them. However, deep within my heart, I was still convinced that God was with us and that He would work it out according to His will. After several hours in the air, we arrived safely at our destination and tried to adjust quickly to our new living quarters.

Occasionally, I accompanied Morris to his treatments. One morning, I was overcome by curiosity and requested permission to get a close-up look as he prepared for treatment. It looked very scary. He had to lie completely still in a white box that was molded to fit the contours of his body; it reminded me of a coffin. The actual treatment was painless and only took a few minutes.

From time to time, I traveled from Huntsville to Loma Linda to be with Morris. It was during one of those visits that I attended the Loma Linda Medical School graduation since some of the graduates were former Oakwood students. As I was getting dressed, my thoughts drifted to the next day when I would leave Morris behind and return to work. My heart was filled with deep sadness. Then, out of the blue, I heard soothing music coming from the Christian radio in our room. "Thou wilt keep him in perfect peace whose mind is stayed on Thee"; "I am weak, but thou art strong"; "All the way my Savior leads me; What have I to ask beside? Can I doubt His tender mercy, Who through life has been my guide? Heavenly peace, divinest comfort, Here by faith in Him to dwell; For I know what-e'er befall me, Jesus doeth all things well" (Frances J. Crosby, 1875); and "Great is Thy Faithfulness," were some of the songs that ministered to my soul. As I hummed along, the heaviness of my heart gradually subsided. My worry vanished and was replaced by hymns that God had sent to dispel my fear and anxiety. Here again, my amazing Heavenly Father had reached down and encircled me with the warmth of His love and peace.

Sitting on the plane the next day, I found myself humming some of the same hymns that I had heard the previous day. I knew that, although thousands of miles would separate Morris and me, God was in control, and He would watch over us and keep us safe from harm.

Time moved along swiftly and soon, we were nearing the end of the first month of Morris' treatment, and, in a few days, the second month's rent would be due. For two days, we walked the streets of Loma Linda in sweltering heat in search of a cheaper apartment within walking distance of the hospital, but we found none. It was Friday afternoon, and the rent was due in a couple of hours. I was disappointed that God, knowing our limited finances, didn't help us find a cheaper apartment. We accepted the fact that Morris would have to stay where he was.

I was preparing to return to Huntsville when Beulah called to give me the phone number of our mutual friend, Chidi Izeogu, about whom I had inquired earlier that morning. I knew if Chidi found out that we were in the area and hadn't called her, she would be unhappy; so, I called. She was surprised to hear my voice and came immediately to see us. We told her why we were in Loma Linda, and I was taken aback by her unexpected response: "Why don't you come and stay at my place? I have an extra bedroom with a private entrance no one is using." I was speechless! I could hardly believe what I'd just heard since we hadn't mentioned anything about our search for a cheaper apartment.

Immediately, I began to pack the clothes I was planning to leave behind for my next visit while Morris sat nearby with furrowed brows. Still in shock, he turned to Chidi and asked, "How far do you live from here? I don't want to have to rent a car to go to my treatments." "Don't worry about a car; my son's car is in the parking lot of the apartment complex, not too far from Loma Linda. You can use it," she responded. I was overcome with joy and excitement and tried hard to refrain from shouting. Although my faith in God had wavered, He had come through for us again in a grand way.

That afternoon, I left for the airport praising God and singing "Glory to God in the highest; great things He has done!" By the time I arrived home, Morris had called with the

129

news that Chidi had helped him to move to her apartment. Two days later, she traveled overseas leaving him with the apartment to himself. I continued to visit him as often as possible.

Morris was the recipient of God's blessings in different and unexpected ways. Midway through his treatment, he became concerned because he was not experiencing any of the side effects associated with the treatment, such as tiredness, nausea, and weakness, as some other men did. So, he asked his physician if she was sure they were administering the right treatment. "Of course," she replied. There was no doubt in my mind that this was an added blessing from a loving Father to His son, Morris. In fact, he felt so good that he volunteered as a part-time librarian at the Loma Linda University library.

Before long, his treatment was completed, and we finalized plans to return to Huntsville. Exactly six weeks after he moved into Chidi's apartment, she returned from her overseas trip on a Thursday afternoon. Friday morning, Morris and I boarded the plane for Huntsville. That's what I call perfect timing, ordained by a perfect God who looks out for His imperfect children.

The night before our departure, Morris gave Chidi a thank-you card along with a check to cover six weeks' rent. She refused to take the check. She said that, when she recalled how God had orchestrated a series of circumstances to answer our prayer, it brought tears to her eyes. The day that I had called Chidi just to let her know that we were in town, she had been outside her apartment on her way to school to complete a few items before traveling overseas. She heard the phone ring but didn't want to take the time to go back inside to answer it. However, God impressed her to do so, and she obeyed. It was because of her obedience and God's intervention that our living arrangements changed drastically just in the nick of time. God used Chidi as the conduit through whom His blessings flowed to us in the form of a rent-free apartment.

It's interesting that, while I was complaining silently about how God had not answered our prayers, unknown to me, He was quietly putting situations and people into place for our prayers to be answered. He worked it all out according to His timetable. His timing is incredible, always perfect; never too late, nor too early. My favorite scripture, Jeremiah 29:11, comes to mind. The *Message* Version of the Bible puts it this way: "I know what I am doing. I have it all planned out—plans to take care of you, not abandon you, plans to give you the future you hope for." I am grateful for the many wonderful miracles God performed on our behalf. My heart cries out: "The Lord is righteous in all His ways, Gracious in all His works. The Lord is near to all who call upon Him, to all who call upon Him in truth" (Psalm 145:17, 18, NJKV).

When we started out on our journey to Loma Linda, I never imagined that God would bring something beautiful from this dreadful situation, but He used this valley season of our lives to bring me into a closer fellowship with Him. My prayer life had been enriched and deepened as I prayed and read God's precious words more frequently. He blessed my family and me immensely and gave us "beauty for [our] ashes" (Isaiah 61:3, NKJV). Also, from Morris' health crisis, my writing and speaking ministries were birthed. "And we know that in all things God works for the good of those who love him" (Romans 8:28, NIV). My husband's health challenge and subsequent treatment took place in 1999. Not only did he regain his health, but, to this day, he continues to be in excellent health. I praise the good Lord for His mercy and favor.

Ellen G. White wrote the following quotation more than a century ago, but it's still relevant today. "You may have no remarkable evidence at the time that the face of your Redeemer is bending over you in compassion and love, but this is even so. You may not feel His visible touch, but His hand is upon you in love and pitying tenderness" – *Testimonies for the Church*, vol. 3, p. 323.

Some years following Morris' health challenge, Chidi moved back to Huntsville. We attended the same church, so we saw each other frequently. Morris and I traveled out of state and upon our return, we learned that she was hospitalized. We visited her and took the devotional book, *Colors of Grace*, as a gift. It contained the story of how God had used her to perform a miracle for Morris. I read the story to her and mentioned that it was read on a Christian radio station in Maryland. I told her that my friend, Nevilla Adjahoe, had called me earlier that morning to listen to my story being read by the station manager during his interview with the editor of the book, Ardis Dick Stenbakken.

I told Chidi that her kindness would touch thousands of lives around the world. A huge smile covered her face as she held the book close to her chest and said, "Shirley, this is the best thing that has happened to me since I have been in the hospital. Thank you. God has been good to me. When I get out of the hospital, I am going to share my testimony during Prayer meeting at the Oakwood College Church."

We listened as Chidi tried painfully to share recent experiences she had had in her store. For many years, she had taught in public schools; later, she decided to pursue other interests and opened a store that she managed. She said that, sometimes, customers wanted to make purchases, but didn't have enough money. From the kindness of her heart, she allowed them to have the item for whatever they could afford.

She told the story of a customer who wanted to purchase a piece of furniture but didn't have enough cash. She was impressed to let her have it for the amount of money she had. Later during the week, the lady returned and handed Chidi more money than she owed her and expressed gratitude for Chidi's kindness. Chidi told her, "I can't take your money; it's too much." But the woman insisted, "You've been very kind to me; keep the extra to help someone else just as you helped me."

A few days later, a young man came into the store and told Chidi that he wanted to attend church, but didn't have a suit. She helped him select a nice suit, but, he didn't have enough left for a shirt. "You can't go to church without a shirt," she informed him and proceeded to select three shirts. She told him that he no longer had an excuse not to go to church. Chidi's eyes lit up as she said, "Shirley, whenever I help somebody, God always sends customers to increase my sales and make up for more than what I gave away. He does it for me all the time. When I get out of the hospital, I am going to share my testimony at the Oakwood College Church. God is so good to me."

Chidi spoke of how God had blessed her to help many people and also of her plans to build a home for orphans in her village in Nigeria. Before leaving, we prayed and assured her that we believed God would perform a miracle for her as He had done for Morris and me. We parted on that note.

Not too long after our visit we learned that Chidi's condition had worsened. Then, much to our dismay, we received the awful news that she had passed. Her husband, children, family, and everyone who knew her were devastated. We questioned how something so horrible could happen to someone so kind, caring, compassionate, and loving.

Chidi's life was like a beautiful garden whose fragrance perfumed the air. Now, it had come to an abrupt end. Sadly, she didn't live long enough to share her testimony, but, amazingly, God worked it out so that it could be told. It began around 2:30 one morning; I became restless and couldn't sleep. It seemed like a persistent voice was ringing in my ear: "You must share Chidi's testimony; get up and write it down." I was tired and wanted to sleep, so I ignored the voice, but it refused to go away. I pondered how I would share her testimony and thought that maybe I could submit it for publication in one of the devotional books published by the Women's Ministries Department of the General Conference of SDA.

Reluctantly yielding to the voice, I got out of bed and began to write. The first few lines consisted of words of a familiar hymn written by Joseph M. Scriven in 1855: "What a Friend we have in Jesus, all our sins and grief to bear; what a privilege to carry everything to God in prayer."[6] I found out from Chidi's husband a few days later that this was her favorite song. After completing the story, I went back to sleep.

The following day during lunch time, I went to the cafeteria and happened to stand in line behind Dr. Craig and Jan Newborn. We chatted briefly, then, he asked, "Are you going to be at prayer meeting tonight?" I said, "Yes." "Would you please share Chidi's story during testimony time?" he asked. His words startled me, given what had transpired earlier. But, instead of accepting the invitation, I began to make excuses, "I don't like to do stuff up front; I become nervous, and my heart beats fast." "Your friend, Chidi, wanted to share her testimony but didn't get the opportunity to do so. You must do it for her," he responded. I shared with him my early morning experience. This series of events was remarkable because Pastor Newborn had little knowledge of Chidi's story outside of a few details I had mentioned to him briefly the previous day. It's incredible how God, at times, arranges so many different events from various directions and perspectives simultaneously.

I shared Chidi's story at prayer meeting and, later, gave a copy to her husband, which was printed as part of the funeral program and also taken to Nigeria where she was buried. Chidi is gone, but I believe her kindness and beautiful life will continue to live on in my heart and in the hearts and lives of her loving family and the many people whom she touched through her caring spirit. She allowed God to use her as a conduit of blessing. I, too, want to be a channel of blessing.

One day soon, God will wipe away all tears from our eyes, there'll be no more pain, nor death. Yes, He'll make all things new (Revelation 21:4, 5). "Weeping may endure for a night, But joy comes in the morning" (Psalm 30:5, NKJV).

My Near-Death Experiences

In spite of God's blessings, it seemed that Satan was working overtime to take our focus away from our blessings. For some time, I had experienced a severe allergic reaction to the smell of cologne, bleach, air fresheners, cleaning chemicals, or anything with high alcohol or chemical content. Previously, the only thing I was allergic to was chloroquine. At the onset of these allergies, whenever I was exposed to fragrances, my throat tightened, and my voice became hoarse.

As time passed, my reactions worsened, and I began to experience a rapid heartbeat, suddenly-elevated blood pressure, and irritating sounds in my ears. On some occasions, I had to be taken to the emergency room because my symptoms mimicked those of a heart attack. It was a frightening experience. Fortunately, the tests for heart disease were negative.

It was a tough period for me. People wear cologne and perfume all the time, and it was difficult for them to understand how someone could become so seriously ill just from the smell of these substances, especially when the scents were so aromatic. I had no control over my work environment and felt helpless to do anything about the perfumes and colognes my colleagues wore.

The first memory I have of experiencing an allergic reaction to anything other than chloroquine occurred when my office assistant and I were eating lunch in the President's office. We didn't expect Dr. Reaves to return to his office until later in the afternoon, but, to our surprise, he came back early. We had been eating curried food and wanted to eliminate the odor before Dr. Reaves reached his office, so Rhonda sprayed an excessive amount of air freshener in the room. Shortly afterward, my throat began to tighten; the strong smell of the air freshener had triggered some respiratory distress. From that day on, my reaction to air freshener worsened with time.

On another occasion, Morris and I were attending a conference at a hotel near Oakwood's campus. Everything went well until bedtime when I began to experience difficulty breathing. My face became hot and sweaty. The smell of air freshener coming through the vent triggered my allergies and, soon, I was in respiratory distress, again. It was a frightening experience. We dressed quickly and left the hotel. The fresh, crisp air outside brought a measure of relief, but we decided not to return to the room and went home, instead.

This episode caused my husband great concern. The next day, he called my brother, Halstead, a physician, and explained what had happened. He also expressed his concerns about my health. Halstead suggested talking with my family doctor about performing 24-hour tests to discover the reason for these unusual reactions. Dr. Benjamin Fail, my doctor, accepted Halstead's recommendations, and I was admitted to the hospital. Various tests were administered, and everything seemed fine until someone entered the room to visit my roommate. The smell of her cologne triggered a reaction, and more tests were ordered.

While I awaited discharge orders, Ngozi called to find out the results of the tests. The nurse happened to be in my room at the time and went to check my chart. She returned hurriedly with the horrific news that one of the tests revealed a right pulmonary embolism, and that they would have to transport me immediately to the cardiac care unit. Unaware of the seriousness of my condition, I reached for my clothes in the closet. Quickly, the nurse called out, "We can get your clothes later; we've got to get you to the cardiac care unit right away!"

There, I received orders not to get out of bed nor to move around. "You can't take a shower. Call the nurse if you need to use the bathroom." Don't do this, and don't do that! Instantly, my tranquility and stability changed, and my life seemed to be disintegrating right before my eyes. My hectic, fast-paced, always-on-the-go lifestyle came to a screeching halt. Without warning, my supposedly well-fortified figurative walls of protection came crashing down around me. And to make matters worse, I had no control over what was going on. Have you ever faced a similar situation? Let me tell you; it was terrifying!

What does a person do in times like these? Quickly, the realization of the fragility of life struck me. We are here one moment, and the next we could be gone. So often, some of us walk around with a sense of invincibility and immortality, just "strutting our stuff," unaware that it's only the breath that God has breathed into our bodies and His abundant grace that keep us alive. When that breath returns to Him, life ceases, and we are as dry grass.

The cardiologist, Dr. Warren Strickland, ordered many tests but was unable to identify the cause of the embolism positively. A few days later, he inserted a Greenfield filter into my right groin to eliminate the possibility of future clots. By then, I was feeling overwhelmed by my unexpectedly long hospital stay. What was supposed to be a 24-hour procedure had now stretched into long, dark days and darker nights. I found myself teetering on the brink of despondency and helplessness.

A little past midnight, I was sitting, alone, on a chair in my hospital room with my right leg propped up on the bed. I was unable to sleep and wallowed in self-pity. This caused me to question God. "Why me?" I asked. My right arm was adorned with long, plastic IV tubes dangling from a pole that prevented free movement. Dark clouds of anxiety, fear, and loneliness descended upon me like torrential rains and penetrated my tired body to the core. It seemed like there was no way out.

I hated the nights most of all. I had difficulty sleeping and frequently prayed for morning to come. Worse yet, every time I began to doze off, lab technicians would come in and poke my sore arm in their effort to extract my blood. I knew that this was necessary to check the therapeutic level of the blood thinner that had been administered, but I still felt like a soldier in a battlefield hospital, bruised, scarred, and powerless to improve my lot.

Every night, when visiting hours were over, I watched my husband slowly and sadly leave to return home, alone. Here was the love of my life, my protector and faithful companion unable to do anything to ease my discomfort or fears. I realized that this ordeal was hard on him, too. Feelings of intense homesickness began to invade my mind. Then, unexpectedly, warm tears welled up in my eyes and began to trickle down my cheeks. I felt like the psalmist, David, when he wrote, "In my distress I called upon the LORD. And cried out to my God; He heard my voice from His temple, And my cry came before Him, even to His ears" (Psalm 18:6, NKJV).

As the morning began to dawn, in its quietness, I heard sweet music playing on the radio Shirley Scott had loaned me a few days earlier to help ease my loneliness. All of a sudden, it was as if God was speaking to me through familiar songs like: "Tell Jesus" by John W.

Peterson. The lyrics began to comfort me. "Tell Jesus when the way is dark before you and the path is hid from view; when you grope with steps uncertain, and you know not what to do. . . Tell Jesus, blessed Jesus. He has grace to meet your need."

The powerful words of a song written by Annie Johnson Flint deeply touched my soul, as well. It says, "He giveth more grace when the burdens grow greater. He sendeth more strength when the labors increase. To added affliction, He added His mercy; to multiplied trials, His multiplied peace. His love has no limit; His grace has no measure. His power has no boundary known unto men for out of His infinite riches in Jesus, He giveth and giveth and giveth, again." I am grateful to God for these songs in the night that ministered to my lonely heart and broken spirit.

Amazingly, He also sent comforting Scripture: "Fear not for I am with you; be not dismayed, for I am your God. I will strengthen you, yes, I will help you, I will uphold you with My righteous right hand" (Isaiah 41:10, NKJV). In His love and compassion, my God had custom-made songs and scriptures to minister to my soul. Yes, when we walk through our dark tunnel of suffering and pain, we can be assured of God's presence. He has promised never to fail or abandon us, and I'm living proof.

Before dozing off that early morning, my heart was soothed by W. O. Cushing's song, "Under His Wings, I am safely abiding; though the night deepens and tempests are wild., Still I can trust Him; I know He will keep me. He has redeemed me, and I am His child. Under His wings, under His wings, who from His love can sever? Under His wings, my soul shall abide, safely abide forever."

While vacationing in Barbados, I got a first-hand demonstration of what it means to be under God's wings. One evening, as I sat on my sister's front porch, I watched in astonishment as roosters and hens flew up branches of tall trees to hide among the thick foliage. I was curious about why they did this and asked Cynthia why. She explained that they used to sleep under the tree, but night predators often attacked them, so they started flying to the top of the trees out of the reach of predators.

Another time, I observed a mother hen with her two little chicks. They looked so tiny and helpless that I wondered how they would make it to the top of the trees. The mother hen flew from one branch to the next highest branch, and, as she rested, she made clucking sounds to which the little chicks responded by making their way to the top of the tree in the same way that their mother had. And then I saw how the mother hen spread out her wings and tucked her chicks snugly under her. That's how our Heavenly Father securely covers us under His powerful arms away from the master predator, Satan. From this object lesson, I understand that God protected me with His wings that unforgettable night so long ago, and I am grateful. The psalmist, David, puts it succinctly in Psalm 91:4: "He will cover you with his feathers, He will shelter you with his wings. His faithful promises are your armor and protection" (NLT).

Looking back on what had transpired earlier during the hospital admission process, I must admit I was ashamed of myself. I recalled that the clerk had asked me if I wanted to be admitted to a private or semi-private room. I told her she'd made a mistake, that I was an outpatient and was not to be admitted. Against my objections, she insisted that my doctor had ordered that I be admitted. After completing the paperwork, she instructed a Red Cross volunteer to escort me to a semi-private room upstairs.

We reached the room, but I continued to complain that it was a mistake. Before leaving, the volunteer calmly said, "Ma'am, relax; everything will be all right. Just put your stuff in the closet, and make yourself comfortable." I was neither ready nor willing to put my belongings in the closet because I didn't want to be charged for a room I had no intention of using. Well, I'm glad they ignored my protestations and followed my doctor's orders. I thank God for His grace toward me, even in my foolish stubbornness.

Quietly sitting on my bed, I reflected on my near-death experience. Satan had tried to snatch me from my family, but God rescued me from his grip. In my pit of despair, I allowed clouds of self-pity and gloom to obscure my ability to see God and His providential leadings clearly, and I failed to recognize that His protective hand saved me from the jaws of death.

People die from pulmonary embolisms; it usually happens quickly and with no warning. A living, vibrant person with everything to live for is simply taken from this life without ever having been sick and without being able to bid farewell to their loved ones or to make any preparations whatsoever. Not only had I been given warnings, but my life had also been spared. I would have many more years to enjoy my husband, children, grandchildren, loved ones, and friends. I would recover and do those things that others, who had been taken suddenly, could not.

Shamefully, I bowed my head in humility and profound gratitude for the blessing of life I had received. I felt sorry for the ungrateful way I had behaved. Suppose I had been discharged from the hospital and gone about my regular duties? The clot could have, and more than likely would have, dislodged causing a stroke or instant death. In fact, Ngozi told me of her friend's mother who died of a pulmonary embolism while sitting at her dining table during the same week that mine had been successfully eliminated.

More tests were ordered, but the doctor was still unable to identify the reason for either my severe allergic reactions or the embolism. One more test was ordered, which involved a tilted table. At one point during the test, the technician placed the table, on which I was strapped, in a vertical position. Shortly afterward, I began to feel faint, and my body went limp. In my last moments of consciousness, I called out, "Nurse, help me!" I remember her hurrying toward me, and in an instant, I blacked out.

As I regained consciousness, I became aware of medical personnel hovering over me, patting my cheeks, and asking me questions to get a response. "Lord, please don't let me die," was my heartfelt cry. Almost imperceptibly, I heard the technician tell someone that my blood pressure had dropped significantly, and my pulse was down to 40. From the looks on the faces of the medical personnel, I knew something was seriously wrong.

The nurse transported me back to my room as exhaustion engulfed me. Later that evening Eveythe, my friend, called to check on me. She said that my speech was slurred, and it was difficult to understand what I was saying. My life hung precariously near death, but, with God's help, I survived my terrifying ordeal. Lovingly, He lifted me from the jaws of death and laid His healing hands upon my body; and O, the joy that flooded my soul. Something happened, and I know He touched me and saved me, one more time.

If someone asked me if I believe in miracles, my answer would be, "I certainly do!" God performed one miracle after another and saved my life twice within a few days. Job was right when he said in Chapter 5, verse 9, that "He performs wonders that cannot be fathomed, miracles that cannot be counted" (NIV).

I consider my near-death experiences to be wake-up calls. I was rushing through life at breakneck speed doing this and that, thinking that I was Mrs. Superwoman; but I wasn't. God allowed these experiences to slow me down and to teach me that He was in control and that He had plans for me. No one enjoys pain, heartache, sickness, or grief; and, while He does not often literally cause them, He uses them to get our attention and to teach us that He's the Boss and that, no matter the circumstances or situation, He is always there to help us.

I remained at the hospital for fifteen days, long enough for me to reflect on God's mercy and grace. From this traumatic experience has emerged a sweeter, deeper, more spiritual relationship with Jesus. It was His plan for me to soar higher spiritually and to grow stronger in my journey of faith. He showed me how much He loves and cares for me and that He is with me, no matter how devastating the situation. I am learning to lean on Him and to trust Him day by day. Additionally, He gave me many opportunities to encourage fellow travelers who are experiencing challenging times to hold on to the firm and unchanging arms of our loving Savior. I'm learning that the battle is not mine, it's God's.

One of my delights after returning home from the hospital was reading the more than 75 get-well cards that came during my illness; they ministered to my heart profoundly and showed me how much people loved and cared for me. I can say, unequivocally, that, out of an awful encounter, God has brought great blessings, and these well-wishes were certainly among them. Yes, He's an all-knowing God who sees the end from the beginning, and He knows what He's doing.

Ellen White penned these powerful words that support my experience in her book, *Ministry of Healing*, pages 144-145: "Often those who are in good health forget the wonderful mercies continued to them day by day, year after year, and they render no tribute of praise to God for His benefits. But when sickness comes, God is remembered. When human strength fails, men feel their need of divine help. And never does our merciful God turn from the soul that in sincerity seeks Him for help. He is our refuge in sickness as in health. God is just as willing to restore the sick to health now as when the Holy Spirit spoke those words through the psalmist. And Christ is the same compassionate physician now that He was during His earthly ministry. In Him there is a healing balm for every disease, restoring power for every infirmity." (Published by Harvestime Books, 1999).

David, the most prolific writer of praise in the Bible, wrote in Psalm 118:17-19, 21, "I didn't die. I lived! And now I'm telling the world what GOD did. God tested me; he pushed me hard, but he didn't hand me over to Death. Swing wide the city gates—the righteous gates! I'll walk right through and thank God! Thank You for responding to me, You've truly become my salvation!"

Over time, I've learned that life is filled with swift transitions that often occur with no advance warning and no time to prepare or execute our plans. Some years after the above episode, I was faced with yet another major health. I was scheduled for outpatient surgery and, unfortunately, I had, once again, allowed fear and anxiety to creep into my heart. The future seemed bleak because the lab report indicated the possibility of cancer. Questions without answers permeated my thoughts: What if the results revealed I had cancer? What will happen to me? Will I become so ill that someone will have to take care of me? How will my family handle this challenge? Will I have to undergo chemotherapy or radiation treatments? Will I die?

I arrived at the hospital at the appointed time, and after settling into the outpatient pre-op room, I opened the devotional book, *Bouquets of Hope*, and was surprised to see the title, "Lord, help me!" Those words poignantly expressed the sentiments of my heart. The text read, "He will call upon Me, and I will answer him; I will be with him in trouble; I will rescue him and honor him" (Psalm 91:15, NASB). WOW!

Reassured by those comforting words, I asked God to be with the surgeon and me during the procedure. Then, it happened: I felt the warmth of God's peace—sweet peace, wonderful peace—surge through my anxious body. The presence of my all-powerful Heavenly Father was in the room, and he assured me that He was with me. He spoke positively, "I will be with you in trouble, and I will rescue you and honor you." Instantly, His promise ministered to me like a soothing balm. You can't imagine the joy that I experienced. The lyrics of a song written by Lieutenant Colonel E. H. Joy came to mind, "All your anxiety, all your care, bring to the Mercy-seat, leave it there; never a burden He cannot bear, never a Friend like Jesus." It's so wonderful to have a special Friend like Jesus.

A few minutes before I was transported to the operating room, Dr. Cherryl Galley and Pastor Lloyd Wilson of the Oakwood University Church prayed with Morris and me. Dr. Galley commented, "Shirley, you have a glow on your face!" When I looked in the mirror nearby, I saw it, apparently placed there by my merciful God.

Following the procedure, the surgeon awakened me with these words, "You'll be happy to know everything went well; there is no evidence of cancer." I shouted, "Praise the Lord!" Words are inadequate to express my joy for what God did for me.

Reflecting on my journey, I am convinced that God allowed certain afflictions to enter my life as part of His plan for my spiritual growth and enrichment. I have learned over the years that, when things have gone well, I haven't been as earnest and fervent about my prayer life as I have become since experiencing hard times. I would forget to pray, to study the Word, or to seek to know God on a deeper spiritual level, and I would start to believe in myself instead of in the power of the Almighty God.

"Praise the LORD! Oh, give thanks to the LORD, for He is good! For His mercy endures forever" (Psalm 106:1, NKJV).

Chapter 14

Testimonies and Testimonials

God sometimes works silently, behind the scenes, unknown to us, to fulfill His plan for us. What follows is an example of what I mean by that.

I received a call from Dr. Cherryl Galley, head elder at the Oakwood University Church at the time, inviting me to speak at Wednesday night prayer meeting. My first reaction was, "No way, get someone else. I am not a speaker." Sensing my reluctance, she responded, "Think about it, Shirley." Later in the week, when she asked if I had made my decision, I looked at her with uncertainty. In her calm and Christ-like manner, she said, "Shirley, just share your testimony; it's all God asks of you." How could I not share my testimony when He had done so much for me?

A few hours before I was scheduled to speak, nervous feelings flashed through my body. As I was leaving the house, my then-four-year-old grandson, Nikolas, called. I mentioned that I was on my way to speak at Prayer Meeting and was feeling scared. His response eased some of my nervousness, "Don't be scared, Gramma; Jesus will help you. I'm praying for you." After hearing such beautiful words of assurance, I drove to church with a smile on my face and a song in my heart. Would you believe it? That night was the first time I'd ever spoken in front of an audience without feeling nervous. It can only be attributed to God's grace called upon by Nikolas's prayer. At the conclusion of the message, individuals commented that they were blessed by my testimony. Dr. Derek Bowe and others suggested that

I share my testimony with a larger audience in the form of a book. Their comments confirmed what I had been mulling around in my head for some time.

In the book, *Patriarchs and Prophets,* Ellen White writes on page 211 that, "The path where God leads the way may lie through the desert or the sea, but it is a safe path." Because of experiences with my husband's medical condition and my illnesses, I began to share my testimony of God's presence and incredible miracles on our behalf. Well, here I am many years later, and God has provided numerous opportunities for me to share my testimony in person, through sermons, as well as articles which have been published in devotional books and church-related magazines. God's grace still amazes me!

I'm blessed to receive local and long distance phone calls, emails, and cards from women commenting on how they have been encouraged and inspired by reading my devotional articles. My friend, Dr. Janice Browne, shared this experience, "Shirley, thank you for my birthday gift." I perked up right away because I was unaware she had celebrated a birthday. "What birthday gift?" I asked. She shared her story that, on the morning of her birthday, she had felt alone because her husband had traveled on conference business and was unable to celebrate this special day with her.

As she read the devotional article for that morning, she said that she began to weep, it had touched her so deeply. She continued that the greatest surprise came when she reached the end of the article and saw that I had written it. She commented, "God read my heart and provided what I needed through a dear friend. Thank you, Shirley." I, too, am richly blessed by the many heartwarming devotionals of other women.

In the Fall of 2006, God had a wonderful surprise awaiting me that almost slipped through my fingers. I was cleaning out my garage early one morning when I got a call from Shirley Scott, Director of Women's Ministries for South Central Conference at the time, inviting me to speak for Sabbath vespers at the women's retreat in Gatlinburg, Tennessee. Her request caught me off-guard. Without giving it a thought, I blurted out, "No way, are you crazy?" She scolded me and insisted that I didn't have to respond right then, that I should pray about it and get back to her later in the day. But I didn't.

When she called back that evening, I came up with all kinds of excuses, which she refused to accept. Finally, she said, "God impressed me to give you this assignment, and I'm just carrying out His wishes." Of course, now, I had to accept.

I had never attended a women's retreat, but, for some unknown reason, I had decided several months earlier to attend this one and had submitted my application and deposit in advance. I was excited and looked forward to a weekend filled with blessings, inspiration, and empowerment. This was all before I knew that I would be called upon to speak. Now, things were about to change! I had to prepare to give the Vesper thought.

While searching for an important document on my desk, I came across the retreat brochure, which had pictures of the two main speakers. These women were seasoned, professional speakers. Right then, I suffered an anxiety attack. What had I gotten myself into? I picked up the phone to tell Mrs. Scott to find someone else, but there was no response. Desperately, I ran downstairs to her office; she wasn't there! All my efforts to find her that day were unsuccessful.

Several days later, when I saw her, she was busy and didn't have time to talk. So, I reluctantly resigned myself to the fact that this assignment was God's doing, and He would help me. I prayed that He would use the message to bless and minister to the attendees. My desire was to give them a new glimpse of God's love and remind them that He has a beautiful plan for their lives.

The date for the retreat arrived quickly, and I traveled on the bus with other attendees to the Park Vista Hotel nestled in the beautiful scenic mountains of Gatlinburg, Tennessee. With my registration completed, I proceeded to the non-smoking room I had requested only to find out that a strong smell of cigarettes had invaded the room. This would be a challenge for me because of my allergies. I requested another room; unfortunately, the people who could help were busy assisting with registration. They promised to fulfill my request as soon as possible.

The evening and the next morning went by without any change. In the meantime, I was faced with an additional challenge—seminar rooms, elevators, and several women attending the conference had the strong smell of cologne. To avoid the odor on the elevators, I sometimes used the stairs.

It was late Friday afternoon when a hotel employee transported my luggage to a new room. As I entered, I was assailed by the strong smell of air freshener. It seemed that I had gone from the frying pan into the fire. Apparently, in their effort to camouflage the smell of cigarettes in the room, they had sprayed an excessive amount of air freshener. I opened the balcony door to let in fresh air, but the air was too cold. Lacking the courage to request another room, I decided to stay.

The darker the night became, the more my anxiety level increased. From past experience, it seemed that more bad things happen at night than in the day. Now, I was gradually losing my voice and becoming burdened by hopelessness. I took an extra dose of allergy medicine, although I was concerned that it might cause me to oversleep. I covered my nose with a damp towel to help reduce the smell.

Although I tried to be brave, frightening thoughts began to consume my mind. I cried out, "Lord, I am scheduled to speak for vespers tomorrow, and I can hardly talk. Please don't let this happen to me. You know I didn't want to speak in the first place. Here I am in this room alone unable to reach my husband, and I don't know the cell number of anyone attending the conference on whom to call in case of an emergency. Please help me!"

All kinds of what-if scenarios kept surfacing: "What if I have a severe allergic reaction in the night and my blood pressure skyrockets—as it had done several times before? What if my heart begins to beat too rapidly? What if I have difficulty breathing? What if I have to be taken to the emergency room?" So many what-ifs with no answers! My faith was being tested far beyond my comfort level, and I found myself buckling under self-inflicted worry. Sleep evaded me, so I covered my body from head to toe with the bed linens as I petitioned God to have mercy on me.

The next morning, I could only speak in a whisper. During my devotion, I asked God to help to regain my voice. He heard and answered my prayer. Miraculously, my voice began to improve little by little. I attended Sabbath School and the worship service but tried to avoid mingling with people, because I didn't want to talk too much and risk losing my voice, again.

Approximately 20 minutes before it was time for vespers, I went downstairs and sat outside the conference room to gain my composure. Shortly afterward, a woman exited the room and picked up the phone on the table across from where I was seated and asked if she could be connected to my room. I went to where she was and inquired, "Are you looking for Shirley Iheanacho?" "Yes, do you know her?" she replied. I told her I was she. We greeted each other, and she escorted me to the front of the room.

It was time to speak. With trepidation, I stood before the audience. Humbly, I bowed my head and thanked God aloud for His goodness and asked Him to have mercy on me, a sinner; to remove my fear, take center stage, and let the words I speak bless and minister to the attendees. My voice had not completely returned, but it was audible. I felt the Holy Spirit nudging me on as I spoke. My hoarseness was evident when I sang: "He giveth more grace when the burdens grow greater; He sendeth more strength when the labors increase, to added affliction, He addeth His mercy; to multiplied trials, His multiplied peace." Even with my vocal challenges, the audience understood the message.

Naomi's story, as recorded in the book of Ruth, was the focus of my message. I related how God had given her victory over her bitterness and pain, how he had turned her tragedy into a thing of incredible beauty, and how He had taken her from her dungeon of obscurity, poverty, and bitterness to a place of high honor in His eternal hall of fame. God revealed triumph in the face of tragedy.

It all began when Naomi traveled with her wealthy husband, Elimelech, and their two sons, Mahlon and Chilion, to Moab, a pagan country, in search of food because of the severe famine in Bethlehem, the city in which they lived. They settled comfortably into their new home and adjusted well to their strange environment, unaware that tragedy lay ahead. Elimelech became ill and died. Naomi's tragic loss struck her like a thunderbolt. Without warning, she had been thrust into widowhood, as well as what we would call single parenthood. Broken and grief-stricken, she continued with life as best she could comforted by the presence of her two precious sons.

Some years later, Mahlon and Chilion fell in love and married two beautiful foreign women, Orpah and Ruth. Naomi's joy was renewed, but it was short-lived because tragedy struck, again. This time, it was Naomi's two most precious gifts, her sons, who were snatched from her by the cold hand of death. Her pride, joy, and financial and societal support were gone. In those days, a woman alone without a man to protect her, provide for her, or speak to her in public was an outcast, all but shunned by the entire patriarchal society that surrounded her. Overnight, the life Naomi once knew as a woman of means was in shambles; her lofty dreams were shattered, and her comfortable life of prominence came to an abrupt end. Like some of us do when hard times knock us down, she questioned why this happened to her family.

It's hard to understand how one family could suffer so much tragedy. After all, Naomi was a wonderful woman who loved and served the Lord and her family faithfully. Now, she was husbandless, sonless, comfortless, destitute, needy, and robbed of her sunshine and happiness. Her pain was very deep. Her focus on her tragic loss caused her to become weighed down by a thick wall of bitterness. Have you ever been in such a tunnel of darkness? Then, you understand what she was going through. Even if you haven't, it isn't hard to imagine, to some extent, the agony and suffering Naomi experienced.

Naomi's future in Moab looked bleak. One day, she heard the good news that God had blessed Judah with plenty of food. Embittered by her situation in Moab, she made the decision to return to her home with her two daughters-in-law. They hadn't traveled very far when Naomi decided that she should let these two beautiful young women return to their hometown where, perhaps, they might find husbands to care for them. She urged them to go back, but they insisted on staying with her. The deep and abiding love that they had for her showed that she must have been a great mother-in-law.

In the end, the pull of home was too strong for Orpah, so she tearfully kissed Naomi goodbye and returned to her home in Moab alone. Ruth, loyal and faithful, remained with Naomi vowing to accept her family and stay with her till she died. Her passionate and heart-warming words have resonated down the corridors of time to all who know her story: "Where you go, I will go,. . . Your people shall be my people and your God my God and where you die, I will die" (Ruth 1:16, 17, ESV). These beautiful words remind me of similar vows that I took more than 47 years ago when I married my wonderful husband, Morris.

Trudging along the dusty road to Judah, Naomi may have recalled the time she first traveled to Moab with her family. At that time, she was a woman of status; beautiful and rich. She had everything any woman could desire: a loving and caring husband; in time, two handsome sons; wealth; and an exalted position in society through her marriage to Elimelech. Never, in her wildest imagination, did she dream that such tragedy would befall her family.

The farther Naomi and Ruth continued on their journey, the heavier Naomi's burden of pain and shame might have become. The road ahead seemed long and the terrain arduous, but they were not alone. God, the Divine Master Protector and Planner, was with them, protecting them from any dangers that lurked nearby.

They finally arrived in Bethlehem. The people were excited and happy to see them and gave them a grand homecoming welcome, but Naomi allowed bitterness to overtake her instead of feeling gratitude to God for bringing her back home safely. Another meaning of the name Naomi is joy, but she was, decidedly, joyless, and everyone around her knew it. Ruth 1:20-21 sheds light on how Naomi felt in this time of tragedy and loss, emotional upheaval, and physical uprooting: "Don't call me Naomi any longer! Call me Mara because God has made my life bitter. I had everything when I left, but the Lord has brought me back with nothing. How can you still call me Naomi, when God has turned against me and made my life so hard?" (Holy Bible, *The African American Jubilee Edition*, Contemporary English Version, American Bible Society, New York, 1995, 1999).

Sadly, bitterness and self-pity clouded Naomi's vision, and she blamed God for her misfortune. She failed to see that, though unknown and unseen by her, He was putting people and circumstances into place to bring about His glorious purpose for her life. Through a series of God-ordained events, Boaz, Naomi's relative, met Ruth, who, in obedience to Naomi, had been gleaning food from his field. He was impressed by her loyalty and dedication to Naomi. According to the custom of the day, Naomi advised Ruth how to approach him, and the stage was set for them to bring to fruition God's plan for them. Boaz proceeded to invite his male next of kin to purchase the property along with Ruth because the custom was that the male next of kin would marry the young widow. If he wasn't interested, the next male relative, in this case, Boaz, could freely marry her. Boaz's relative did decline, paving the way for Boaz to marry Ruth, which he did.

To this happy couple, a beautiful baby was born. "Then the women said to Naomi, 'Blessed be the LORD, who has not left you this day without a close relative; and may his name be famous in Israel! And may he be to you a restorer of life and a nourisher of your old age; for your daughter-in-law, who loves you, who is better to you than seven sons, has borne him.' Then Naomi took the child and laid him on her bosom, and became a nurse to him'" (Ruth 4:14, 15, 17, NKJV). According to the biblical account, the neighborhood women gave this handsome baby boy the unique name, Obed, which means "to serve."

Naomi's heart was filled with joy. Because Naomi's daughter-in-law had married into her family, again, making it possible for Naomi to regain her place in society. God had lifted her from the worst experience of her life to occupy a place of high honor and recognition again. The greatest honor of all was that, through the ancestral line of Obed (David's grandson), Jesus, the Savior, and Redeemer of the World, was born. How beautiful! Naomi's story began dismally, filled with hopelessness, but God turned it into a happily-ever-after ending. The victorious latter part of her life is a testament to the awesome love and care of our great God Who continually monitors our affairs and works everything out for our good. Only He could have orchestrated such an incredible and awe-inspiring series of events!

One of the lessons that Naomi's story teaches us is that, when we are faced with hardships and disappointments, and the going gets tough, we should trust God to bring us through victoriously. He's in control. He has the power to bring about great outcomes from the most horrific situations, all to His honor and glory.

Some of us, like Naomi, are in a far-off country, overcome by the loss of a loved one, failing health, loss of job and property, children in jail, mounting bills, foreclosures, no money, and more. We suffer from deep pain, frustrations, discouragement, and depression. The journey back home is not always easy. There may be obstacles and dangers to overcome. However, don't waste time fretting and complaining; it only deepens the pain and causes us to dwell on the negatives and turn our eyes from our wonderful Heavenly Father. I recall a song my grandson Nikolas used to sing when he was a little boy. It went something like this, "Don't pray and worry. . . Just pray, and, then, leave it there." Now, that's good advice!

During my message, I shared the way in which God orchestrated something amazing for my daughter, Akunna, and taught her an incredible lesson about prayer and His faithfulness. When she began graduate school, she was enrolled in an intense four-week summer session in preparation for her graduate program, which would start in the Fall. After attending a few classes, she realized that the material to be covered would be difficult to grasp over the course of a full semester, much less in a month in the summer. It was tough; some students dropped the class, but she said that failure was not in her vocabulary and that, without a test, there can be no testimony. She continued to attend class and complete her assignments. She prayed and persevered, although the visiting professor casually suggested that she could always drop the class.

One day, she was impressed by the Holy Spirit to put the following quotation by an anonymous author on the cover of her assignment notebook: "How to Handle Your Problems." It states: "Prayer is the answer to everything in life. It puts us in touch with divine wisdom, which knows how to adjust everything perfectly. So often, we do not pray in certain situations because, from our standpoint, the outlook is hopeless. But nothing is impossible with God. Nothing is so entangled that it cannot be remedied; no human relationship is too strained for God to bring about reconciliation and understanding. No habit so deep-rooted that it cannot be overcome; no one is so weak that he cannot be strong; no one is so ill that he cannot be healed. No mind so dull that it cannot be made brilliant. Whatever we need, if we trust God, He will supply it. If anything is causing worry and anxiety, let us stop rehearsing the difficulty and trust God for healing, love, and power."

Akunna was surprised a few days later when her professor read the statement aloud in class and asked her if she believed it. She told him that she did, and the students laughed. At the end of the summer session, she was shocked to learn that she had made the highest grade in the class on the final exam. This convinced her, beyond a shadow of a doubt, that God had done this for her. In His faithfulness, He had taught her an unforgettable lesson of what prayer, faith, perseverance, and trust in Him can do.

At the conclusion of my talk, many women commented about how the message spoke to their hearts and how they were blessed. Praise the Lord! I, too, was spiritually blessed and returned home jubilant. I talked so much about my spiritual blessings that Mrs. Scott asked me to write an article about the weekend's activities. The article, titled "Living the Victorious Life," was published in the February 2007 issue of *Southern Tidings Magazine*. That was one more unexpected blessing that God provided for me.

My Heavenly Father continued to extend His hand of blessing and, later that year, I was featured for a week on the program called "Women of Excellence" broadcast on the Huntsville, Alabama, radio station WJOU 90.1 FM. This program was sponsored by the late Minneola Dixon, who was the Oakwood University archivist at that time. I was also among more than 20 women honored by Gwen Baker at Gwen's Legends Ball, an awards banquet for lifetime achievement. God is so good; His blessings are new every morning. As long as there is breath in my body, "I will lift Him up and bless Him at all times; His praise shall continually be in my mouth" (Psalm.34:1, NKJV).

"For I know the plans I have for you," declares the LORD, "plans to prosper you and not to harm you, plans to give you hope and a future" (Jeremiah 29:11, NIV).

Chapter 15

Reflections on Death and Dying

enry Wadsworth Longfellow wrote these poignant words in his poem, "The Rainy Day": "Into each life some rain must fall. Some days must be dark and dreary." It was true then, and it is still true today. Difficult times are inevitable. Each of us, at some point in our lives, will experience them. Sometimes, they come without warning when we least expect them. Since we can't predict the form they will take, we are often caught off guard. That's how it was with my friend, Maureen.

We were prayer partners and had set aside specific days of the week to pray for our children and others. We designated Thursdays as our "Praise Days." We had just completed our prayer and praise time together, and I was making up my bed when the phone rang. It was Dr. Galley. "Shirley," she began, "I have bad news for you. Rajeeni was killed in a car accident, and the pastor and his wife are on their way to tell Maureen." I was stunned, and screamed, "No, no, are you sure it's not someone else with the same name? Maureen and I just finished praying for her. You'd better make sure that this information is correct before the pastor goes to her house." "Yes, it is correct; her relative has identification from her purse," she responded.

Shortly afterward, the phone rang. It was Maureen. She was distraught and uttered these wrenching words, "Rajeeni is dead; she was killed in a car accident in Atlanta. The pastor and his wife came to give me the news." Even though I had already been given the news, it was still hard to accept. Only a few minutes before, we had prayed and asked God to be with Rajeeni during her job interview that was scheduled for that morning. Tears rolled down my cheeks as I replayed in my mind the horrific news that struck a hard blow to my heart. I shared it with my husband, and he, too, was shocked.

My dear friend and prayer partner's life had been turned upside down. One of the questions that raced through my mind was, "How will Maureen withstand this tragedy?" You see, Rajeeni was her only child; her pride and joy. She was beautiful and brilliant, kind and caring, and had done extremely well in school. She had completed her law degree, passed the bar, and was looking forward to her job interview that morning. Everything was going perfectly for her; then, suddenly, tragedy struck, and Maureen's life took an unexpected turn. Her hopes and dreams for her daughter were shattered into a million pieces. There were a hundred "whys," and no answers for them.

Morris and I went to be with Maureen. When we arrived at her house, we expected to find a screaming, out-of-control, brokenhearted mother. Instead, my friend was relatively calm and composed, although with a tear-stained face, as she contacted family members and began making final arrangements for her beloved daughter. She paused to listen, again, to the voicemail that her daughter had left a few days earlier, "Hi, Mom, how are you doing, Good Looking?" There was deep anguish and pain as Maureen muttered, "I will never hear her voice alive, again."

Later in the week, as we talked, she said, "I have been praying for the Lord to do whatever He had to do to save my daughter. I didn't mean for Him to take her, but He chose to. How can I be mad at Him? How can I turn against Him when He's done so much for me these many years? It's His call, and I must trust His wisdom. His ways are faultless, and He knows what He's doing. I have memorized and repeated God's precious promises for years. I have to believe that He meant it when He said that "When you pass through the waters, I will be with you, and through the rivers they shall not overflow you, when you walk through the fire you shall not be burned. Nor shall the flame scorch you, for I am the Lord your God" (Isaiah 43:2, NKJV).

Maureen mentioned that, after hearing the horrific news, she fell on her knees and asked God to give her strength to get through her nightmare and to let her testimony be one of praise and glory to Him instead of bitterness and anger. "He knows my endurance, and He will not give me more than I can bear. His grace is sufficient for me. 'Whenever I am afraid I will trust in Him'" (Psalm 56:3, NKJV), she said. Day by day, God continued to comfort, strengthen, and sustain her through her grief.

Maureen and I had shared devotional time together around 5:30 a.m. for some time. I thought that, in this dark season of her life, she wouldn't have the time or the desire for our regular prayer session. Every morning, between 5:15 and 5:30, she would call, and I would brace myself for an outburst of anger against God, but I'm happy to say that I waited in vain. Morning after morning, she shared what He told her in their private moments together.

The day of the funeral came, and I didn't know what to expect. Maureen mentioned that, during her personal devotion that morning, she had asked God to talk to her. Upon opening the Bible, her eyes were drawn to the scripture in Isaiah 44:21, "You. . . are my servant; I have made you;. . . I will not forget you" (NIV). Yes, her faithful God wrapped His loving arms around her and assured her that His presence was with her and that He will not forsake her. What beautiful words to receive from her Friend, Jesus!

The Oakwood University Church was packed with hundreds of people, young and old and all ages in between. Many had traveled from around the country and overseas for this solemn occasion. The service was unforgettable. Something happened that was unusual: Maureen stood up in the pulpit and shared her testimony. It was not only compelling, heartfelt, and inspiring, but it had a great impact on everyone in attendance. As a result, she received numerous calls and visits from people who were deeply moved by Rajeeni's life and Maureen's testimony and who, because of them, rededicated their lives to Jesus that afternoon. Many were encouraged and strengthened.

Maureen spoke of how blessed she was by the outpouring of love, prayers, and support from friends and strangers. Among the many letters she received was one from a man who was incarcerated in Atlanta, Georgia. He wrote that he never reads obituaries, but Rajeeni's picture caught his eye. His words comforted and encouraged Maureen's heart. She was impressed by his thoughtfulness and that he had taken the time to write to her. One added blessing that brought her much joy was hearing from some of Rajeeni's friends that the Sabbath before her tragic accident, she had publicly recommitted her life to God at the

Berean SDA Church in Atlanta, Georgia, where Dr. Carlton P. Byrd had pastored before becoming the pastor of the Oakwood University Church. Maureen is eternally grateful to God for this wonderful blessing.

What was most surprising to me was that when Maureen was experiencing the valley of the shadow of death, her faith in God never wavered. In fact, it became even stronger. She has been able to weather the storm and to manage her grief and pain with courage and strength, leaning on her loving and compassionate God. I believe that her faith, hope, and trust were securely anchored in the Solid Rock, Christ Jesus, long before this tragedy struck; so, when violent winds tried to blow her to pieces and to uproot her faith, she found refuge in Jesus, her faithful Companion.

She shared that, during one of her private devotions, like Job, she questioned God and invited Him to talk to her. Again, she opened her Bible and was drawn to a text already marked in Deuteronomy 29:29, "The secret things belong to the Lord our God. . ." (NIV). She said, "God is in the control tower; He doesn't have to explain anything to me. He doesn't have to get my permission to do anything He wants to do. He knows what He is doing. I ask Him for peace and serenity. I must be faithful so I can see my child again." In her moments of reflection, she found herself reading the book of Job from which she gathered new insights and glimpses into Job's life, and how he remained unmoved in his love for God.

Although Rajeeni's life ended abruptly, she continues to profoundly touch the lives of young and old alike, some physically and others spiritually. Before her tragedy, she had signed up to be an organ donor, and, although it was emotionally painful for her mom to carry out her wish, she did. Maureen was happy when she received a call from the organ donation office several months later with the great news that several people had been recipients of Rajeeni's selfless generosity. Her gift to others continues and underscores the significance of her life. Death is not the end! Yes, God can use death as much as He can use life, sometimes more.

Life is unpredictable, and the unexpected can disrupt your entire life and leave you permanently heartbroken. How does one cope with a time of tragedy and profound personal loss? To whom do you turn when your joy and reason for living have been utterly destroyed?

Where do you go when you are in the valley of the shadow of death? How do you prepare for the swirling storms of life?

Over the years, Maureen and her Heavenly Father have had a very intimate and personal relationship. Every morning, for years, she had arisen early to share her innermost thoughts with Him and to listen to what He had to tell her through His Holy Word. Maureen had invested her time in God's Word and in communion with Him, and it paid off a thousand-fold in her hour of need. Through it all, she had the peace and calm that could only have come from her connection with Jesus.

Like the Psalmist, David, Maureen cried out to God: ". . . I will cry to you when my heart is overwhelmed; lead me to the rock that is higher than I. For you have been a shelter for me, a strong tower from the enemy" (Psalm 61:1-3, NKVJ). God heard her cry, and became her mighty Fortress, her strong Deliverer, her Rock in a dry and weary land, her Comforter and Balm in Gilead (Psalm 18); her refuge in her time of the storm, and her El Shaddai, "perfect sufficiency."

We have all witnessed hurricanes or tornadoes or earthquakes or floods at one time or another and have heard the loud, wailing noise of sirens warning of impending danger. We've kept our eyes glued to the television set and our ears to the radio to listen to weather forecasts. We have seen people hurriedly board up their homes, secure their property, and/or purchase food and other survival essentials because they have been warned that something was coming. Then, dark storm clouds begin to gather, the lightning flashes, the thunder rolls and roars, the earth shakes, and the rivers rise, but they are protected, fortified, and ready. However, these potential catastrophes sometimes come unexpectedly, without warning and without time to prepare. As a result, we have witnessed destruction, devastation, and death. Just as we can't wait till we are drowning to learn to swim, neither can we wait until the storm is in our backyard to board up our windows and purchase emergency supplies. We must prepare in advance.

God never promised that we would go through life without problems, but He's promised to cover us with His arms of protection. Deuteronomy 33:12 puts it this way: ". . . The beloved of the LORD shall dwell in safety by Him; and the LORD shall cover him all the day long, and he shall dwell between His shoulders" (KJV). What a beautiful promise.

It's almost inevitable that, at some point, tragedies will enter our lives; torrential rains and howling winds, rumbling earth and rising waters may assail us and threaten to destroy us as well as our faith in God. No one is exempt; no one is left unscathed. My storm is coming, and so is yours. We don't know when or where or how, or what form these events will take. I pray that, like the apostle Paul and Maureen, we can say with confidence: "For I know whom I have believed and am persuaded that He can keep that which I have committed unto Him against that day" (2 Timothy 1:12, NKJV). May our faith in God be strong and our lives living testimonies to Him.

Maureen has experienced deep and lasting pain, but she is confident that, with God's help, her heart will sing again on that glorious resurrection morning when the skies shall unfold, and Jesus returns to retrieve His children. She looks forward to seeing her beloved daughter, again, when God shall wipe away all tears, and there'll be no more death. What a glorious day that will be. I want to see my loved ones, too. May God continue to uphold, comfort, and keep us in His loving care until that great day.

"I know that my Redeemer lives, And He shall stand at last on the earth; And after my skin is destroyed, this I know, that in my flesh I shall see God, whom I shall see for myself, And my eyes shall behold and not another. How my heart yearns within me?" (Job 19:25-27, NJKV).

Chapter 16

A New Season of Life

"To everything, there is a season and a time to every purpose under heaven. He made everything beautiful in its time" (Ecclesiastes 3:1, 11, NKJV). After more than 77 years of combined denominational service, 43 for Morris and 34 for me, we had arrived at a new season of life called retirement. It is with profound gratitude and praise to God for His wonderful miracles and countless blessings that we reached this significant milestone. All glory to God!

Our employment at Oakwood University officially came to an end the summer of 2007. In April of the following year, we, along with other retirees, were honored for our years of service to the University and the Seventh-day Adventist Church. It was a delightful occasion. Each retiree was presented with a plaque and a tribute book of letters from former colleagues, students, administrators, faculty, staff, family, and friends. My eyes were filled with tears as I read the many letters in my tribute book. I was especially touched by the one from our daughters.

The following is an excerpt from the letter written by Ngozi, Chioma, and Akunna: "On behalf of all the student workers whom you mentored and students you invited to your home for Sabbath lunch, we express our gratitude. Some of these individuals were international students, and others were overcome with homesickness. You helped them to adjust to a new environment. We are thankful that you offered free storage space in your garage during summer breaks for students to store their belongings. We applaud you for providing free taxi service to and from airport terminals, bus stations, and to and from doctor's and dentist's appointments. We commend you for all of those times you stopped to listen to a mother's worried plea for her child or went out of your way to check on a particular student in response to a parent's concern or your own. . ."

Sharon Perguson, a former student worker, wrote: "Thank you for modeling for me the essence of gracefulness, tact, professionalism, and integrity. Thank you for standing in the place of my missionary parents, thousands of miles across the ocean. Thank you for forgiving my mistakes, (and they were many) and giving me ample opportunities to 'try again.' Thank you for being more than just a boss, but making me part of your family. Thank you for opening up your home to me and sharing all those wonderful meals Mr. Iheanacho cooked!"

From Janice Whaley: ". . . Next to my parents, you had the greatest influence in my life. It was you who molded my work ethic when I used to work for you as a student assistant in the president's office. It was you who taught me the importance of professionalism and respect of peers. Now as a healthcare executive, I look for and cultivate these traits in my employees. You commanded excellence no matter how small the task. . ."

My former ASWA student, Ekele, penned these words: "Shirley, you were an astute and disciplined teacher who taught with a passion. You instilled in me, and I believe the rest of your students, the value of perseverance and dignity of labor. You are endowed with a beautiful singing voice, and you also encouraged me to sing more so as to enhance this natural gift God has given me. As a young woman, you were, and still are, my mentor. You made me appreciate various deep values of womanhood as I watched you respect your husband, cook, dress, nurture, and teach your very young daughters. You were not just my teacher, but you were also very open and as friendly and firm as a big older sister. You taught us, students, to maintain a good posture, walk briskly and smart, to smile and be friendly, and to have a good spirit and a sense of humor."

Margaret Scott Angelo, a parent of an Oakwood graduate, wrote this tribute: "Mrs. Iheanacho's warm, welcoming smile was among the first to greet us upon arriving on campus in August of 1999. Her personality was just as inviting as she did everything in her power to help my son transition from family and friends to a new little town, hundreds of miles away from home. This was only the beginning of what would turn out to be a lifelong relationship. Mrs. Iheanacho became a surrogate mother to my son Jonathan. What peace of mind I had knowing that there was someone my son could turn to in my absence. . . the invitations to Sabbath lunch for a hot and tasty home-cooked meal, finding Jonathan's first roommate, and raising funds when Jonathan needed $1,450 to graduate. Don't ask me how, but she managed to secure the amount in one afternoon from this person and that person. The acts of kindness are endless. Oakwood had its own Mother Teresa. A humble miracle worker, and indeed an angel missing in heaven disguised as the wife of Mr. Iheanacho."

The late Dr. Garland Millet, Oakwood University's fifth president, commented, "Your priceless service to Oakwood and the church have contributed greatly to the Lord's work, including valued service administrating two of the highest offices at Oakwood (including those of the president and provost). Your vigorous ringing bells in the bell choir, singing in the choir, or just representing Jesus as a genuine Seventh-day Adventist Christian have not gone unnoticed."

Travel Adventures

The year 2008, our first full year of retirement, ushered in a season of relaxation, excitement, adventure, and travel. We visited the sick-and-shut-in and healthcare facilities on a weekly basis. I served as an elder, prepared for speaking engagements, wrote articles, edited books, and articles, played with the hand bell choir, sang in the church choir, etc. There were no dull moments.

We traveled far and near visiting with family and friends. Among the first places we visited was our former home in Ionia, Michigan, where Morris began his professional career as a librarian, where Chioma was born, and the city from which we left to serve in Nigeria. Our friends, Dr. Darrel and Anna Jean Opicka, were celebrating their 50th wedding anniversary, and their children invited us to be part of the celebration. We were happy to return and to see so many of our friends, who were still attending church and serving God faithfully.

As a surprise to Anna Jean, Joyce, her daughter, asked me to sing two songs for the Sabbath worship service. Unknown to Anna Jean, I had rehearsed with a friend, Gisella

Knowles, so, when I stood up to sing, Anna Jean was surprised. Later, she told me that the music brought tears to her eyes. Following the worship service, we joined in a sing-a-long with Anna Jean as organist; Vernice Hatcher Storey, pianist; and a guest violinist. We recalled precious and happy memories of years gone by as we renewed our friendship and shared past experiences. During the potluck following the service, two couples reminded me that I had sung at their weddings several years before. Precious memories, how they linger!

On our way to the hotel, Chioma, Nikolas, Morris, and I drove around the neighborhood where we had lived. Our former home is still beautiful and continues to boast a well-manicured lawn. The little trees Morris planted in the front yard are now towering to the sky. Thoughts of the years spent in that house came flooding back as we drove around the block. I recalled Ngozi and Chioma, as little children, lying in the sun on the lush green grass in our backyard. When I asked, "What are you all doing?" Ngozi nonchalantly responded, "Mom, I'm trying to get a suntan!" I told her she already had a permanent suntan. I assume that they were imitating their Caucasian babysitter. I also recalled one of our neighbor's young sons who innocently asked, "Ngozi, why is your skin so dirty." He was unaccustomed to seeing Black people, so he didn't know that it was her permanent color and not dirt.

We still treasure fond memories of Ionia, but, looking back on our journey, we wouldn't trade our experience in Huntsville for anything. When we were called to Huntsville, we were unaware that our Omniscient Father, Who knows the end from the beginning, in His wisdom, placed us in a larger vineyard of service to be ambassadors of His grace, goodness, and mercy. He blessed us immeasurably and provided countless opportunities for us to interface with and touch the lives of some of the most delightful students, faculty, staff, and others who crossed our path. For this, we give God our deepest heartfelt praise, gratitude, and honor!

Our next big trip took us to Barbados. We were happy to see my mother and other family members. We enjoyed beautiful moments together, but there was some sadness, as well. Many familiar faces of church members who had had an impact on my life as a young girl were no longer there. Some were sick, and others had succumbed to death. I missed them. As we travel the road of life, changes can occur rather abruptly, and we never know what's awaiting us around the corner. We pray daily that God's hand of mercy and protection would be on us and our loved ones as we continue on this journey.

Later in the year, we traveled to beautiful Alaska on a seven-day cruise. It was exquisitely stunning as we observed breathtaking glaciers, deep blue fjords, and magnificent mountain views. We reveled in the splendor of God's majesty as far as our eyes could see. There was plenty of delicious food, too! Although we enjoyed our dining experiences, we didn't neglect our exercise.

One morning, at the conclusion of devotion, I asked God for a witnessing opportunity. Later that day, we went to the dining hall, and, after selecting our breakfast, we were looking for a place to sit when a couple invited us to join them. We happily accepted their invitation, greeted them, and sat down. Morris offered the blessing, and, as soon as he finished, the lady said, "Thank you. This morning, I asked God to let me meet some Christian people, and He has sent you." We had a delightful time together. God heard and answered both of our prayers.

During our cruise, I experienced a stark reminder of how quickly things can change. I had just completed my devotion and looked out the cabin window in time to capture a beautiful panoramic view of majestic mountains, evergreen trees, fluffy white clouds floating across the bright blue skies, and the golden sun shining in its brilliance, causing the waves to sparkle. It was an awe-inspiring moment, and I stood there captivated by its grandeur.

Some hours later, when I looked out the same window, I was shocked to see that dense fog had eclipsed the mountains, water, trees; my once-breathtaking view had been obliterated without warning. I couldn't help but think that this was a perfect depiction of life; one moment, all is well, and the next, our dreams can be obscured in ways that make us feel that they never existed. It is encouraging to note, however, that, no matter how much the scenes of life change, we have Someone Who is constant, our Special and Faithful Friend, Jesus. He never changes; He remains the same yesterday, today, tomorrow, and forever! That's good news!

Upon returning from our Alaska trip, we unpacked, repacked, and, along with other church members, boarded a bus headed for the Three Angels Broadcasting Network (3ABN) camp meeting in West Frankfort, Illinois. What a spiritually-rewarding treat it was! We were privileged to meet many individuals we frequently watched on 3ABN: Danny Shelton, John and Angie Lomacang, Dona Klein, C. A. Murray, Shelley Quinn, Jill Morikone, and many others. We enjoyed glowing reports, inspiring messages, and sweet music. Chioma and Nikolas joined us later. Nikolas had a good time visiting booths and collecting souvenirs. Later, he traveled back with us to Huntsville where he spent his summer vacation.

We were not at home long before we were on the road, again, this time to Andrews University for my 40th Alumni Homecoming Reunion Celebration. Morris, who also attended AU, Chioma, and Nikolas accompanied me. Upon entering the campus, a gorgeous picture greeted our eyes! The entrance was new and exquisitely beautiful.

At the invitation of a friend, we attended worship service in the newest building, the Howard Performing Arts Center, instead of the Pioneer Memorial Church, the church we had attended as students. As we walked into the auditorium, we were surprised by the large number of lovely Black faces that comprised a portion of the choir performing on the platform. We were mesmerized by their melodious voices as joyful musical praises ascended heavenward and blessed our hearts. Looking around the congregation at those in the packed auditorium, I was fascinated by the beautiful sea of skin tones with every shade of brown and black. It was evident that change had come, and it made my heart jump for joy!

Later on, Chioma accompanied me as I took a stroll down memory lane. We visited Nethery Hall where I first saw Morris back in 1967. From there, we walked to the steps of the James White Library, where he and I had had our first conversation. What cherished memories!

Of course, I could not leave the campus without visiting Lamson Hall, my home-away-from-home for three years. Walking down the stairs and around the corner to my first room, Room 10, I was saddened to see that there was, now, a sign on the door which read: Storage #10. And to think! No one consulted me before desecrating "my" room! Nevertheless, I will always treasure fond memories of the great and mischievous times I shared in that room with my roommates Thelda, Sherrie, Joy, and Gloria.

As we continued our stroll through pathways leading to the many old and new buildings, my thoughts turned to days gone by. I thought about my teachers, Ms. Hannah, Ms. Degner, Don Jacobsen, Clarence Richards, and, especially, Ms. Benson. Ms. Benson taught me voice lessons for a semester and encouraged me never to refuse an invitation to sing. I reminisced about dorm and church worships, the beautiful organ music by Dr. Becker, the lifelong friendships that began here, and, best of all, the place where I met my beloved husband.

Standing outside the Pioneer Memorial Church, I couldn't help reflecting on the goodness of my Heavenly Father and His innumerable blessings over the past 40 years of my life since graduating from Andrews in 1968. Pausing for a moment on the walkway, I had flashbacks of the day I received my degree. I was a 27-year-old woman without a clue that God had incredible plans for me. Now, there I stood, a 68-year-old retiree with a husband of 38 years, 34 years of denominational service, three adult daughters, two grandsons, a four-year mission service assignment in Africa, and many published articles in devotional books and recognized church magazines. I am humbled each time I reflect on what my wonderful God has wrought in my life. My soul shouts for joy, "Oh, give thanks to the LORD, for He is good! For His mercy endures forever" (Psalm 118:1, NKJV). Words are inadequate to express my gratitude for all the wonderful things He has done for me.

All too soon, our visit came to an end. We had enjoyed ourselves immensely. So many beautiful and priceless memories still lingered in my mind! One of those memories occurred when we returned to our hotel room. As we drove through the village near the campus, I was unaware that Nikolas was listening to my conversation about the times his grandfather took me to the local eatery where we ate good food and drank root beer. He was puzzled by this revelation and finally said, "Gramma, I didn't know that you and Grampa used to drink beer." I quickly explained to him that there are two kinds of beer: alcoholic and non-alcoholic. What we drank was non-alcoholic." "Oh, I see; I thought you all drank beer," he responded with a smile.

One of the things that I miss the most since retiring from Oakwood is the daily chats I had with students. Somehow, though, God continues to provide opportunities for me to share His love and words of encouragement with fellow travelers. I am not very brave when it comes to talking about my faith, but, after watching my friend, Brenda Walsh, on 3ABN talk about her book, *Passionate Prayer*, and how every morning she asks God to send someone with whom she can witness, I began to pray a similar prayer quietly. It's amazing what God did.

I was sitting in my hotel room working on my book when the housekeeper, Carmen, entered. She greeted us, then walked over to the bed and began to change the linens. When she spotted my Bible and a devotional book on the nightstand, she picked up the Bible and held it close to her chest and said excitedly, "A Bible! You Christian?" "Yes, I am," I answered. "Thank you, I Christian, too!" she replied. She said that she was exhausted and had not gotten much sleep the night before because of a very painful family crisis. We talked, and I prayed with her. She hugged and thanked me several times. I encouraged her to continue to pray and read her Bible and told her that God hears and answers prayers and that He would help her.

A few days passed, and Carmen returned to clean the room. As she entered, she asked, "You Adventist?" I said, "Yes." Excitedly, she told me that, a few weeks before, she had attended meetings conducted by Mark Finley, an international evangelist, who was holding evangelistic meetings at Forest Lake Academy in Florida. Both she and her son attended the meetings and enjoyed the preaching and Jennifer LaMountain's melodious singing.

I told her that I watched the same program in Huntsville, Alabama, on the 3ABN channel, and was also blessed. Her face lit up when she said that her son accepted the message presented by Pastor Finley, but she was still struggling with her job situation. Then, she said, "My son tell me, 'Ma, you read Bible and do what Bible say do, and Jesus will help you.'" I told her it was awesome advice.

On the day of our departure, I gave her a new devotional book, *Grace Notes*, and a thank-you card. She was elated. She said, "Thank you, I no read much English, but my son know much English; he will help me." I thank God for providing another opportunity to share my faith.

Orlando is one of our favorite places to vacation because we get to visit with our long-time friends, Joseph and Uche Okike, Ivan and Grace VanLange, and Thelma and Eugenia Prime. We cherish these memorable times.

Rarotonga, Australia, and New Zealand

Visiting other countries is exciting. There are interesting places and people and many opportunities for learning more about their cultures and history. In September 2009, Morris and I had the unique opportunity to be part of a 42-member tour group that visited the countries of Rarotonga, Australia, and New Zealand. This once-in-a-lifetime adventure was invigorating, fascinating, and spectacular. The historic sites and scenes were breathtaking, but they can in no way compare to the great beauties awaiting us in the earth made new. 1 Corinthians 2:9 tells that "Eye has not seen, nor ear heard, Nor have entered the heart of man The things which God has prepared for those who love Him" (NKJV).

We traveled by airplane, bus, glass-bottomed boat, amphibian vehicle (so called because they are a means of transport that is viable on land as well as on (or under) water), and train. We climbed steep mountains and rode on sky rails. What splendor to sit high in the skies and view the magnificent artistry of our Omnipotent Father. The psalmist David writes: "The heavens declare the glory of God; the skies proclaim the work of his hands" (Ps. 19:1, NIV).

As far as our eyes could see, we were greeted by imposing jagged mountains; gloriously dazzling waterfalls; gorgeous valley gorges; lush, green, dense forests; miles of verdant pastures with many roaming animals; and vast expanses of ocean. This created a panoply of grandeur, and magnificent beauty that caused my heart to cry out: Our God is a great God!

We had the opportunity to witness the shearing of a sheep. It was fascinating to watch the shearer rapidly move the sharp shears up and down the sheep's body without the sheep making a sound. This event brought to mind the text in Isaiah 53:7 that says that Jesus "was led as a lamb to the slaughter, and as a sheep before its shearers is silent, So He did not open His mouth" (NIV).

We visited a penguin colony, wildlife centers, kiwi vineyards, and the Great Barrier Reef. We enjoyed watching the indigenous people dance and sing, and we listened as they shared the rich and fascinating history of their country. We saw koalas, fish, and animals of all colors, shapes, and sizes. We even got to feed kangaroos and other wildlife. The bus took us to a high peak, and it was exhilarating to watch skiers course merrily down stunning, snow-covered mountain slopes.

Another captivating experience was visiting the glow worm caves in New Zealand. Walking through these fascinating caves, we came face to face with stalactites hanging down from the cave ceiling and stalagmites growing up from the cave floor creating sculptures of exquisite beauty and majesty. We stood transfixed as we savored the moment. Our guide told us that many renowned singers had sung in the cave, and he invited our group to sing. As we sang the much-loved hymn, "How Great Thou Art," the tuneful music rang through the caves, a powerful demonstration of praise to our awesome God, Creator of the heavens and the earth.

To get the best view of the brilliance of the glow worms, we traveled in darkness on a river at the bottom of the cave. No lights were allowed, so it was pitch black. The guide told us to look up. What a spectacular view we had of thousands of glow worms illuminating the darkness! Like the glow worms, though we are surrounded by a world of darkness, God's beautiful light can still shine brightly through us to illuminate the paths of others.

One of the highlights of our trip was our visit to the campus of Avondale College and the former home of the late Ellen G. White, an early Adventist pioneer, who had lived in Cooranbong, Australia. We met some of the old missionaries to the South Pacific islands and listened as they shared stories of their missionary ventures for God and of His providential leading in the affairs of His church and their lives.

Over the years, I had heard about the Sydney Opera House in Sydney, Australia, where T. Marshall Kelly, a family friend, had sung decades before. We finally got to see this extraordinarily unique and impressive structure. It was an enjoyable experience.

Downtown Sydney was extremely busy and captured our attention right away. The streets were teeming with people hurrying and scurrying in every direction. I was surprised at its hectic pace. At each stoplight, it seemed as if a tidal wave of individuals was anxiously waiting to cross the street. As the traffic light turned green, everyone quickly dashed across the street. I was curious to know where everyone was going and mustered the courage to ask a passerby if there was a special event going on. "That's the way it is on Mondays in downtown Sydney," he responded. I wondered if these people ever have a quiet moment to think about the God in heaven Who loves and cares for them. Morris and I continued walking, staying close to each other to avoid getting lost in the crowd.

From Australia, we traveled back to New Zealand on the last rung of our three-week tour. The sites, scenes, and stories we saw and heard were fascinating. There were too many for me to tell all of them. However, I must tell of one unfortunate experience that remains vivid in my memory. It happened the day of our departure from New Zealand.

We arrived at Auckland Airport two hours ahead of our departure time. Long lines of passengers waiting to check in had already formed. I was haunted by the feeling that my luggage was heavier than the allotted weight restrictions. The attendant instructed Morris to put his luggage on the scale; as usual, his was below the prescribed limits. To lighten my luggage, I decided to pull out a few items and put them in my carry-on before putting my luggage that was to be checked on the scale. It weighed three kilograms, or slightly less than 7 pounds under. At that point, I should have returned the items I'd removed, but I wasn't thinking. I was more concerned about the larger luggage. To our surprise, the attendant didn't ask us to weigh our carry-ons as they usually do in New Zealand, so I thought that it was a blessing. She processed our travel documents and instructed us to go upstairs to the departure gate.

We were about to enter the security line upstairs when another attendant called out for all passengers to come to the area where she was standing to weigh our carry-on luggage. Instantly, my heart sank, and I could feel a hammering in my chest. "How am I going to get out of this?" I thought. Nervously, I watched my husband place his carry-on on the scale. Of course, it was under, as always. With trepidation, I put my carry-on on the scale and, sure enough, it was over. The attendant told me that I would have to throw out the excess or go back downstairs and send it through as a check-in. To go back downstairs and have to wait, once again, in the long lines and to find my checked luggage was out of the question. Since my husband's luggage was below, I transferred some items to his, which, now, caused his to be over, so a few pieces had to be removed.

Unwillingly, I went through my luggage and began to discard some of the contents, but it was still over the weight limit. Much to my shock, the attendant asked me to put my personal handbag on the scale, too. In more than 50 plus years of air travel, I had never had to weigh my handbag. Unbelievably, it was overweight, too. The attendant hastily informed me: "Three kilos are allowed for handbags, and yours is five." Hearing those words was quite disheartening, I became fearful that I would have to rid my bags of items that I valued.

By this time, I was flustered. With a stern look and a voice devoid of emotion, the attendant kept insisting that I throw out more items or take them downstairs to be checked in. I stood there, embarrassed and humiliated. I didn't have the courage to look at Morris' face because I knew that, by this time, he was not only embarrassed but angry. Other passengers were waiting in line to weigh their luggage, and I was holding up the line. I pleaded with the attendant to let me keep some of the things, but her voice seared through me like a knife, "Make up your mind what you want to do; they have announced the departure of your flight, but you can't take those things with you!" Humbly, I stood before her clinging to a pair of slippers in one hand and a gift for my mother in the other, pleading with her to let me go. Somehow, God worked on her hard heart, and I was allowed to go.

With the luggage hurdle behind us, we headed for the very long security lines. Anxiety and fear coalesced inside me as we headed for the gate. I wondered if we would make it to the plane on time, but I dared not utter a word. We passed through the first security checkpoint without any alarms, unaware that we still had two more to go, further heightening my stress level. "Lord," I pleaded, "Please, help us make our flight." The distance to the gate was very long, and there were no trains or buses to take us there. We walked hurriedly, and I sometimes ran, too. Breathless and exhausted, we arrived at the gate. Boarding had already begun. Embarrassment washed over me, again, as some of the passengers looked in my direction. Only a few people of color were in that large airport, so, needless to say, we stood out. I wanted to hide, but there was no hiding place down there.

Finally, we boarded the plane. Almost breathless, I sat down to begin the 10-hour-journey from New Zealand to Los Angeles. As I sat quietly on the plane, I had an immediate flashback of my horrible ordeal. I could still hear the unrelenting voice of the attendant: "Your luggage exceeds the weight allowed. You can either throw the excess in the trash container or go back downstairs and check it in, but you can't take it with you." Thoughts of an old Bible story about an unknown woman referred to in the Bible as Lot's wife kept tumbling through my mind. In her heart, she too was clinging to her things even though she was going away from the doomed city with her husband. It pained her very much to let them go. So, after having been admonished by the angel not even to look back, for one brief, unguarded moment, she yielded to temptation and took one last glance backward. Because she had disobeyed and because that backward glance indicated her lack of commitment to God and His will and her longing to return to the corrupt city, she was instantly turned into a pillar of salt. She lost all of her worldly possessions, lavished lifestyle, and, ultimately, her life. Like Lot's wife, my heart was clinging to my stuff; I didn't want to let it go.

In the stillness of the moment, my mind fast forwarded to judgment day that's coming soon upon the earth. I saw myself standing at the gate of heaven pleading with the judge to let me go through. In my mind, I could hear His voice solemnly say, "Sorry, Shirley, there is no room in heaven for you. You are overweight with the sin of selfishness, covetousness, greed, an unforgiving heart, and material goods. We have no room in heaven for such stuff. Depart from me!" Sorrowfully, I envisioned myself standing before the Judge of the Earth, being weighed in the balance, and found lacking the necessary attributes to enter heaven.

One day soon, I believe that this scene will be real. The Bible tells us in 2 Cor. 5:10, "For we must all appear before the judgment-seat of Christ, that each one may receive the things done in the body according to what he has done, whether good or bad" (NIV). I asked myself the question, "How shall I stand in that great day?" How shall you? Shall we be found before Him lacking and with all our sins forgiven? Or not? The choice is yours. . . and mine. I pray that all will be well with our souls and that we will hear the wonderful voice of Jesus proclaim, "Welcome home! Enter into the beautiful mansion I have prepared for you."

Travel to Nigeria

For more than 33 years, I had dreamed of returning to Nigeria, and my dream finally became a reality in February 2013. It was an exhilarating and memorable experience. However, the circumstances surrounding our return were sad. The purpose of our visit was to attend the funerals of two of Morris' loved ones. However, in the midst of our sadness, God brought joy to our hearts.

Our flight landed safely at the airport in Lagos, Nigeria, after a 14-hour flight. We waited for several hours before transportation arrived to take us to the campus of Babcock

University, formerly ASWA. The 45-minute drive from the airport to Babcock University took more than three hours because of the unusually high volume of traffic. Traffic laws are often ignored in this part of the world, and drivers take chances that could be tragic. We were appalled to see two-lane roads become five lanes, with vehicles coming extremely close to each other. It was frightening, and I braced myself for a collision at any moment. From my observation, three things are necessary to be an adept driver in Nigeria: an aggressive spirit, brakes in excellent working condition, and a loud horn.

After what I consider the scariest and most stressful drive of my life, we reached Babcock University without any mishaps. Before entering the campus, we had to pass through tight security complete with armed guards. As we drove in, we noticed that nothing looked familiar. What had been forest when we left in December 1979 had been replaced by massive buildings, new roads, a new entrance to the university, faculty housing, etc.

Morris & Shirley at Babcock University

We had a good night's sleep and, after breakfast, we began a tour of the campus. Everything looked new. The house in which we had lived was almost unrecognizable except for the trees I had planted along the driveway in 1976. The little schoolroom where our children had been educated had been moved to a different location and had been replaced by a large school building that housed hundreds of students.

Because of the university's high enrollment, the church had become too small to accommodate the students, so chapels had been built. We stayed at the home of Dr. Rowland

Nwosu, Director of Missions, and a friend from our days at ASWA where he was a student. He invited me to speak at vespers and Sabbath worship service in one of the new chapels which seats approximately 650. It was indeed a special moment as we watched and listened to hundreds of students vibrantly sing songs of praise during the worship service. We marveled at the new three- and four-storey dormitories and other buildings. We stood in wonderment at how the campus had dramatically changed, but we welcomed the progress that had been made in our absence.

Approximately 10,000+ students and a high percentage of non-Adventists (80%) attend the university, making it necessary to employ seventy full-time pastors to attend to the spiritual needs of the students.

We spent a few days on the campus before traveling by plane to eastern Nigeria to attend the funerals of Morris's relatives: Mrs. Festa Anyatonwu and his mom's brother. Following their retirement, Papa and Mama Anyatonwu had returned home to Nigeria to live. Several years later, Papa had unexpectedly become ill and passed away. Mama always urged us to come for a visit. Some weeks before her death, she had invited us to come home for the Christmas holidays. Unfortunately, she became ill and died shortly after extending that invitation. We were deeply saddened, but will always cherish beautiful memories of her loving, kind, generous, and caring spirit.

This was my first visit back to the village after more than 33 years. It was quite a memorable experience to see Morris' family and friends after such a long absence. We were elated to see each other again; a woman was so happy that she kept on repeating, "Shirley, Shirley, welcome, welcome!" She reminded me of my first visit and how I had greeted everybody of all ages with the same greetings specifically reserved for seniors. We both had a hearty laugh. I was blessed to be with Morris' family, but I missed his mom's presence.

After spending several days in Aba and the village at the home of Morris' only remaining uncle, Clement Iheanacho Onwulata and his hospitable family, we returned to Babcock University, where, providentially, Morris was reunited with his best friend and classmate, Dr. James Kio, along with another classmate. These three men constituted the second group of students to enter the Adventist College of West Africa in the early 1960s, and they had graduated together in 1964. This was the first time they had been together as a class since graduation.

Morris' Class of 1964

It was thrilling to listen to them recall stories from their college years. They shared fond memories of the early pioneers and how they worked tirelessly in the development of the school. Dr. Nwosu interviewed them and aired it later on his TV network. Another thing that worked out perfectly for us was that the retired chancellor of the University of Ibadan, the person writing the history of Babcock University, was on campus, and he sat in on their conversation. He, too, was fascinated by their stories.

Time flew by swiftly and, before we knew it, two weeks filled with cherished reminiscences and great fellowship had passed, and we headed back to Alabama. We thank God for the opportunity to, once again, visit and spend time with family and friends in Nigeria, and for the golden opportunity we had to serve on that beautiful campus many years before.

"Praise the LORD! For it is good to sing praises to our God; For it is pleasant, and praise is beautiful" (Psalm 147:1, NKJV).

Chapter 17

Global Missions Adventures

*O*ften, we human beings think that we have the most brilliant plans mapped out for our lives. Then, God shows us His plan that is, many times, just the opposite of what we had in mind. We tell ourselves that His plan will in no way fit into ours. Then, reality sets in, and we recognize that God is the perfect Master Planner and Controller and has the power to do and help us to do whatever He wills. He can turn us around from whatever direction we've decided to go in and give us new and better plans. He never forces us to do anything; however, if we choose to embrace His will for us, He sends us on our way, or, actually, His best way.

This was my experience some years ago when Morris expressed his desire to participate in a Maranatha Volunteers Missions Project. His interest was piqued by Dick Duerksen's exciting and inspiring Maranatha Mission Stories on 3ABN. At the conclusion of one of the episodes, Morris expressed his desire for us to go on a mission trip, and, right away, he began his online search for information about the upcoming Maranatha Volunteer Open Team project. Only one was available at the time, and it was in Maputo, Mozambique. He said, "Let's go on this mission project." I thought to myself, "No way am I going half-way around the world on a mission trip." Morris had delayed his retirement date so we could retire together and travel. We had plans of things we wanted to do, but Mozambique was not on my agenda.

Now, I was faced with the challenge of telling him that I didn't want to go because of what I considered three valid reasons: (1) Mozambique was halfway around the world, and political unrest flanked the area. (2) Airfares were exorbitant; and as new retirees, we had to watch our budget. (3) Health concerns regarding my severe allergic reactions to the smell of alcohol, chemicals, and strong fragrances evoked fear in me. I dreaded becoming ill so far from home.

When I mentioned to our daughters the reasons why I didn't want to go, their responses were the same, "Why don't you tell Dad?" I didn't have the heart or the courage to tell him. In the meantime, Morris proceeded with his online search regarding the project and the requirements to enter Mozambique. He filled out the necessary application forms and mailed them to Maranatha Volunteer International office and Mozambique Embassy along with the required fees.

Whenever the subject was mentioned, I remained silent, quite unusual for me, but, deep in my heart, I silently prayed that God would allow something to happen to change Morris' mind. Little did I know that, while I was praying this prayer, God was working behind the scenes in Morris' favor.

First, He began by using our seven-year-old grandson, Nikolas, who overheard me tell my friend, Kaven Ible, that I didn't want to go to Mozambique. He said, "Gramma, you are like Jonah!" When I asked him what he meant, he proceeded to tell me the entire Jonah story with such fervor that I became fascinated with his vivid picture of Jonah running from God. He stated the fact that God loved the people of Nineveh and gave them a second chance. God loved Jonah and also gave him a second chance. He concluded that God loves us, too, and gives us a second chance (Jonah 2 and 3). Wow! Was God speaking to me through this little boy? Was He giving me a second chance to reconsider my decision? I felt a twinge of guilt gnawing at my heart.

For two weeks, we were busy traveling, and no mention was made of Maranatha or Mozambique. I concluded, wrongly, that Morris had changed his mind. Then, out of the blue, he announced that we should book our flights because it was getting late, and airfares were going up. I was not excited. However, reluctantly, I decided to go with him and began to make plans to travel to Mozambique.

Several days after mailing our visa applications, Morris had been browsing through his Maranatha folder and realized that he'd forgotten to enclose our passport pictures. "Great!" I thought this was an answer to my prayer. My heart was happy! Not daunted by this set-back, Morris asked me to contact the embassy to inform them of the oversight. I did, and the officer told me that our passports and visa applications had been returned because of the missing items. She advised that if we returned them immediately, along with the photos and a copy of our itinerary, it would take ten business days to process. It was already June 23.

Amazingly, something happened that brought about a complete transformation in my heart. God turned me around from a reluctant participant to a willing volunteer, fully accepting of His plan. He tore down my self-made red light of fear, doubt, and inadequacy, and replaced it with His green light of excitement and enthusiasm at the prospect of going to Mozambique to share His message of love with the children in the villages of Mucatine and Celula 5. He knows the plans He has for each of us, and how to work them out perfectly, as well as how to overcome the obstacles that we place in His way.

July 7, the day before my 68th birthday, was the major turning point in my decision. I had awakened early but lay in bed still thinking about our plans to go to Mozambique and mulling over my reluctance to accept Maranatha's request to lead out with Vacation Bible School (VBS). I decided to have my personal worship but, instead of reading my devotional book first, as my custom was, I picked up the Sabbath School Adult Lesson Study Guide titled *"Agents of Hope: God's Great Missionaries."* Providentially, the Bible study guide opened to September 20, the last lesson for the Third Quarter. My eyes were drawn to the title, "'Here Am I! Send Me': The Prophet Isaiah." I reread it. Was the Lord trying to tell me something? The memory verse seemed to be conveying the same message: "Also I heard the voice of the Lord, saying: "Whom shall I send, and who will go for Us?" Then I said, 'Here am I! Send me'" (Isaiah 6:8, NKJV).

Some statements in the lesson made a profound impression on me. One was that God had transported Isaiah through vision into the heavenly throne room and had given him the experience of a lifetime. It was so profound and heart-wrenching that Isaiah cried out, "Woe is me! For I am undone; because I am a man of unclean lips, and I dwell in the midst of a people of unclean lips" (Isaiah 6:5, NIV). Isaiah realized his unworthiness in the presence of the Almighty God.

I got a sense of my unworthiness and found myself asking God to forgive my sins, to cleanse me of my selfishness, and to make me a vessel fit to share His love with His children in Mozambique. He had placed a solemn responsibility on my shoulders, and, like Jonah, I was trying to run from it. I needed a renewing of my mind first, like Isaiah; then, and only then, could God use me.

As I read further in the lesson, I was touched by this statement: "Isaiah does not respond because he believes he knows that he will do a good job. And he does not respond because it is a task that appeals to him (he does not even know what the task is). Isaiah responds because he knows that, although he is unworthy, God is worthy. Although he is powerless, God is all powerful. Although it may not be a mission he would have chosen for himself, it is a mission God has chosen."

On the same page, Gary Krause, the author, went on to say that "If we are willing, God gives us the power we need to accomplish the mission He gives us. . . What, if anything, is holding you back from doing more for the Lord? What changes must you make? How can you learn to rely on God's power and not your gifts, whatever they are?" (Adult Sabbath School Bible Study Guide, "Agents of Hope: God's Great Missionaries," Pacific Press Publishing Association, 2008, p. 107). Those soul-stirring words seemed aimed directly at my heart. I was stunned. God had spoken loud and clear!

Still in a daze from this unexpected encounter, I reached for my devotional book, *Heaven's Whisper*. To my surprise, God had a message waiting for me there, too. The scripture read: "Fear not for I am with you;. . .' For I, the Lord your God will hold your right hand, saying to you, 'Fear not, I will help you'" (Isaiah 41:10, 13, NKJV). After reading these two verses, I was impressed to read the entire chapter. When I read the following words, I became convinced that God's wishes for me were clear: "But now, thus says the Lord, who created you, O Jacob, and he who formed you, O Israel. Fear not for I have redeemed you, I have called you by your name, you are mine. When you pass through the waters, I will be with you, and through the rivers, they shall not overflow you; when you walk through the fire, you shall not be burned, nor shall the flame scorch you. For I am the Lord your God, The Holy

One of Israel, your Savior, I gave Egypt for your ransom, Ethiopia and Seba in your place. Since you were precious in my sight, You have been honored,. . ." (Isaiah 43:1-4, NKJV).

God was relentless in his pursuit of me, and there was no way of escape. I had been reluctant to accept the leadership of the VBS because of my feelings of inadequacy. Now, in simple, clear words, He promised to hold my right hand and to help me. The lyrics of a hymn I used to sing many years ago flashed through my mind. "It may not be on the mountain's height, Or over the stormy sea; It may not be at the battle's front My Lord will have need of me; But if by a still, small voice he calls To paths that I do not know, I'll answer, dear Lord, with my hand in Thine, I'll go where you want me to go" (lyrics to this verse by Mary Haughton Brown).

God was still not through with me. Later in the week, Shirley Scott came by with birthday gifts. Included was Stormie Omartian's book titled, *The Power of Praying: Help for a Woman's Journey Through Life*. I opened it and was surprised when these were the first words that I saw: "Know His Plans for you. You never know when you will step into the moment for which God has been preparing you. And it is not just one moment; it's many successive ones. It doesn't matter whether you are a single career woman or a married lady with nine children under the age of ten; it doesn't matter whether you are nineteen or ninety, God is preparing you daily for something great. He wants you to be willing to let Him purify you, fortify you, and grow you up in Him. But you have to play by the rules (pp. 34, 35). I was amazed and profoundly moved by these words.

Glancing at page 34 I read, "God has great plans for you. He has important things He wants you to do. And He is preparing you daily for your destiny right now. But you have to trust that He knows the way and won't hurt you in the process." Continuing on, I read this solemn prayer: *"Lord, show me what You want me to do today to be a blessing to others around me. Specifically, show me how I can serve my family, my friends, my church, and the people whom You put in my life. Keep me from getting so wrapped up in my own life that I don't miss the opportunities to minister Your life to others. In Jesus' name I pray"* (p. 34). Harvest House Publishers, 2004. I was deeply touched and even more convinced that God was speaking directly to me.

Honestly, I was impressed that this series of events was not just mere coincidences, but divinely-appointed incidents designed by God for His unworthy daughter, Shirley. He wanted to do a new thing in my Christian experience and growth. I realized that His plan for me was beyond my comprehension.

Our Heavenly Father has a way of going ahead of us and orchestrating situations and circumstances long before we are aware of what's happening. Because time and space do not constrain Him, He has already made provision before the beginning of time! Two years before this, during one of our visits with Chioma and Nikolas, God had begun to prepare me for this assignment. Morris and I were invited by Debbie Agard to assist with VBS at the Hinsdale SDA Church in Illinois. Little did I know, at the time, that God was preparing me for this. In Prov. 16:9 (NIV), the Bible declares that: "In his heart, a man plans his course, but the LORD determines his steps." I can testify to it!

Well, after the guilt trip that Nikolas took me on, the "Here Am I" jolting, and the penetrating words about God's plans for me, I willingly surrendered my life to God and accepted the responsibility of leading out with VBS. Now, I *was* excited! With renewed vigor, I began preparations for my mission venture. I sought advice from various children's ministries experts, attended VBS programs in my community, and purchased VBS supplies. Every morning before beginning my devotion, my prayer was, "Lord, speak to me today." After that July 7 encounter, God spoke words of assurance, affirmation, and encouragement to me daily through Scripture and devotional readings.

Initially, Mrs. Mary Barnett, Maranatha Volunteer Project Specialist, shared information about Mozambique. I also tried to learn as much as I could about this country which lies along the Indian Ocean and is one of the poorest of all of the African countries. It was ruled by Portugal for many centuries but gained its independence in 1975. However, sixteen years of civil war had devastated the country. It was further crippled by illiteracy, lack of clean drinking water, malaria, and HIV/AIDS.

Portuguese is the official language, but the most common is Emakhuwa, and the villagers speak their own dialects. According to 2006 statistics, life expectancy in Mozambique is 40 years. The overall literacy rate is 39%, but only 17% for women. Agriculture employs 85% of the workforce, many at mere subsistence levels. The crops grown include cashew nuts, sugar, cotton, and cassava. The average yearly income is $350 USD; for pastors, it's $127 USD. The dominant religion is Catholicism.

Mrs. Barnett informed us that, because there was no church structure in the village, the VBS would be conducted outdoors. Upon inquiring about the availability of electricity to play CDs and DVDs, we learned there was none nearby, only a generator at the construction site. What about felt board, felts, musical instruments, supplies, etc.? None! And the biggest surprise was that I would have to bring my VBS supplies. The airline tickets, vaccinations, and malaria medicine had already consumed a sizeable amount of our money, and this would be an unexpected added expense.

Reluctantly, I mentioned to a few church members and friends that we were planning to participate in a Maranatha mission project and asked if they would be willing to contribute VBS supplies. Their response was generous. Also, the Maranatha office contacted other volunteers and requested their help with supplies. Everything was progressing well, or so we thought. Then, unexpectedly, we encountered a major setback. Five days before our scheduled departure, our visas and passports had not arrived, although the Mozambique embassy insisted that they had mailed them eight days earlier.

Our testing time had come. Each of us will experience these times at some point in our lives. How well we handle them will depend upon our personal relationship with Jesus. I sadly admit that I didn't handle mine very well. I allowed anxiety and doubt to, once again, wedge their way into my mind. When God places a responsibility on you, there is no guarantee that you will not encounter roadblocks nor that everything will work out the way you planned it. What He has promised is that He will be with you always, and He keeps His promises.

The delay in receiving our passports and visas caused many questions to surface: Why were our passports and visas taking so long to arrive? Why was this happening to us? Why was God standing by and allowing us to go through this unnecessary stress? Why did He tell me to go and then changed His mind? Question after question engulfed my mind for which I had no answers. We had invested a lot of money, time, and effort into preparing for this trip. Now, it appeared that our dream was about to go unrealized. I doubted that we would be able to travel with so little time remaining and with no passports or visas. Have you ever had a similar waiting experience where you felt as if your patience was being tested to the limit?

I still had no answers, but every morning, during my devotional time, God gave me words of hope and encouragement: "But now. . . the Lord who created you says: 'Do not be afraid, for I have ransomed you, I have called you by name, you are mine'" (Isaiah 43:1, NLT). "Is anything too hard for the LORD?" (Genesis 8:14, 1st part). "Behold, God is my salvation; I will trust, and not be afraid; for the Lord, Jehovah is my strength and my song; he also is become my salvation" (Isaiah 12: 2). Regrettably, I was not paying attention. My faith began to waiver when things didn't work out the way I envisioned they should, but God remains faithful even through our doubts and fears, stubbornness and reluctance.

"The Master Planner" was the title of the devotional reading for Thursday morning, and the scripture read, "You did not choose me, but I chose you and appointed you to go and bear fruit that will last" (John 15:16, NIV). These words were strong, powerful, and affirming. Deep within our hearts, Morris and I were convinced that God was calling us to go, but how could we go when our travel documents were missing?

That morning, we waited with baited breath for the mail carrier. He finally arrived. My heart was pounding so rapidly I thought it would burst through my chest. I peeked out the window and watched as the mailman put the mail in our mailbox. There was no manila envelope from the embassy. A sickening feeling came over me as I watched him drive away. I called out to Morris that the mail had come, but that it contained no documents. We were both disappointed and entertained the thought that, maybe, it was no longer God's plan for us to travel to Mozambique.

We called Mary Barnett to inform her of this latest development. On her advice, we began to put plan B into action to request new visas since it appeared that our other travel documents were lost. Forms were filled out and signed, with pictures, ready and waiting for the arrival of the mail carrier the following day. Our plan B was to send the forms and fees by express mail to the General Conference headquarters requesting their assistance.

Dr. Clarence Hodges, a church elder and scholarships contributor, came by with his donation for VBS supplies. After chatting briefly, Morris shared our dilemma and invited him to pray for us. He prayed that God would intervene and permit the release of our documents so that we could be about His business. Our spirits were lifted, and our hearts encouraged.

The next day was Friday, July 25. I was up early, as usual. What news would the day bring? It was 3:30 a.m.; I picked up my devotional book, and it opened to page 137 (May 8), "In My Father's Arms." The scripture was Psalm 34: 4 (NIV), "I sought the Lord, and he answered me; he delivered me from all my fears." The author of the devotional article, Nelci De Roco Lima, stated that "Whatever may be causing a storm in your life, whatever may be causing us to hear thunder and feel the dark clouds that are leaving us in gloom, we can be certain that God always gives us a promise for each trial. He is ready to extend His hand to us. Serenely protected under His wings, we do not need to fear. Under His wings we are safe. We 'find refuge in the shadow of your wings" (Ps. 36:7, NIV). (*Heaven's Whisper*, Review and Herald Publishing Association, 2007). I was convinced that these beautiful and affirming words were designed especially for me!

"Will our documents arrive today?" I kept asking myself. It was 7:30 a.m. I was too impatient to wait for the mail carrier to come. "I'm going to the post office to wait for it to open," I called to Morris. "I don't think that it opens before 8:30," he responded. By 8:05 my patience had run out, so I called the post office and inquired if mail from the Mozambique Embassy had arrived for Morris Iheanacho. The postal attendant checked but responded that there was nothing. She assured me that the courier was still sorting mail and that she would call me back. There was still a glimmer of hope!

We prayed as we awaited the postal attendant's call. An hour passed with no word. Too anxious to wait any longer, I called again. The same lady answered the phone, and I made the same inquiry. She shouted, "Ma'am, didn't I tell you I would call you back? The courier is still sorting the mail!" "Sorry, sorry Ma'am," I quickly responded. Not long after, the phone rang. I rushed to answer it. It was the same lady, but this time she was calling with good news! Our travel documents had arrived! Inexpressible joy erupted from my heart. Fearing the mail carrier would take too long to deliver our mail, I hastily took off for the post office as Morris called out, "Don't drive too fast!"

I arrived at the post office and identified myself to the clerk. She went to the back and returned with a manila envelope and handed it to me. As I held it in my hand, I lifted my voice and shouted, "Thank You, Jesus," very loudly. People standing in line looked at me in astonishment, but I wasn't bothered. God had heard and answered our prayers. Why had I doubted that He would? Why had I limited His power? "Oh, Shirley, where is your faith?"

Sabbath morning came, and it was time for my devotion. Upon opening my Bible, two pages of praises in the book of Psalm caught my attention. Every chapter rang out with praises from my heart to God Who, in His compassion, great love, and mercy had come through for us, again. "Praise the LORD, Praise the LORD, O my soul! While I live I will praise the LORD, I will sing praises to my God while I have my being" (Ps. 146:1-2, NKJV). "Praise the Lord for it is good to sing praises to our God; for it is pleasant, and praise is beautiful" (Ps. 147:1). Praise the LORD! Praise the LORD from the heavens" (Ps. 148:1). "Praise the LORD! Sing to the LORD a new song and His praise in the assembly of saints" (Ps. 149:1). "Let everything that has breath, praise the LORD." Praise the LORD" (Ps. 150:6). Amen!!

To say that we were elated to receive our passports and visas is an understatement, but, by Monday, we had become overwhelmed by the large volume of supplies waiting to be packed and concern that we would exceed our weight restrictions. Although we wanted to avoid paying extra money, we didn't want to leave VBS supplies behind because the children needed them. God was still at work doing His thing. He sent two friends, Shirley Scott and Sonia Paul, with supplies. They volunteered to pack as they shared ideas and suggestions to help with the mission God had placed on our hearts. They did a terrific job of packing, and this lifted a heavy burden from our shoulders. Without our knowing it, God had gone before us and provided for our needs, even before we asked. I was reminded of the scripture that says "Before [you] call I will answer, and while [you] are still speaking, I will hear" (Isa. 65:24, NKJV).

The morning of our departure arrived, but we remained concerned about the possible excessive weight of our luggage. I took two extra bags to the airport so that DeLoras could take home any items that we might have to remove from our luggage. We arrived at the check-in counter and, with trepidation, we placed our luggage on the scale. Two pieces were seven pounds over the weight allowed, and the other two were seven pounds under. Amazing! Nervously, I quickly transferred items until the last piece of luggage weighed

51 lbs. The attendant was waiting for me to remove the extra pound when I pleaded with him, "Sir, it's only a pound, please let it go." He acquiesced. We had a hearty laugh when everything was completed. With gratitude to God and hearts bubbling over with joy and excitement, Morris and I thanked, and said goodbye to DeLoras and Reggie. Now, there was no turning back. Happily, we boarded the flight to begin our 26½-hour journey of faith to the country of Mozambique.

Our first stop was Atlanta; from there, we continued to Senegal. We were surprised when the plane landed at the Senegal airport because we thought it was a non-stop flight to Johannesburg. I looked out the window of the aircraft and saw armed officers with serious faces board our plane along with uniformed workers wearing gloves. The workers began to check the luggage in the overhead compartments. A twinge of nervousness came over me as I considered the possibility of the plane being hijacked. I mustered enough courage to ask one of the officers if something was wrong. He responded that they wanted to be sure no unidentified luggage was left on the plane before it departed for South Africa. I breathed a deep sigh of relief!

With all the luggage identified, the plane took off for Johannesburg. Upon arrival, we made our way through long immigrations lines. Finally, we boarded the flight for Mozambique. The only blight on our excitement was that Morris and I were assigned seats to the back of the plane when we boarded. I didn't like that because it meant that we would be the last passengers to deplane. Nevertheless, we were happy when the plane touched down at the airport. When the flight attendant announced that passengers could disembark, we stood up and faced the front of the aircraft. We soon noticed, however, that all the other passengers were facing us. It was then that we realized that we would be the first to leave the plane, not the last! Only the government officials on board exited from the front. Of course, we were overjoyed at this turn of events.

My feet finally touched the ground in Mozambique, and what a thrilling moment it was! We had arrived safely! Maranatha staff and Merrill Zachary, Maranatha Mozambique Open Team Coordinator, greeted us warmly, along with Dan Whatley, a volunteer from Alaska. It was late at night when we reached the compound. We looked on in anticipation as the driver stopped at the entrance and a guard opened the gate.

Entering the grounds, we noticed 24 little green tents. Zach introduced us to our home away from home: one of those little green tents we had seen as we entered. We had first choice, and I chose tent #3 because it was positioned a short distance from the restrooms. As we pulled up the zippers to enter our tent, reality slapped me in the face. It was cold and as black as pitch inside. There was no light switch, no heat, no closet in which to hang our clothes, no chairs on which to sit, no bed linens or pillows or blankets, just the two cots that would be our beds. We managed to get our luggage inside and began to search for our flashlight and pajamas. My thoughts turned to Morris. Knowing how meticulous he is, I wondered how he would survive this experience.

Morris standing by our tent

My mind was so obsessed with bringing VBS supplies that I neglected to bring bed linens or warm clothing. The first night, I slept in my pajamas, a nightgown, a T-shirt, and my robe, covered with the jacket I arrived in and the little blanket I asked the flight attendant to let me keep after hearing the pilot announce that it was 50 degrees in South Africa. Most of the night, I shivered from the cold and prayed earnestly, "Dear Jesus, please don't let me get sick or die in this strange place." Thank God, we survived our first night. The next day, we secured warm blankets from Zach. I used one to cover my bed, one as a pillow, and the other to wrap myself. We were on God's errand, and He was fulfilling His promise to take care of us.

Friday, August 1, enthusiastic volunteers gathered in the open-air dining/kitchen facility for breakfast from 6:30 to 7:30. Zach greeted us enthusiastically, and we introduced ourselves. Thus, began our unique bonding process. He explained our mission and taught us a new theme song to begin worship: "I'll live for Jesus, day after day; I'll live for Jesus, let come what may; the Holy Spirit, I will obey, and live for Jesus day after day. I'll work for Jesus, day after day; I'll work for Jesus, let come what may; the Holy Spirit I will obey and work for Jesus, day after day" (Paul Schultz). Morning and evening worships were conducted by Maranatha volunteers who shared their personal, inspiring stories of God's providence and faithfulness.

On our way to the construction site, we sang a chorus to cheer us on our way: "Good morning, it's God's morning, whether skies are cloudy or gray; Good morning, it's God's morning; Hope you have a wonderful day, Hey!" One of the songs we sang for evening worship was "Turn your eyes upon Jesus." Joy flooded my soul as we sang the chorus of this beautiful hymn: "Turn your eyes upon Jesus, Look full in His wonderful face; And the things of earth will grow strangely dim In the light of His glory and grace" (Helen H. Lemmel).

The purpose of this mission trip was to build two churches that would double as community/literacy centers and to conduct a Vacation Bible School in each of the villages of Mucatine and Celula 5. At the completion of worship, 23 volunteers from around the United States and Canada poised themselves to tackle their new assignments. We traveled by bus to the construction site approximately 75 minutes away.

The journey was an eye opener. We were overwhelmed by the abject poverty that we viewed from the bus. Along the road, we saw women and children living in shacks, in indescribably dark slum areas, with their little "homes" surrounded by garbage. Trash lined the streets. I never imagined the degree of poverty that existed in this faraway country. As we traveled on, we saw beautiful houses, too, and wondered at these two extremes in circumstances and living conditions. Many people were walking along the streets; some briskly with large loads on their heads and babies on their backs. Buses were overcrowded with anxious-looking passengers. There were lots of vendors, cars, vans, trucks, and other vehicles along the way, with everybody hurriedly rushing to their various destinations.

We arrived at the construction site and were greeted by smiling, curious children. Most of the volunteers began work on the church building immediately; others checked out the place for VBS. VBS would be conducted outdoors in the open air under large trees with huge welcoming branches.

Mucatine Outdoor Church

The next day was Sabbath, and we worshiped in the "outdoor" church. Many children sat on the ground, and some adults sat on mats. The volunteers and a few village seniors sat on chairs. Sabbath School began with beautiful songs of praise to God. One of the elderly village women appeared to be the song leader; her voice rang out with clarity and sweetness. The voices of villagers filled the air with music as they sang in their native dialect; we visitors joined in English. The local elder conducted an enthusiastic Sabbath School lesson study that was interpreted in English. I presented the children's story during divine worship, which was translated by Sallis, our VBS interpreter. A trio comprised of Maranatha volunteers provided special music, and William Bellot, a New Yorker, preached a profound sermon. We were blessed and gave praises to God for our first Sabbath worship in Mozambique.

Shirley Telling Story

The night before we officially began VBS, volunteers worked tirelessly separating the supplies into two equal stacks for the two sites where the VBS programs would be held. We sharpened scores of pencils until our fingertips turned black, prepared name cards, made dozens of crowns, and performed countless other tasks to ensure that our program would run smoothly. Sunday, around 9:00 a.m., we arrived at the construction and VBS sites. Cheerful and enthusiastic building and VBS volunteers began building the church and reaching boys and girls for Jesus respectively. I didn't quite know what I was doing, but God knew and made up for my deficiency by providing volunteers with the skills of craft making, organizing, etc. We shared our different talents, and God blessed and increased them.

Upon arrival at the "outdoor church," we blew up balloons and decorated trees, punched holes in posters and tied them to trees with colorful yarn. We set up the tables brought from the campsite to hold our supplies. Initially, we were told to plan for 75 to 100 children; fortunately, Sue Davis Lea and her dedicated assistants had prepared more than 100 crowns and other crafts. The first day, we were blessed with approximately 300 children and adults. And so began our VBS in the village of Mucatine.

As I looked into the eager faces of the boys and girls, I saw that some had dirt-streaked faces, hands, and feet, and some were barefooted. Others wore dirty clothes; some were in need of medical attention; and, most poignant of all, little children were caring for their siblings, sometimes carrying one on their backs and another in their arms. Silently, I prayed to God to use us to bless these little ones and their families. Watching the excitement on their faces solidified my understanding that God had sent me here for a purpose: To tell boys and girls how much He loves them and that He sent His Beloved Son, Jesus, to die for them. It is so true that in the words of the beloved children's song, "Jesus loves the little children; all the children of the world, red and yellow, black and white, all are precious in His sight."

Dr. Sheila Hodgson, a colorectal surgeon and one of our volunteers, conducted health talks and taught the children personal hygiene, which included how to care for their bodies and wash their hands before eating. At one point, she asked the children to raise their hands if they had eaten breakfast. To our dismay, only a few hands went up.

I held a few granola bars in my hand to reward children who answered questions correctly. I was shocked when Dr. Hodgson said, "Let's give the kids something to eat." I thought, "Where are we going to find food to feed these many kids?" In no time, Maranatha volunteers came together and willingly gave up their lunches and granola bars. We broke them in pieces, said a prayer for God's blessing and that He would multiply our meager rations as He had done for the multitude (Matthew 14:15-21). We distributed the food to children sitting on the sand, waiting eagerly.

It was a heartwarming experience to watch hungry children extend both hands to receive a small morsel of food, and, then, to see their little faces glow with smiles of happiness as they ate. It was even more gratifying to know that we had, in this small way, been the instruments that God used to ease their discomfort. Again, just as God did for the little boy in the Bible with the two loaves and five fishes, we watched Him do the same with our meager offerings. He multiplied them more than a hundredfold (Matthew 14:20, 21). I must say that His math is quite different from ours. We were blessed, all of the children were fed, and our hearts were touched.

Our VBS program lasted approximately 2 to 3 hours each day and consisted of action songs, Bible stories, memory verses, crafts, and games. It was delightful to hear the sweet voices of the children sing and to watch them as they listened, with deep interest, to the stories of Jesus. At the end of each day's program, we distributed toys, coloring books, crayons, and stickers. The children were glad to receive whatever we had to give them. Some of them decorated their hands and faces with the colorful stickers.

The first day's task was completed, and we thanked God for His abundant blessings. Female volunteers quickly headed for the construction site to assist the men. Around noon, we took our lunch break, which was a welcomed time for everyone. It was a chance to relax and reflect on our mission. We ate sandwiches that we prepared or other foods that Maranatha's chef, Joseph, provided for us in plastic containers. We carried our bottled water and used alcohol wipes generously for cleaning our hands since no running water was available.

There was a decrease in attendance the second day because it was a regular school day; however, more than 80 children were present. We learned that some of them attended school in the morning and others in the afternoon. Adults attend at night. Following the preliminary program, we separated the children who had to leave for school but made sure each child received a gift. This small act made them happy.

The next day, volunteers worked feverishly to complete the first building and prepared to start the second building on Thursday. George Adler, Maranatha Project Director from Alaska, was extremely conscientious and painstaking. He made sure that the bricks for the building were placed in the correct position; if they weren't, they would have to be torn down and restarted. His keen eye quickly detected anything out of order.

The last day at the construction site, Maranatha engineers used a huge truck with heavy equipment to drill a well in the yard of the new Mucatine Church, providing water for the villagers. It was a welcomed and awesome sight to see fresh, clean water gush out of the hole. Volunteers and villagers alike were ecstatic! There is no doubt that this new well will significantly improve the sanitary conditions of the villagers and reduce the distance they have to walk to fetch water.

I was fascinated watching the water as it flowed freely from the well. I thought of the woman of Samaria whose life was changed because of her encounter with Jesus at a well. He touched her heart so deeply that she ran to the village and shared with her neighbors what He had told her. The impact on the people was profound. Her testimony was powerful, and many people came to hear it for themselves. They believed and were converted (John 4:7-42). Silently, I prayed that when the villagers draw water from this well, they, too, will be attracted to the church from which will flow the Living Word of Life, that their lives will be profoundly changed, and that they will return to their neighborhoods and share the good news of salvation.

We all witnessed this miracle of the well and were blessed as shouts of joy, cheers, and other expressions of gratitude ascended to God for this precious gift. It was a marvelous experience to watch the faces of villagers beamed with delight as they danced and sang. God is using Maranatha Volunteers International to provide a better way of life for the villagers of Mozambique. Their futures will be much brighter because someone cared enough to make a difference.

My full day at the construction site was Tuesday. I assisted with preparation of the grounds for the church's dedication, carried unused blocks by hand and wheelbarrow to a pile behind the church, and raked dry grass from around the church. Occasionally, I checked to see how Morris was holding up. It was fun being a part of such a labor of love for these deserving people, and I saw it reflected in Morris' countenance.

Volunteers worked hard to complete the first church building, stopping only to eat. Women from the village were hired by Maranatha staff to prepare meals for the national workers assisting with construction. The food was cooked on makeshift, outdoor stoves that consisted of three large stones on which large pots were placed. Firewood was used to cook the food. Women often relaxed on the ground under a tree nearby while performing other chores. From my observation, it seemed that rice was the main staple in the diet of the village people. I don't recall seeing fish, meat or green vegetables other than cabbage served in the village. However, everyone appeared happy and satisfied with the food.

Work on the first project was completed. A few volunteers remained behind to complete the finishing touches, while Zach and others walked to the village to distribute vegetable seeds for villagers to plant in their gardens. Upon their return, everyone worked enthusias-tically to assemble new benches for Sabbath worship.

New Mucatine Church

Wednesday was our free day. We traveled by bus on an excursion during which we saw beautiful scenery and lavish mansions of the affluent in stark contrast to the many who have so little! We visited the Maranatha warehouse where windows, doors, etc., for churches, are assembled, and blocks are constructed. Production was slow. We were informed that many workers had been laid off because of a shortage of funds. Maranatha's projects in Mozambique have also been affected by the state of the economy in the U.S. We pray that God will impress upon the hearts of people to continue to give so this great work can be completed. We may never know until eternity the far-reaching impact of our efforts.

Thursday morning, following breakfast and worship, we headed for the second con-struction site located in the Celula 5 village, a distance away. When we arrived, I overheard someone mentioned that we would meet in the church. In my mind, I was expecting an actual church building with walls, roof, windows, doors, etc. Instead, the "church" was a collection of passion fruit trees with beautiful, interlocking green branches that served as the roof. The local elder, who was also the owner of the property, lived next door and brought benches for the children to sit on. Several women and children sat on mats on the ground. We decorated the trees and prepared for VBS.

The first day of VBS in Celula 5 presented my greatest challenge. The night before, I had struggled with allergic reactions caused by the smell of the antibacterial wipes and the dust from blocks that were sawed at the first site. I became very ill and had no desire to eat. The medicine I had taken earlier that morning helped to contribute to my drowsiness, and my voice was almost a whisper. It looked as if I would be unable to lead out with VBS. Earlier, on the bus, Zach had requested prayer for me.

The time arrived to begin the VBS. Standing in front of our improvised church, I silently prayed for God to restore my voice so that I could talk and sing clearly enough for the translator to translate. By the time I was ready to begin, my speaking voice had returned somewhat. I discovered that I could sing, as well. It was another wonderful experience of God's miracle-working power. His words, "Call upon Me and I will answer" (Psalm 91:15) were fulfilled right then. I recalled earlier that morning as I sat on the bus on our way to Celula 5, I felt downcast because of my physical condition. I read from the devotional book, *Heaven's Whisper*, "The Best Is Yet To Come" (page 225, written by Cheryl D. Cochran). God used one of my favorite scriptures to convey His beautiful message to me: "For I know the thoughts that I think toward you," saith the Lord, "thoughts of peace, and not of evil, to give you an expected end" (Jeremiah 29:11, KJV). I was gratified to know that my faithful God hadn't forgotten me.

We had a grand time sharing God's Word and His love, singing songs, telling stories, and witnessing to the children and adults. Sue Davis Lea and her fantastic team worked long hours preparing crowns and crafts. The children were treated to granola bars and other snacks, which they loved. God blessed, and we ended our first day at Celula 5 successfully.

When we arrived the next day, we were surprised to see that the outdoor church was remarkably changed. The local elder had decorated it using decorations from colorful advertising magazines. We thanked him for his creativity. On the final day of VBS, we distributed flip flops, cars, toys, stuffed animals, crayons, pencils, pencil sharpeners, erasers, pens, toothpaste, toothbrushes, snacks, coloring books, dolls, etc. You should have seen the faces of the children bubble over with happiness and bright smiles! We were just as elated as they were. The precious seed of God's love has been sown; now, we pray for His extraordinary miracle of growth to multiply them and to bear fruit in abundance. We pray, too, that the children in these villages will be changed because of the love and kindness showed them by Maranatha volunteers.

We concluded the VBS, and women volunteers, once again, joined the construction crew and assisted with the building project. We had the opportunity to witness the drilling of another well at Celula 5. After lunch, the village women were organized in rows and given a number. The older women sat on the ground, and the younger ones stood as volunteers distributed bags of beans and rice to them. Women and children expressed their gratitude with dance, songs of praise, and shouts of joy. What a beautiful and marvelous sight to witness. Some of us joined in the festivities, much to the delight of the villagers.

Distribution of Rice & Beans

Sabbath, August 9, was a high day in the village of Mucatine. It was the official opening of the Mucatine SDA Church/Community Center, and the celebration was grand. High ranking church officials and local government representatives attended this auspicious occasion. They all expressed thankfulness for the project and commented on the beauty of the new edifice. The church was packed with local villagers, church members from other cities, and people from other denominations. The president of the Seventh-day Adventist Mozambique Conference officiated.

The ribbon-cutting and the passing of the church key from the conference president down through the ranks to the lowest level were quite impressive. The Sabbath School superintendent presented an interesting and inspiring program. The children gathered at their former church-under-the-trees for their Sabbath School, and I gave my last Bible story. At the conclusion, we returned to the new church building for the worship service. Special music was provided by young people from a visiting church, and, Maranatha Volunteers sang the dedicatory song written by Anne Ebron Galley, at my request. Victor Allen of Canada inspired us with his profound message and we were blessed.

At the conclusion of the worship service, Maranatha volunteers distributed Portuguese Bibles to villagers. A woman sitting across the aisle pointed to her new Bible and, then, to her eyes. She whispered something in her language. I interpreted it to mean that she could not read. Once again, God had already made provision; with the completion of this new church/literacy center, the opportunity will be available for her and other villagers to attend adult literacy classes.

One of the senior ladies of the Mucatine church presented Zach with four hand-woven baskets in appreciation of our labor of love. This humble gesture moved me deeply. From the little the villagers had, they willingly shared. I was blessed to be one of the leaders who received a basket.

At the end of the service, everyone assembled outside of the church and Maranatha volunteers distributed bags of beans and rice to the women. We were happy to be able to witness this event. It was beautiful to see the excitement and expressions of joy and gratitude on the faces of the villagers.

Thanks to Maranatha International, the villages of Mucatine and Celula 5 will no longer be the same, and neither will its people. With God's help, two new edifices, with fresh, clean running water, will shine as lighthouses in these villages and will serve as worship and learning centers. What a beautiful example of God's love in action. We continually thank Him for the opportunity to serve His people.

My eyes filled up with tears when Sallis, my interpreter, expressed his gratitude and that of Pastor Felipe for the privilege to work with the VBS. He said they learned many things; among them were new songs and how to tell engaging Bible stories. In addition to pastoring both the Mucatine and Celula 5 churches, Pastor Felipe pastors 27 more churches, comprising a membership of more than 1000. He remarked that many more children would attend church as a result of our VBS. I genuinely appreciated the dedication and hard work of Pastor Felipe and Sallis. God blessed our feeble efforts and showered us with one blessing after another.

During the service, Maranatha volunteers contributed a complete Bible story felt set with an accompanying book, a Child Evangelism Kit, a cassette/CD and DVD player/radio combination with batteries, and books. Morris and I contributed funds to purchase chairs for the rostrum. Before leaving, volunteers gave rice and beans to the women, and the children received toys, books, and other goodies.

With our mission completed, we said our thanks and goodbyes for the last time and boarded the bus to return to our compound. As we were leaving the church, I looked out the window and saw a picture that I will long remember. I counted nine children of varying ages sitting on the ground under a large tree eating from one bowl of white rice with their fingers. As far as I could see, there was no meat, beans, or vegetables, but they all seemed contented. Yes, God's children can be found in all parts of the world. In fact, Christ died for all, not some, even if they don't truly know Him and/or if they live in remote places. One of my personal missions is to let others know about these precious ones and to encourage all of us to share our gifts. Let us reach out and make a difference for the kingdom of God.

Volunteers enjoyed a change of scenery as we traveled by bus to Kruger International Park in South Africa. The scenes along the way were magnificent! We saw fabulous, exquisitely-built homes; mansions, indeed. As far as the eye could see were fields of sugarcane miles long, acres upon acres of banana trees, and much more. From the park, we continued our travels via jeep and caught glimpses of God's handiwork in the wilds.

Quite visible as we drove along were tall, stately giraffes, lazy-looking elephants, impalas seemingly always on the alert and ready to run, a lion resting quietly, and strikingly beautiful zebras. There were boars, hyenas, and vultures fighting over an animal carcass. We saw exotic birds, too! Yes, this is my Father's world. How magnificent!

Living in Mozambique for two weeks made me appreciate how blessed I am. I learned to do without ironing my clothes, eating broccoli, talking on the telephone, watching television, shopping in large department stores, driving my car, etc. I bathed in the outdoors in a makeshift shower obscured from view on all sides with black plastic to provide privacy for the bather and opened at the top. Our tent had no hardwood floors nor carpet, no king-sized bed nor expensive furniture, no heat nor air-conditioning, no fancy stuff; just a tent, two cots, and two plastic chairs we borrowed from the dining facility on which we hung our clothes. We used a cord hanging from the ceiling in the middle of the tent to tie our flashlight so that our very dark tent could be illuminated. And, perhaps the greatest miracle of all for us city-dwellers, was that, with God's help, we survived!

We didn't like the sand we brought into our little tent every time we entered, but sand didn't bother the villagers; they sat on the ground and appeared quite comfortable, and children played in it without concern. We partook of three healthy meals each day. Villagers were lucky if they got to eat rice and beans. Some slept on the ground on mats and endured cold nights without warm blankets. They had no toilet to flush their waste, no tub in which to take a relaxing bath, no shower, and no electricity.

On our return home, I couldn't help but reflect on our blessings. Every Sabbath morning, Morris and I are able to drive to church in our car and barely make it to Sabbath School on time, while some villagers walk long distances, some shoeless, to worship under trees. In our home church, the environment is temperature-controlled with beautiful red carpet, stained glass windows, padded pews, and a variety of musical instruments.

We have various versions of the Bible and scores of unread Christian books in every room, including our garage. Many villagers do not even own Bibles, but their love for the Lord drives them to faithfully and sincerely worship Him with all their hearts in the most unwelcome of circumstances. We enjoy so many blessings that seem to be so commonplace that, often, we take them for granted until we see the way others live and the lengths to which they have to go just to worship. Being the recipient of God's extravagant blessings compels me to be even more grateful for what He has done in my life and to reach out and help others in a more tangible way.

God gave us the incredibly unique opportunity to serve as His witnesses in Mozambique. I must confess that a piece of my heart was left behind in the villages of Mucatine and Celula 5. This experience has had a profound impact on my life, and, to think, I almost missed it.

Two pictures remain vivid in my mind: the Bible study guide with the words, "Here Am I! Send Me" and the beautiful children on the first day of VBS with their hands outstretched to receive whatever we had to give them. Like Peter and John in the temple, silver and gold we didn't have, but we tried to share as much of what we had: God's love through our love, happy worship, and physical provisions.

Often times, I find myself reflecting on the song Victoria Miller sang at the Oakwood Church a few days before we traveled to Mozambique: "There is peace and contentment in my Father's house today, Lots of food on His table and no one is turned away. There is singing and laughter as the hours pass by, but a hush calms the singing as the Father sadly cries, My house is full, but my field is empty, Who will go and work for Me today. It seems my children all want to stay around my table, but no one wants to work in my fields, No one wants to work in my fields" (Lanny Wolfe, songwriter and composer).

What a challenge to each of us! We are blessed to live in a land of plenty, and the needs around the world are so great. Let us share our time and our gifts so that others, who are less fortunate, may have a better life as they learn about Jesus. Remember, we only have one life, and it will soon pass away; what is most lasting is what we do for Christ every day.

I am incredibly grateful to Morris for his commitment, dedication, and persistence in pursuing this mission. Without his determination, I would have missed this incredible experience. I am thankful also to the many contributors of time, money, gifts, counsel, prayers, supplies, etc., for the Vacation Bible Schools.

Reflecting on our journey, I believe that God allowed the challenges that occurred with our travel documents, the luggage weight overages, the living conditions in Mozambique, etc., to test our faith and to teach us that He's in control and that nothing is too hard for Him to overcome. Sometimes, I failed His tests, but, day after day, He reached down in love and gave us precious promises, words of encouragement, strength, and hope to guide us on our journey. We are immensely grateful to Him for His amazing, extravagant goodness. He took us a long way from home, gave us the privilege of a lifetime, watched and protected us, and brought us back home safely.

"I will greatly praise the Lord with my mouth; yes, I will praise Him among the multitude" (Ps. 109:30, NKJV).

Mission to Tamale, Ghana

Our next global outreach ministry took us to Ghana, West Africa, where Morris and I teamed up with 25 Maranatha volunteers to build a 12-room elementary school in the city of Tamale in northern Ghana. Although this was my first trip to Ghana, it was the second for Morris. Back in the late 1950s, he, along with other pastors from Nigeria, received training in evangelism when they assisted the late Elder E. E. Cleveland with a series of evangelistic meetings in Accra.

After our 17-hour journey from Huntsville to Ghana, we arrived safely at the Accra Airport where we were greeted by the Maranatha team director, as well as Dr. Seth Laryea and his wife, Florence. Seth was my reader when I taught at ASWA, and he also assisted my husband in the library. He had served as president of Valley View University for 17 years. We were delighted to be reunited with him again. He treated us to a delicious dinner before giving us a tour of the university campus.

The following day, Maranatha volunteers boarded the Starbow Airline bound for Tamale. Ninety percent of the people who live in this city are Muslims, in contrast to the rest of the country, which is predominantly Christian. Despite a difference in religious beliefs, the people get along well. I found it surprising that the churches of these different religions coexist near each other without any problems, unlike in some other countries.

Before we left Huntsville, we were informed that preparation of the construction site had been delayed because the land donated by one of the tribal chiefs had been reclaimed. We learned that land is under the control of tribal chiefs, and a regional chief had granted the church 51 acres, but, by the time Maranatha was ready to build, a new chief was in power, and he reclaimed the land. After much prayer and negotiation, Church officials were able to regain 25 acres.

After a healthy breakfast and worship, volunteers from across the United States and Canada boarded a bus for the construction site. When we arrived, local workers were busy preparing slabs for the building's foundation and putting together materials for the classrooms. The building superintendent gave us an overview of the project, and volunteers energetically began building the school. I was impressed by the enthusiasm and knowledge with which the volunteers tackled the construction of the buildings.

Everyone was involved in the building process: some carried materials from the storage building to the construction site on their heads, shoulders, or hands; others set up metal frames, raised the metal sidings, installed windows and assembled desks and benches. It was strenuous work carrying 10- and 15-foot-long bars and sheets of metal siding in sweltering heat. The inspiration we felt regarding the mighty work we were doing gave us the stamina we needed to endure. Having a relationship with God and knowing He was with us made all the difference.

Our first Sabbath was spent in a village located a long distance from our hotel. Because of a torrential downpour of rain the night before, the roads were covered with water-filled potholes, which made for a bumpy bus ride, but we enjoyed the beautiful sites and scenes along the way. On arrival, we were greeted warmly by church members, as we joined them for outdoor worship under tall, stately trees and bright, beautiful blue skies, with cascading clouds. This lovely outdoor setting gave me a feeling of being more connected to nature and our Creator.

A group of students from the Valley View University Extension School in Tamale provided special music for the worship service, and we enjoyed their enthusiastic singing. I sang "I Believe in Miracles," as the song of meditation and our spiritual coordinator preached. After a hearty lunch, we distributed clothes, shoes, books, crayons, balloons, and other materials to the children. Their bright, captivating smiles verified their appreciation for the gifts they received.

Later, we walked a short distance to the village to meet the local chief and to request permission to distribute rice and beans to the villagers. The chief and his representatives were delighted to see us and to learn about the work we were doing. Permission was granted for us to distribute foodstuffs, and we also got a chance to visit with some of the women in their homes.

I was impressed to ask one of the pastors, who served in another village, what he considered the greatest need of his church. He responded that one of his churches had a membership of 25, but, after a recent evangelistic meeting, God blessed their congregation with 75 new members. Their challenge was the lack of seats to accommodate this increase. Morris and I contributed funds to purchase several benches.

Back at the construction site, our work progressed well, and we forged ahead, eager to accomplish our mission in the allotted time. However, by mid-week, we received the shocking news that the chief who owned the property was planning to stop the construction project. We were concerned because the work was moving forward rapidly, and we were approaching the completion date with optimism. Ron Kedas, Maranatha's Support Leader, asked volunteers to pray about this unforeseen obstacle. He invited the mission president, his executive secretary, and volunteers to accompany him to talk with the chief.

Before entering the chief's palace, Ron informed us of proper protocol. Following the exchange of formalities, he presented a compelling petition to the chief's representatives to allow us to complete the project, and explained that the purpose of the school was to educate all children of the community. He also pleaded for the return of the remaining acres of land that had been repossessed.

We were informed that the chief was in Mecca and that the requests would be presented to him upon his return. One of the chief's representatives spoke very highly of Adventist education. He mentioned that his children had attended Adventist schools and that he was pleased with the education they had received. The village officials were impressed with the presentation and granted permission to continue the project. This good news filled us with joy, and work was resumed with heightened enthusiasm. We thanked God for His intervention!

Female volunteers experienced an added blessing while conducting Vacation Bible Schools in the villages, all of which were well attended. The children were excited and eager to listen to Bible stories, learn new songs, work on crafts and receive gifts. Also, the wives of local pastors were given gifts of African fabric and handbags by female volunteers.

Distribution of gifts in Tamale

Our last VBS was conducted in the village near the construction site. What an impressive sight to see so many children gathering from everywhere with bright eyes and keen anticipation to hear what we had to say or to receive what we had to give. God blessed our efforts, and we thank Him.

The night before our final day of work, a heavy downpour flooded the construction site. When we arrived the next morning, the ground was covered with water and thick, red mud, which made it difficult to get from the bus to the construction site. Surprisingly, the spirit of the volunteers was not dampened; they worked enthusiastically to drain off the water from the site, with renewed determination to complete the project come rain, shine, or mud. Through it all, our faith and trust in God remained intact. Soon, to our great amazement, the sun came out, dried up a lot of the water, and we were able to accomplish our task. Watching God work in our behalf was marvelous So often in our frail human nature, we tend to forget that He is a limitless God Who specializes in impossibilities.

Our last Sabbath in Tamale was very busy. Volunteers visited three churches, sang, and brought greetings. Pastor Fred Agyeibaah, president of North Regional SDA Mission in

Tamale, was extremely hospitable and expressed his deepest gratitude for the work that had been done and the mission of Maranatha Volunteers International. Church members were happy to see us and to learn about our mission.

Earlier in the week, Pastor Agyeibaah had invited me to speak at the Kalpohin Estate SDA Church where he is a member. It was inspiring to hear church members sing the opening hymn, "Because He Lives." This song has special significance for me. Many years before when I taught at the Adventist Seminary of West Africa, Alfred Adonu, a Ghanian student, asked me to sing this song at his wedding. I suggested the *Wedding Prayer* or *The Lord's Prayer*, but he insisted on "Because He Lives." I told him that it was not a song that is usually sung at weddings, but he said that it was the one he wanted. I acquiesced.

Some years later while attending a library association meeting with my husband at Andrews University, we were happy to meet Alfred and his young family. He was pursuing graduate studies at the time. During our conversation, he reminded me that I had sung "Because He Lives" at his wedding, and how much it had meant to him and his family through all of their trials and tribulations. He said, "Because Jesus lives, I can face every today and every tomorrow with confidence and courage, no matter what comes my way." What a powerful testimony!

The Lord blessed, and the service went well. Glory to God! Volunteers returned to the hotel for lunch and later traveled to the village near the construction site one last time to distribute VBS supplies, rice, and beans.

One of the highlights of our mission was the dedication service for the classrooms. Workers and volunteers assembled in one of the classrooms that had been completely furnished with desks, benches, and decorations. In the beautiful, candle-lit room, we sang songs and shared testimonies of God's goodness and blessings. Our Spiritual Coordinator made brief comments and invited us to form small groups where we anointed each other's hands with oil and prayed for God's continued blessings on our lives and hands as we work for Him. It was a solemn time of reflection, praise, thanksgiving, celebration, and rededication.

Looking back on our journey, I am filled with gratitude when I think of how God brought 27 strangers together, from different corners of the world to this community to share His love and to spread the Good News that He is coming again. As we built classrooms in His honor and reached out to the surrounding villages and communities, we prayed that we would make a difference and influence lives for His kingdom, and He answered our prayers. According to President Agyeibaah, "Because of the work of Maranatha volunteers, we now have our school that will be owned and operated by Seventh-day Adventists, and we can choose our teachers." We give honor and glory to God. He did amazing things for us, as well as for those to whom we ministered.

After completion of our mission project, volunteers traveled to Cape Coast and Elmina Castles where we toured many of the rooms where slaves were housed before they were shipped to countries in the Caribbean and the Americas. It was a heart-wrenching experience to walk through the rooms where hundreds of slaves were crammed, and some eventually died from diseases. We listened as the tour guide told horrific stories of the days of slavery. Praise God, in Christ, we all are free.

We cherish warm memories of our visit to Ghana, and we thank God that, one more time, He granted us the opportunity to contribute, in our small way, to the advancement of His work in Ghana. We are truly humbled that we could be His ambassadors in a foreign land.

Changuinola, Panama

One of our most fascinating experiences was our mission trip to Changuinola, Panama, January 27 to February 9, 2015. We landed safely at Panama Airport and were transported to a hotel nearby to spend the night. The next morning, we boarded a small airplane headed for Changuinola. We arrived at the beautiful Bocas del Toro where Morris and I teamed up with a cohesive team of more than 70 volunteers from diverse backgrounds, cultures, socioeconomic status, religious affiliations, etc. Some were nurses, physicians, professors, painters, builders, dieticians, farmers, retirees, Hindu, Baptists, librarians, and more. The purpose of our mission was to build churches, conduct medical and animal clinics, and share the love of Jesus with boys and girls through Vacation Bible Schools. This was the largest group of volunteers with whom we had participated.

Within a few hours of our arrival, the VBS team began to sort out the huge variety of clothes, toys, supplies, and materials generously donated by volunteers and churches in the

U.S. Other volunteers prepared for the various projects for which they had signed up. It was a pleasant experience to work with such a team of happy and exciting volunteers.

Let me pause here and share a few statistics about Panama that might interest you. It is a very picturesque country located in Central America and is bordered by Colombia and Costa Rica. At one point, we walked across a bridge from Panama into Costa Rica. Seventy-five percent of the population is mixed Spanish and Indian, West Indian 14%, Caucasian 10%, Indian 8%. The dominant religion is Roman Catholicism, and Spanish is the official language. The literacy rate is approximately 94.1%.

The Panama Canal is the top tourist attraction and the most significant generator of revenue. It was fascinating to watch large ships as they were guided through the canal's Miraflores Locks. I learned from family members that my dad's brother, Allen Howell, helped to build this massive structure decades ago. There are more than 309 Seventh-day Adventist churches and 170 companies in the country with a total membership of 76,250. Maranatha Volunteers have built more than sixty-five churches.

All volunteers were involved with the mission either building or painting churches, VBS, medical or animal clinics, and, of course, the preparation of delicious meals. Morris worked with the construction and kitchen crew. A typical day began with breakfast at 6:30 a.m. (Our prayer team, of which I was a member, met at 6 a.m.), followed by worship. Around 7:30 a.m., the construction crew traveled by bus to the various building sites. One of the sites was inaccessible by land, so volunteers had to use a dug-out boat. Between 8:00 a.m. and 8:30 a.m., VBS and medical teams boarded vans for the villages. After a busy day, we assembled at 5:30 p.m. for dinner followed by worship. During this time, group leaders shared experiences of God's blessings and the progress of different projects.

It was amazing that although it rained almost every day, God held back the rain long enough for the construction crew to build two churches, paint two old churches, inside and out, over a six-day period, to His glory and honor.

More than 580 patients were seen by the medical team, and five Vacation Bible Schools were conducted in four different locations. With the help of our wonderful 12-year-old interpreter, Jonathan, approximately 500 children listened to Bible stories, learned new songs, and worked with crafts. At the end of each VBS, children received clothes, toys, school supplies, etc. The timing for the VBS was ideal because summer vacation for students begins in mid-December and lasts until the end of February. Additionally, animal clinics were conducted by a local veterinarian where turkeys, dogs, pigs, and other animals were vaccinated.

VBS kids in Panama

Our first Sabbath in Changuinola, Maria Molleda, Project Support Coordinator for Maranatha, invited me to preach at Iglesia Adventista Finca 12 located in the province of Chiriqui. When we arrived, the church was packed. Chairs had to be placed in the aisle to accommodate the overflow. As I entered, I became overwhelmed by the number of worshippers in attendance. Of course, this made me more nervous; I expected a little church with older people; also, I didn't speak or understand Spanish. Fortunately, I had an excellent interpreter, 14-year-old Abielene, and God blessed the message and song as well as the congregation. What an awesome God we serve!

I consider this mission trip my busiest, most productive, and spiritually rewarding. In addition to serving on the prayer team, I presented two devotionals for worship, assisted with VBS, preached at two churches and experienced God's mighty power as I watched Him work in marvelous ways to perform many miracles. He blessed our efforts exceedingly abundantly above all that we could ever have imagined.

One of our first miracles began the day following our arrival. Maria took the medical doctor who would supervise the medical clinics to the health department to obtain permission to conduct the clinics. She invited the VBS leader and a few others to come along to see the sites for the VBS.

After meeting with the health department officials, Maria told us that they experienced some challenges because the credentials of the doctor should have been submitted to the health department two weeks in advance. However, this had not been possible. After pleading her cause, the health director granted permission on condition that a local doctor signed off on it. This was necessary in case any problems arose, the Health Department would have the name of a local doctor whom they could contact.

Maria knew a doctor who conducted a clinic, so she didn't foresee a problem; however, when she contacted him, he declined. It was Friday afternoon, and the clinic was scheduled to begin the following Sunday. The churches would have to receive the announcements about the clinics by Saturday so that people could plan to attend.

Maria phoned a few people about her request but was unsuccessful. This created some concern because it was getting late, and we still hadn't seen the VBS sites. We prayed for God to work it out soon. Maria phoned a friend and explained her dilemma. He gave her the name of a young man who knew doctors at a local hospital. Maria called and explained the situation. He gave the name of a doctor who willingly consented. God worked it out one more time, just in the nick of time.

The second miracle that impressed me that God moves in mysterious ways occurred a few days after our arrival. Glen, one of the volunteers, asked me to pray for him, because he was experiencing a serious health challenge, and he felt he should return to the U.S. Morris and I were sad to hear this. We, along with the prayer team, prayed for him daily. His condition improved, and he teamed up with the construction crew. It was at the building site that he met a young man named Junior. Everyday Glen observed that this young man from a nearby village looked intrigued as he watched them work, so he handed him a drill and asked him to help. Junior took the drill and began to work enthusiastically. His quick response and willingness impressed Glen.

Glen had a special Bible that he brought from the States to give to a local person. While working with Junior, he was impressed to give it to him. During their break, Glen handed the Bible to Junior and called him "Pastor." Junior was amazed to hear the word "Pastor."

He told Glen that all of his life, his dad had always dreamed that he would be a church pastor. As he grew older, he had left that idea behind because he didn't agree with his dad. However, when Glen called him "Pastor," it rekindled that desire in his heart to become a pastor. God had a special assignment for Glen, and He used him to accomplish His purpose for Junior. Isn't that amazing?

The morning of our last VBS, our team was scheduled to leave early for the new site because it was a farther distance. Maria had requested that we conduct a VBS in that neighborhood because of a "Macedonian call" (Acts 16:9, 10) that she had received to come and help them.

The time to depart arrived, but no van neither the driver was available, and we were becoming a little anxious. Finally, Isis, our driver came, and we left. On our way, she stopped at a supermarket to purchase items for VBS. Providentially, she met a friend from Nigeria whom she wanted me to meet. Isis brought her to the van and introduced us. We learned that she was a doctor and director of one of the programs at the Health Department. Maria mentioned her earlier visit to the Health Department and her efforts to find a doctor to sign off on the project. The doctor gave Maria permission to use her name in the future along with her business card. Before leaving she commented that she is usually at work at that time, but, for some reason, she left her house later. We told her it was a miracle that God did so we could meet her. He's an on-time God who works in mysterious ways.

We finally reached our destination, and the children were waiting with eager anticipation. They sang songs, worked on crafts, and listened to Bible stories. Everyone was delighted to receive gifts. This was our largest VBS.

One of the things that generated a lot of happy faces at the Vacation Bible Schools was the picture taking. Debbie, one of our volunteers, took pictures of the children and gave them a beautiful handmade frame in which to put it. It was fun to watch them creatively decorate their picture frame with stickers and show it to their family and friends.

On the last Sabbath, everyone was enthusiastic about the dedication of the new Las Tablas SDA Church. We traveled about an hour to get to the church. It was full with people and some looking in from outside. We enjoyed wonderful Christian fellowship as we sang songs of praise to God and listened to an inspiring sermon by the pastor. God blessed me with the lyrics for the dedicatory song, which was translated into Spanish. We all sang lustily in our own language. The song was sung to the tune of the old hymn, "Take my life and let it be," but with new lyrics specific to our mission. "Take this church, and let it be dedicated Lord to You; Take its pastor and members, too; Use them mightily for You; Use them mightily for You. Bless and use us; keep us true, ever faithful Lord to You. When you come, again, some day, take us all to live with you, Take us all to live with you." Amen! It was a beautiful experience to witness the pastor and church members beam with satisfaction and joy as they expressed their gratitude and appreciation to the volunteers for their brand new edifice.

Las Tablas SDA Church Dedication

At the conclusion of the service, volunteers donated a keyboard, a guitar, clothes, toys for the children, and funds to assist with the completion of the adjoining building that would house the children's Sabbath School and other ministries.

We thank God for allowing us to complete our mission, and we pray that He will bless and multiply our efforts. With our mission accomplished, volunteers flew to Panama City where we visited the Panama Canal and other historic sites. Morris and I had made plans to stay an additional week in Panama to enjoy the warm sunshine and to visit places of interest.

We mentioned our plans to Maria, and she invited me to speak at a church and offered to arrange a tour of the city for us.

It was an incredible experience to observe how God worked behind the scenes to bring people together and to use them to execute His plans. It all began when Maria was planning for another Maranatha Mission project. She visited the owner of a new vegetarian restaurant to request her services in preparing meals for the next group of volunteers. It was there that Maria met Glory who had volunteered to assistant her friend at the restaurant that same day. Maria inquired if Glory was available to accompany two missionaries, Morris and me, on a tour of the city, and she agreed. Maria also gave her the name of a man who could provide transportation.

Glory wanted to use her car, but it needed some repairs, so she took it to a friend who is a mechanic to have it checked. While waiting, she saw a longtime friend, Isaac, the brother of the mechanic, sitting in his taxi. They had been baptized together in 1983, and she had not seen nor talked to him for about 15 years. Although Maria had given Glory the name of a person who could provide transportation, Glory felt impressed to ask Isaac, instead, and he gladly consented.

The next day, Glory and Isaac picked us up at the hotel. Our first stop was the Museum where we viewed many artifacts and relics of old buildings. While we were walking around outside, the sun became extremely hot, so we returned to the taxi. Soon after we sat down, black ants started crawling out from where Morris was sitting; I tried desperately to kill them, but they were multiplying. They crawled on our hands and clothes, and from the Maranatha wide-mouthed water bottle Morris took from the seat. Fearing they would bite us, I told Glory to tell the driver to stop so we could get rid of them.

When Glory looked back, she saw ants crawling all over the bottle Morris was holding, so she said, "Give me the bottle; I am going to pray and rebuke these ants." She took the bottle and got out of the car. We tried unsuccessfully to kill the ants, so Morris and I got out of the car. Isaac was nervous because he had never experienced anything like this before. Glory returned the bottle to Morris. "Here, the ants are gone, I rebuked them," she said. Morris took the bottle, and more ants started crawling out from the nozzle. We got rid of them and returned to the car. Glory asked me to pray, and I prayed that God would make the ants go away. Isaac mentioned that the ants might have entered his car when he parked it under a tree in the parking lot. Still flustered from the incident, he asked Glory if we wanted to continue the tour or go back to the hotel. We continued and had a great time viewing the beautiful sites of the city.

When we returned to the hotel, Glory told us that Isaac mentioned that many things were going wrong in his life: his daughter was in the hospital, his wife's brother had passed two days earlier, and he had suffered a heart attack recently. He believed that God was permitting these afflictions to happen to him and his family because he had abandoned the church. He told her that he was convinced that God used the black ants to talk to him and that he had made up his mind to return to church and take his family with him. We were happy to hear these words. Morris paid Isaac and prayed that God would bless him and his family in his decision to return to church.

I am baffled every time I recall this incident. How did so many black ants get from the tree into the car and to the nozzle of the water bottle is mind-boggling. Only God knows. Another amazing thing was how they appeared and disappeared so quickly. Later in the tour, when we stopped to take pictures, Isaac checked the back seat where we were and found only two ants. It's astonishing how God brought together strangers from near and far to one place to fulfill His plan for Isaac's life. He indeed moves in mysterious ways His wonders to perform (William Cowper, 1731–1800).

I'm convinced that our decision to extend our stay in Panama was God-ordained. In addition to being a part of Isaac's story, God worked it out for me to sing and preach at the La Chorrera SDA Church. Karvin Dill, a pioneer of La Chorrera Church, picked us up at the hotel and drove us to his home where we spent the weekend with him and his lovely wife, Esteria. We enjoyed great fellowship together. The Lord blessed, and the service went well. At the conclusion, members greeted me warmly and expressed their gratitude for the message and music. God blessed one more time.

A young physician stated that she had planned to go to a retreat that Sabbath to escape the festivities of carnival, but she was happy she came to church, instead. She was encouraged and inspired by my story of God's answer to prayers on Akunna's behalf. She shared that when she completed medical school, she was unable to take her medical boards because they were administered on Sabbath. God worked it out for her to take them the following year. She admitted that she was a little anxious awaiting the results. I reminded her of Jeremiah 29:11, that God knows the plans He has for her, and that He is able to work everything out beautifully.

During this mission trip, I was incredibly blessed to meet two remarkable women: Diane Zachary and Tanuja, both from Canada. Diane (Di) was the wife of Merrill, our team leader. The first time we met, she mentioned that she knew me right away because her husband had talked about me when he returned from his mission trip to Mozambique.

Di had a warm, caring, effervescent personality, and a contagious smile. Although she was experiencing a serious health challenge, she was still able to bake more than 140 dozen cookies and other goodies for 70-plus volunteers. She and her husband had served as Maranatha volunteers since 1995 and had traveled the world building churches and schools along with participation in medical and community projects.

During one of our worship sessions, Di shared an inspiring testimony that blessed everyone. I encouraged her to write her story so it could be published and bless a larger audience. She promised she would. Following her return to Canada, she became very ill and was hospitalized for several weeks. She was diagnosed with inoperable, non-curable pelvic cancer. Di loved the Lord very much and had a strong desire to share Jesus. Her husband said that, even in her weakened state and under palliative care, she was still determined to complete Bible studies she had started with some individuals a few months earlier. She did. What a powerful testimony of a godly woman who was committed to sharing her faith and to using what she had left, even on her death bed.

Sadly, Di passed before she could write her story, but her testimony will live on in the hearts of those she touched so profoundly. We continue to pray for Zach in his valley season of life.

Tanuja and I worked together with VBS. She loved the children very much and didn't hesitate to hug them whether clean or dirty. She gave them toys, candy, clothes, money, etc. She mentioned that she grew up poor in Guyana, and made a promise to the Lord that, if He blessed her with a better life, she would help poor children to have a better life, too. The Lord answered her prayer in an unusual way and blessed her with a very loving, kind, and generous husband. She said that, although he is not a Christian, he encourages her to go on mission trips, provides the funds for her transportation, and gives her money to help needy families. Tanuja has participated in more than 15 mission trips with Maranatha and other volunteer organizations as far away as China, India, and Nepal.

Recently, she called to tell me that she had just returned from a mission trip to Cuba. I commended her on her global outreach ministries and encouraged her to keep on sharing the gifts God has given her to make a difference in the lives of children around the world. She said, "Sister Shirley, after my devotion this morning, the Lord told me to call you. I now see why. You energized and encouraged me. I have something to tell you, I'm not a Christian; I'm a Hindu, but I love the Lord very much. He's my friend." What a beautiful testimony!

Just ordinary people, yes, God uses ordinary people; people just like Di and Tanuja to do extraordinary things for Him. I count it an honor to have met these lovely women. We only have one life and time is fleeting by. What really matters is what we do for Christ.

"How beautiful upon the mountains Are the feet of him who brings good news, Who proclaims peace, Who brings glad tidings of good things, Who proclaims salvation, Who says to Zion, "Your God reigns!" (Isaiah 52:7, NKJV)

Chapter 18

What's Left?

*A*s Oakwood University retirees, we receive invitations annually from the president to attend the Faculty/Staff Colloquium. It was during one of these events several years ago that Pastor Henry Wright, the devotional speaker, spoke on the topic "What Do You Have Left?" It was a soul-stirring message that impacted me profoundly. During the night, my thoughts drifted back to his words: "What do you have left?" Reflectively, I began to consider what I had left to offer as a retiree. I used to sing solos and hadn't sung for a long time. Over the years, I've been haunted by the thought that I might lose my ability to sing because my voice has been adversely affected by my allergies. In the stillness of the night, I whispered a prayer, "Lord, whatever I have left, please use it to glorify You." Well, let me tell you how quickly God answered my prayer and provided an opportunity for me to sing.

It was the Sabbath morning following Colloquium, and I was sitting in my Sabbath School class when Dr. Eveythe Cargill, one of the Sabbath School superintendents, entered and sat beside me. It was unusual for her to visit my class, so I asked, "What are you doing here?" "I have prepared my Sabbath School program for next Sabbath, but don't have special music, and my husband suggested that I ask you to sing a solo," she replied. She also mentioned that she had thought of asking me to sing, but was afraid I would refuse. She continued, "Would you please sing a solo for Sabbath School next week?" Upon hearing her unexpected request, it seemed a battle began to rage in my head, and a voice was shouting,

"Say, 'No.'" Another voice softly whispered, "What do you plan to do with what you have left?" Dr. Cargill had no idea what was going on inside me. "Say, 'Yes.'" "Say, 'No.'" In the midst of these voices pulling me in opposite directions, these poignant words, again, came to mind, "Shirley, what are you doing with what you have left?" Without further hesitation, I said, "Yes, I will sing." She was surprised but happy. As she walked away, I thought, "Shirley, what trouble have you gotten yourself into?"

I decided to sing the song, "I Believe in Miracles." I considered it a perfect song to sing, because I had been the recipient of God's wonderful miracles thousands of times. During the week, I rehearsed with Dr. Cherryl Galley and Mrs. Winifred Rivers and was encouraged by their positive comments.

When I awakened that Sabbath morning, deep fear gripped my heart. I opened the devotional book, *Grace Notes*, and these words captured my attention: "Fear not for I am with you, Be not dismayed for I am your God. I will strengthen you, yes, I will help you; I will uphold you with my righteous right hand" (Isa. 41:10). It was a humbling feeling to think that God knew and filled my need even before I called upon Him, and He ministered to me through these much-needed words of encouragement.

Before leaving for church, I called Nikolas, my prayer warrior grandson, to pray for me. He was asleep, but his Mom said excitedly, "I can pray for you!" She prayed a heartfelt prayer that God would use my voice to bless the people who would hear me sing. On my way to church, I prayed, "Dear Father, Thank You for Your words of encouragement; please take control and use my voice and song to minister to someone today, in Jesus' Name, Amen."

My heart began to beat rapidly and loudly as I awaited my turn to sing. I was concerned that the audience could see the movement in my chest. Although I tried hard to maintain my composure, at one point, I became overwhelmed with nervousness. Silently, I prayed, "Lord, You promised to help me, so please, don't let me down, now!" As I was about to stand up to sing, I felt a calmness come over me. God had instantly replaced my fear and nervousness with His wonderful peace. My husband remarked later that I was very calm without a trace of nervousness.

Yes, God heard and answered our prayers and kept His promise to help, strengthen, and uphold me, and He used my voice as my witness for Him. Many individuals commented that they were blessed by the song, even 96-year-old Sister Jackson made similar comments. God is so good!

On other occasions, I have experienced God's willingness to help me when I step out of my comfort zone and use what I have left for Him. Early one morning, after my devotion, I prayed that He would put someone in my path to whom I could witness. Later that day, Morris and I went on our morning walk, and I thought no more about my prayer request.

Customarily, I greet people and wish them a great day as we walk. On this particular morning, I saw a man walk from his house to his car; I greeted him with my cheery, "Good morning, sir; have a great day!" He said thanks and, then, began to tell us that he was on his way to the hospital to visit his daughter who was very ill and had almost died the night before. He mentioned that she had diabetes, and the doctors were planning to amputate her right leg. During the night, the nurse had given her medication to relieve her pain, and she had experienced a severe allergic reaction to it. He said he saw her eyes roll back in her head, and he screamed for the nurse to come. He watched helplessly as the medical team transported her to the ICU.

As he was talking, a little voice whispered in my ear, "You need to pray for this man's daughter." Without hesitation, I said, "Sir, let's pray for your daughter right now." Standing in the driveway of this total stranger, Morris and I bowed our heads, and I thanked God for sparing his daughter's life and petitioned Him to have mercy and to touch and restore her according to His will. The gentleman thanked us, and we continued on our walk. I surprised myself that I could do something like that in public.

Later in the week, we traveled to Maryland to visit Akunna. Upon our return, we resumed our walking. Turning onto a busy street, we saw a gentleman, whom we often greeted, sitting on his porch. As we approached his house, he got up and walked briskly toward the end of his driveway. By the time we got there, he greeted us with a big smile and said, "I told my wife that there is a nice couple who greets me every morning when they pass by, and I don't even know who they are, but I am going to find out. I didn't see you all for several days and wondered about you."

We told him our names and that we were retired and enjoyed walking and traveling. He mentioned that he had retired several years ago, and had plans to travel with his wife.

Unfortunately, due to complications with her diabetes, both of her legs had been amputated, so their dream of traveling had been shattered. My heart reached out to them and, right then, I said, "Let's pray for her." We bowed our heads, and my husband prayed for this stranger and his wife. Our new friend seemed surprised by our gesture, but he expressed his sincere gratitude. Another day, we stopped to chat with him. He was delighted and said, "You don't know what a joy it is when someone stops by or waves; it makes me feel good." We inquired how his wife was doing and wished them well. A few days later, I gave him the devotional book, *Sanctuary*, as a gift for his wife. His face lit up with a smile as he thanked us.

Morning walks are delightful, and, as can be seen from the examples above, they give us the opportunity to meet many new people. Two other people were a traffic police officer and a cook from a nearby middle school. I met the police officer on the street and the cook in the parking lot of the school. On several occasions, I greeted them and sometimes chatted briefly. I felt impressed to share a women's devotional book with them, so, later in the week, I gave one to each woman. They were grateful for the gifts.

On another morning, I prayed my usual prayer that God would put someone in my path to whom I could witness but didn't see the possibility of having a witnessing encounter because the only place I was planning to go was to my handbell rehearsal. So, I went about my chores without realizing that God had a witnessing opportunity for me even on this day.

Around mid-morning, the phone rang. The voice on the other end sounded like a very distraught old man. He said, "Tell Jerry that they canceled my cataract surgery, and I have to go back home. I don't know what I'm going to do." I felt sad, so I said, "Sir, I am so sorry, but you called a wrong number." He apologized, but, before hanging up, the idea came to me to pray for him, so I told him, "Sir, let me pray with you before you go." I prayed that God would bless him and work out everything well for him with his surgery. "Thank you, Ma'am; you must be a Christian," he responded. "Yes, I attend the Oakwood University Church." He stated that he was a Christian, too and that he attends the First Baptist Church.

A little curious about what phone number he was trying to reach, I asked him. To my surprise, he called out my number. I believe that his call was God-directed in answer to my prayer. If we are willing, we can always count on our Heavenly Father to open the door of opportunity for us to share Him with others. It's amazing how profoundly blessed we are in return.

Not long ago, we were visiting Ngozi's church in Georgia when I received two unexpected surprises. The first was a young lady who greeted me in the lobby after the worship service. She looked familiar. Probably noticing my hesitation, she quickly told me that many years before, when she was a student at Oakwood, she did her secretarial internship in the President's office and that I was very nice to her. "In fact," she continued, "when I graduated in 1985, you gave me a gift which I still have." I was surprised when she pulled out a beautiful gold and black business card holder from her handbag and showed it to me. "Are you sure I was the one who gave you this gift?" I asked her. She assured me that I was and, that over the years, she had often thought about me and how kind I was to the students.

Nearby, a young man was waiting to talk to me. I greeted him, and he told me that I might not remember, but, about two years earlier, he and his family had Sabbath dinner at Ngozi's home when Morris and I were visiting. He said that I spoke with excitement and fervor about my Christian experience and how God had blessed me throughout the years, and how my enthusiasm had rubbed off on him. Later, he made the decision to give his life to God and to be baptized. The day of his baptism, he told Ngozi to let me know that it was my Christian witness at her house that had influenced him to take this step.

It's amazing how God continues to provide unique witnessing opportunities and, in the process, gives me spiritually rewarding experiences. Here's an example: Dr. Clarence Hodges, a fellow church elder, mentioned that he would be unavailable for a few days and asked Morris and me to visit the six nursing homes/rehabilitation centers where he ministers weekly. We agreed, and he gave us the names of 25 residents, along with brief comments about each one, to acquaint us with them. A few days later, we set out on our mission, unaware of the blessing that awaited us.

We arrived at the room of the first resident but were told to wait in the hallway because her nurse was attending to her needs. While waiting, I observed some residents sitting on their wheelchairs in the hallway near the front of the nurses' station looking weary and forlorn. I asked the nurse supervisor for permission to sing a few songs, and she readily consented. When I announced the first song, "Blessed Assurance," the nurse raised her hand

and shouted, "That's my favorite song. I gotta hear this!" It was an invigorating experience to listen as some of the nurses and residents joined in singing. We sang at the other nurses' stations, too, and brought smiles to the residents.

Later in the week, we drove several miles to visit the fifth facility. We stopped at the nurses' station to inquire about the room number of the resident we had come to visit. The nurse informed us that she had been admitted to the hospital. Disappointed, I walked away, but I silently complained that we had wasted our time and gas to travel so far and she was not there. As we walked through the hallway to leave the facility, I observed several senior women sitting on wheelchairs in a room. Not wanting to leave the facility without ministering to someone, I asked the supervisor if we could sing a few songs, and she consented.

Morris and I shared encouraging words with them. However, what brought the greatest response and brightest smiles from the residents was the song, "If You're Happy, and You Know, It Clap Your Hands." You'd be amazed at how quickly these senior citizens came alive as they clapped their hands and sang loudly, "AMEN!" Employees as well as visitors stopped to listen. From the smiles on their faces, it was evident that they were enjoying the singing. One resident, who was hunched over in her wheelchair, raised her head slightly and said, "Thank yah, thank yah!" The supervisor and residents thanked us and invited us to come back.

We were about to exit the building when we noticed some residents and their family members sitting on the front porch. I requested to sing a few songs, and they agreed and sang along with us. By the time we concluded the first song, a long black van had driven up in front of the facility, and the driver called out: "Hello, Ma'am. I work at Valley View; a few days ago, you all sang for the residents over there. We enjoyed your singing very much. You all are doing a good job; keep it up. Thank you very much. I wanted to tell you how much we appreciated what you are doing, but you left before I had the chance to. Thank you." She sat in her van as we continued to sing; then, as quickly as the van had appeared, it disappeared. We prayed with the residents and their family members on the porch and left.

Walking slowly to our car, I reflected on what had just occurred. The nursing facility where the lady in the van works is located in another city many miles away. What was the likelihood of her coming to this facility at this particular moment if God hadn't orchestrated it? I believe He wanted to teach me a valuable lesson: It's not about me, my time, or my gas. It is that He wants to use me to share His love with those who need it and, by doing so, bring joy and cheer into their lives. That, in the process, we get to honor and glorify God, Who has done so much for us, is an added bonus.

God rewarded our efforts more than 100 percent. Instead of ministering to the one person we initially intended to visit, we witnessed to more than 30 residents, family members, and caregivers. His blessings didn't stop there. He continued to bless our outreach ministry by opening a door for Morris and me to visit a few nursing care facilities regularly.

I experience much joy when residents and staffers join in singing or express their gratitude for our ministry. At the conclusion of one of our visits, the lady lying on her bed turned her head toward me and, with a beautiful smile, said, "Thank you, darling!" Not only are the residents appreciative, but the nurses and custodians often express their thanks and call us the "sweet singers."

Dr. Hodges, his wife, Yvonne, Morris, and I were singing in the room of a resident when a young woman with tear-stained face walked in from across the hallway and asked us to sing a little louder for her mom to hear because she was dying. We told her we would come to her mom's room. We completed our visit and proceeded to the room. Her mom was lying in bed, motionless, with her eyes half opened as her daughter tenderly caressed her cheeks and whispered, "I love you, mom."

I asked the daughter if she had a favorite song she wanted us to sing, but she didn't, so I suggested the chorus, "Heavenly sunshine, heavenly sunshine, flooding my soul with glory divine." I felt it was appropriate because of the bright sunlight shining through the window. The young woman turned to her mom and said, "Mom, you know that song; you used to sing it!" Her mom's voice remained silent, but the daughter sang along as tears rolled down her cheeks. We read scripture and prayed. Before leaving, the daughter, her mom's roommate, and the nurse standing nearby thanked us.

On another occasion, Morris and I had just finished eating Sabbath lunch when we received a call from Dr. Hodges. He informed us that a request had come to the Oakwood University Church for a choir to sing to a dying patient at a hospital. Since it's hard to secure a choir on such short notice, he suggested that we try to get a few people to sing. A short time later, we joined Dr. Hodges at the hospital and were escorted outside the patient's room by a nurse who introduced us to the doctor. He explained the situation and invited us to come into the room where a man was lying on the bed surrounded by family members. One of them requested that we sing "Amazing Grace." We sang a few more songs and Dr. Hodges led out with Psalms 23 and 91.

It was a heart-wrenching experience to watch the gentleman take his last breath as tears flowed down the cheeks of his wife and loved ones. I was profoundly impressed by this family's demonstration of love for him. They hugged and thanked us for ministering to them in their time of need. One of the older ladies came to where I was standing and hugged me. Then, she rested her head on my shoulder and wept. I had never witnessed anything like it. We prayed with the family before leaving the room. I thank God for using us as conduits through whom His love flowed to this family in their valley experience.

Recently, we experienced immense happiness during our visits to two nursing care facilities. Residents were seated in wheelchairs in the lobby near the nurses' station. Morris, Shirley Blake, Flore Hamilton, and I had decided on a few songs we would sing. However, when we got to the station, another song popped into my mind, so I sang the words lustily, "I have a joy, joy, joy, joy, down in my heart." Immediately, some of the residents raised their heads and began to sing; one of them, especially, sang to the top of her lungs. This was unusual because she usually sits quietly and listens. Nurses, as well as the janitor, joined in singing; we sounded like a mini-choir. We sang a few more songs and, as we finished singing, residents clapped and said, "Thank You, come back." One of them shouted, "Sing some more; we enjoy your singing!"

We visited with some of the residents in their rooms, then we traveled to another facility. As we entered, I noticed that some residents were being wheeled to the lobby area where about 25 had gathered there. I decided to sing the same song. One of the residents jumped up from her wheelchair and began to sing very loudly with the accompanying movements. The nurses looked on in astonishment. We sang familiar songs like "If You're Happy, and You Know It, Clap Your Hands," "Heavenly Sunshine," and "Jesus Loves Me; This I Know." During this last song, I heard a deep bass voice. When I looked around, I saw an elderly man with a disfigured face sitting alone singing to the glory of God. Yes, Jesus loves us all.

In addition to the nursing home ministry, God has given me two new passions: sharing devotional books with women I meet during my travels or on my morning walks, and encouraging women to write their personal stories of God's love and goodness. As a result, 21 women's devotional articles have been published in the General Conference women's devotional books with more pending. Maple, a new author, was so elated to see her name in a recent devotional book that she called to thank me. "Sister Iheanacho, I didn't know I could write, but you kept insisting that I should just write, and I did. Now, I hold a book in my hand with my name in it. Thank you very much for being so persistent. I can't hold back the tears." Elder T. Marshall Kelly, a retired pastor and singing evangelist, called to express his appreciation for encouraging his wife, Jean, to write a devotional article. Although she passed before her story was published, her testimony of God's faithfulness lives on to minister to the hearts of her family and many readers around the world. We give thanks to our Almighty God.

It's amazing the doors God opens in some unusual ways to use what I have left. Not long ago, He used my jacket. Here's how it happened. My husband and I were returning from spending our vacation in Hartford, Connecticut with our friends Fyneboy and Margaret. We stopped at the Atlanta airport to change planes, and while waiting, a Caucasian woman walked up to me and said, "Your jacket is beautiful, and you are too." I told her thanks that in my senior years, I try to wear colorful clothes to make me feel youthful. We chatted a little and then she said, "I got good news today. I no longer have cancer. I am keeping my fingers crossed that it doesn't return." Just then I saw her crossed her fingers. I thought, "Keeping your fingers crossed won't stop your cancer from returning." I felt impressed to pray for her, so I said, "Let's pray about it." Standing in the airport with people hurrying and scurrying everywhere, we held hands, and I prayed. Afterward, she hugged and thanked me. Her face glowed as she kept repeating "Thank you." I told her to hurry along before she missed her flight. As she walked away, I surprised myself at what had just occurred. I never thought I would have had the courage to pray for someone in an airport. If you're willing, God provides the moment. He's truly awesome!

Even at the age of 76 plus, God is not finished with me yet. Mrs. Lucy Cort and Dr. Lela Gooding, officers of the University of the Southern Caribbean University Huntsville

Alumni Chapter, extended an invitation for me to be the guest speaker for the chapter's 25th anniversary. I responded by giving them the names of excellent speakers. Their response was: "No, we want you."

God had placed a solemn responsibility on me! Daily as I prepared, I asked Him to forgive my sins, speak to me, first, then speak through me to His people. And He did far beyond my expectations. The title of my message was "I have called you by your name; you are mine." At the conclusion of the service, several individuals mentioned that the message spoke directly to their souls. Some were dealing with serious personal problems, and they were encouraged to give their problems to God and trust Him to handle them because He is the world's greatest problem-solver. A young OU male student said, "I was not planning to be here today, but I'm glad I came. Thank you for your inspiring message. I was blessed." On my way to my car, a lady greeted me, "Thank you very much for your sermon. As you were speaking, tears flowed from my heart that only God could see. He gave me the answer to something I am dealing with. Thank You." I thanked God for using me, His broken vessel, one more time, for His glory and honor.

USC Alumni 25th Anniversary

A ministry through which I have been tremendously blessed is the South Central Conference Women's Ministries Teleconference Prayerline called "Morning Manna." It was started by Elder Clementine Collins in 2010. Six days weekly, beginning at 5:30 a.m., approximately 50 to 75 people call in from around the country to listen to profound and inspirational devotionals and to share praise testimonies and prayer requests.

I am energized as I listen to the powerful and heartfelt testimonies of God's abundant blessings and miraculous answers to prayers, as well as the dynamic speakers. Twice monthly, I serve as a ministry leader/moderator and, occasionally, as a speaker. Three times annually, I am assigned to provide speakers and prayer warriors for a week. It was on this Prayerline that I met my two fantastic prayer partners: Elder Clementine Collins and Elder Marilyn Wallace. They have prayed my family and me through many dark valley experiences. I thank God for them, as well as other Spirit-filled prayer warriors like Sister Adams, Sister Crockett, Sister Francis Harris, and many others whose heartfelt prayers daily ascend like sweet incense to God's throne room.

Fellow traveler, what are you doing with what you have left? I pray that God will put the desire in your heart to use whatever it is to bless others and to make a difference for His kingdom. He is able to do far beyond what you could ever imagine. You, too, will be blessed, and your heart will be filled with indescribable joy as a result.

Yesterday is gone forever, and tomorrow may never come. So, don't delay. Begin today! Let the fragrance of God's love flow through you to touch others. Make a difference!

"Bless the LORD, O my soul; And all that is within me, bless His Holy name. He has done great things; praise His holy name. Bless the LORD, O my soul, And forget not all His benefits" (Psalm 103:1, 2, NJKV).

Chapter 19

Gratitude and Highest Praise to God

I have reached the final chapter of my book, and it's with a sense of profound gratitude, heartfelt appreciation, inexpressible joy, and deep humility that I say "Thank You" to my Mighty and Wonderful God for all that He has done for me, and for His incredible plans for my life. He's the One who has brought me this far, and what an incredible journey it has been! It's amazing to think that He had every step planned long before I was born. I thank Him profusely for all that He has done in my life and for blessing my latter days greater than my beginning.

Taking a reflective look back, no way, in my puny imagination, could I have envisioned my life turning out this way. If someone had ventured to predict my future when I was a young girl in Barbados, they would have been wrong. Yes, I am the recipient of God's love, mercy, and faithfulness. His magnanimous grace still amazes me. Today, I can testify that He's been so good to me! The song, "Great is Thy Faithfulness," has new meaning for me.

My Savior has brought me a long way these many years. He has been my Guide step by step, moment by moment, day after day, through dangers, toils, and cares, through mountains steep and valleys deep, and in shady green pastures, so rich and so sweet. I stand in awe of His divine presence. Can I ever doubt His tender mercies Who through life has been with me? No! He has proved Himself strong and has carried me in His powerful arms when my strength failed, and I couldn't keep on going.

God has been my Rock in a weary land, my Shelter in the storms of life, my Protector, my Provider, my Problem-solver, my Miracle-worker, my Mighty Fortress, my Song and my Salvation. He's my Balm in Gilead, my Lifter-upper, my Comforter, my Divine Healer, my Battle Fighter, my Way Maker, my Deliverer, my Compassionate, Merciful, Sin-pardoning Savior, my Alpha and Omega, and my Omnipotent and Holy God. Without Him, I would be nothing; without Him, I would certainly fail. I give Him thanks, glory, adoration, honor, and praise. He's marvelous! I just can't explain it, but I can say Glory! Hallelujah! Praise His Holy Name from whom all blessings flow!

Through all my trials and triumphs, twists and turns, bruises and bumps, ups and downs, He's been there for me. He's never failed me, yet. What seemed impossible I saw my God do. My heart cries out in wonderment and humility: "How great You Are!" I lift my voice in total praise to thank Him for the peace He gave me in my valley experiences, and for bringing me safely over the rough side of the mountain. He continues to be my source of strength and joy. As long as I live, I will love Him and sing praises to my God. I humbly pray for His continued guidance as I press on the upward way, confident of His presence and the assurance that He'll keep me till I arrive safely at my destination— heaven—because He's my Navigator.

Honestly, the journey hasn't been easy. Life can be hard with its thorns and thistles. Walking through my dark valleys, the physical and emotional trials at times, have felt insurmountable and I have succumbed to doubting and complaining. But God walked with me and rescued me every time and brought me through victoriously. He has never failed to keep His promises to strengthen, help, and uphold me (Isaiah 41:10, NKJV).

God has a great plan completely mapped out for each of our lives. I encourage you to give Him your life as you hold on tenaciously to His unchanging hand. Interruptions, heartaches, disappointments, and pain are inevitable, but keep your eyes on Jesus! Confidently trust in Him. He will make a way for you where there seems to be no way. I know from experience that it is not always easy to trust God. Sometimes, it is a lot easier to say than to do, but don't ever give up on Him. You are His precious possession, and He will never give up on you.

Pray perseveringly; He hears and answers prayers. In your weakness, claim his precious promise to "bear you up on wings of eagles and give you strength" (Isaiah 40:31). "Be strong and of good courage, do not fear nor be afraid of them, for the LORD your God, He is the ONE who goes with you. He will not leave you nor forsake you" (Deuteronomy 31:6). "In all your ways acknowledge Him, And He shall direct your paths" (Proverbs 3:6).

My God is real and faithful. I know. "Once I was young, and now am old. Yet I have never seen the godly abandoned or their children begging for bread" (Psalm 37:25, NLT). Thank You, Father, for Your precious promises that encourage us as we journey on the road of life.

As I close, I want to give special tribute to my husband, Morris, to thank him for his faithfulness, love, support, untiring assistance with this book, and for taking me around the world and giving me the adventure of a lifetime. I thank God for choosing him for me and for sustaining our marriage more than 47 years. Morris has stuck with me through thick and thin, sickness and health, in sadness and in laughter, in good times and bad, and the overwhelming challenges of life. I am thankful for his love, wisdom, support, for enriching my life so profoundly, and for the opportunity to participate in Maranatha Volunteers Global Outreach Ministries, sharing God's love and making a difference in our travels nationally and internationally. How can I say thanks for all that he has done for me? To God, I give all honor and glory. Today, I pledge to be Morris' faithful companion till death do us part and to give myself to God so that He can continue to use me to make a difference for His kingdom.

Morris & Shirley

Thank you, dear Reader, for taking the time to read my story. It is my hope that something in this book has energized, encouraged, or inspired you as you journey on the road of life. I pray that heaven will shower you with favor as you abound in God's grace.

As we part, I commend you "to Him who is able to keep you from falling, and to present you faultless before the presence of his glory with exceeding joy, To the only wise God our Saviour, be glory and majesty, dominion and power, both now and ever. Amen" (Jude 24-25, KJV). Until we meet again, "The LORD bless you and keep you; The Lord make His face shine upon you And be gracious to you; The LORD lift up His countenance upon you, And give you peace" (Numbers 6:24-26 NKJV). AMEN!

"Looking for that blessed hope, and the glorious appearing of the great God and our Savior Jesus Christ" (Titus 2:13, KJV).

About the Author

*S*hirley C. Iheanacho is a native of the beautiful paradise island of Barbados. She is a wife, mother, grandmother, elder, author, missionary, international speaker and traveler, prayer warrior, encourager, philanthropist, hand bell ringer, choir member, and a retiree. In addition to the many hats she wears, she and her supportive and wonderful husband, Morris, visit nursing care facilities to minister to the sick and shut-in. They also participate in global outreach mission projects as far away as Mozambique, Ghana, and Panama.

She is a graduate of Caribbean Union College (now University of Southern Caribbean, Trinidad) and Andrews University where she received her B.Sc. degree. She has also attended Alabama A&M University and Oakwood College. Her productive career spans more than 40 years, 34 of which as an employee of the Seventh-day Adventist Church organization.

Shirley and Morris have been married for more than 47 years and are the proud parents of Ngozi Bolton, Chioma, and Akunna; and grandparents to two handsome teenagers: Nikolas and Timothy.

End Notes

THE POWER OF PRAYING® Copyright © 2004 Stormie Omartian. Published by
Harvest House Publishers Eugene, Oregon 97402. www.harvesthousepublishers.com.
Used by Permission

CPSIA information can be obtained
at www.ICGtesting.com
Printed in the USA
LVOW04s1220250517
535612LV00002B/2/P

9 781498 498586